WINE Q & A

A collection of trivia designed
to make learning about wine
fun and easy.

Gordon B. Sullivan

WINE APPRECIATION GUILD PRESS

SAN FRANCISCO

Wine Q. and A., a collection of trivia designed to make learning about wine fun and easy.

Text copyright © 2023 Gordon B. Sullivan

Wine Appreciation Guild
an imprint of
Board and Bench Publishing
www.boardandbench.com

Editorial direction by Annika Dougherty
Design and composition by EndLight

ISBNs
978-1-935879-96-1

Library of Congress Cataloging-in-publication is on file with the Library of Congress

DEDICATION

This book is dedicated to Joanna, my beloved daughter and best friend.

You are an indescribable gift from God, made in His image and for His glory.

Your beauty and brilliance make both your heavenly father and earthly father proud every day.

Continue helping others including the less fortunate, in your chosen field.

You are so loved, Joanna.

AMEN

FOREWORD

The world of wine can be a vast and intimidating place for those new to it. There have been many books written on the subject over the centuries, and many of these books are challenging to learn from, written in a dense, overly detailed, and often pedantic fashion. The book that follows this introduction is nothing of the sort. Beginning with Gordon Sullivan's original foray into wine, first as a banquet wine waiter and later chef sommelier at The Breakers in Palm Beach, Florida, followed by a decades-long long career with Southern Glazer's Wine and Spirits, Wine Q. & A. is a fun and fascinating read and learning tool written in a question-and-answer format that promotes knowledge retention.

Gordon covers not only the world of wine region by region, touching upon appellations, grape varieties, personalities, history, geography, climate, and soil, but also includes a good grounding in viticulture and winemaking as well. And for good measure, he includes a chapter each on the French brandy regions of Cognac and Armagnac as well as one on sake, subjects that he is also passionate about.

Suitable for beginners as well as those with more advanced wine knowledge, Wine Q. & A. is a must have for anyone studying for a wine certification program, planning a career in wine, or simply someone who enjoys drinking wine and wishes to learn more about it.

À votre santé!

Eric Hemer, Master of Wine, Master Sommelier
SVP Corporate Education, Southern Glazer's Wine and Spirits

ENDORSEMENTS

"I've known Gordon for more than 40 years during his time at Southern Glazer's Wine & Spirits. He joined our Company as a wine salesman in 1978, working in our restaurant wine division in Palm Beach, Florida. He dedicated himself to his role in sales for 27 years, becoming well known and respected in the market, and in 2005 was promoted to luxury wine brands manager in Palm Beach. His commitment to sharing his knowledge of wine throughout his career made a great impact on both the customer accounts he served and among his colleagues. Gordon's passion for wine and the industry comes through in his innovative approach to wine education as he uses trivia to share his extensive knowledge. Whether you are a novice looking for an introduction to wine, or a Master wanting to enhance your expertise, this book takes you through an easy to digest and fun to read wine journey around the world."

Mel Dick
President Wine Division/Senior Vice President
Southern Glazer's Wine & Spirits

Gordon was employed by our organization for more than 4 decades. During his tenure, he was involved in wine sales, and wine education for our consultants and managers, as well as the trade. Realizing the need for the next generation, he has devised a new concept in wine education. His concise learning technique combines single-sentence wine trivia questions, with single-sentence educational explanations as answers. This exhaustive research may revolutionize how people absorb wine facts and data. I recommend this innovative learning format for the wine industry, the hospitality industry, wine novices, and knowledgeable wine consumers as well.

Wayne Chaplin
CEO of Southern Glazer's Wine & Spirits

I first met Gordon over 40 years ago in Palm Beach, Florida. He was my sales consultant from Southern Wine & Spirits, and assisted me in compiling my restaurant wine list. He was extremely helpful, and taught me about wine in my early years as a chef/restaurateur. Gordon has remained diligent in the wine trade all these years, and has devised a new way to learn about wine in this book. I recommend this publication as a learning tool, for novices and well-seasoned servers and managers.

Chef Thomas Keller

Men and women who hold great passion and can both articulate it as well as educate others in that passion are exceedingly rare. My friend Gordon Sullivan is one of those rare people. We may, if we are incredibly lucky, get to meet such a person once or twice in a lifetime, or even get to know them. In reading Gordon's book, I am not only inspired but humbled by his knowledge and passion. This work is a must-read for those who love wine or are even thinking they may find the vinous world worth studying. And in the reading, you will get to know this passionate man just a little bit better, as have I.

Indeed, In Vino Veritas!
Greg La Follette
Founding winemaker of Marcelle and GLF Wines

Gordon Sullivan is a perfect person to write a treatise on education, love and appreciation for wine and the culture that surrounds it. I worked with Gordon for many years and always looked forward to our time together. His interest, sociability, knowledge and, importantly, lack of pretension made it a pleasure. It didn't hurt that he always had a comfy Cadillac too. For myself, as well as those we both sold to and worked with, Gordon's easy manner, breadth of information, and love of his subject make him an easy person both to learn from and to be around.

Dan Goldfield
Winemaker / Partner
Dutton-Goldfield Winery

I've known Gordon for over forty years, and he is by far the most knowledgeable wine person I have ever met. Throughout my entire restaurant career, especially with my partner Burt Reynolds at the Backstage Restaurant & Jazz Club in Jupiter Florida, Gordon has been a big part of my wine successes. He always assisted me in composing great wine lists and server training classes. He has composed a unique wine education book, useful for the next generation of trade personnel and hobbyists.

Bruce Nierman
Owner, Gallery Grille, Jupiter Florida

"I am pleased and honored to be writing this personal reflection and endorsement about my dear friend, Gordon Sullivan. My team and I, were coming off an incredible 20-year career in the highest levels of professional motorsports with personal victories at the 24 hours of Daytona and the 24 hours of Le Mans… but I was now completely enamored with starting over in the wine business… which was a very humbling experience. One of the things, that keeps you going, when you are questioning your core decisions, is when you meet someone truly special. Gordon had an incredible ability to see the "big picture" and his knowledge of the industry is encyclopedic. He quickly saw and understood how our previous success in an incredibly challenging business could translate over and how committed we were to try to replicate it here…. others never even understood. He is a motivator, an educator and helped me to see clearly to the next steps. I have been around the globe so many times and 30+ years on the road and it's exceedingly rare that you meet someone who is this incredibly talented and diverse and is also genuine, patient and kind. Gordon's knowledge of wine, regions, nuances of the industry and most importantly to me "the big picture of it all". how he was able to gently tie it together and handed it to me, gave me inspiration and motivation to continue forward. Gordon is an inspiration and a truly bright light in this crazy world we live in as well as a "Must Have" for all restaurant servers, managers, industry personal, hobbyists, collectors, etc. because it is "The Real Deal" written by "The Real Guy". one of the absolute best in the business. It is with sincere respect and appreciation that I'm sharing this personal memory. Good luck Gordon on everything you do… for all this you have helped along the way… we're all with you now on your journey & behind you all the way my friend!!! And we will try to do our small bit to "pass it forward"…

Kevin Buckler
CEO, The Racers Group - Five-time International Endurance Racing Champion
CEO, Adobe Road Wines

CONTENTS

WHY ANOTHER WINE BOOK – WHY NOW?

One check on my decades long bucket list has been to compose a *wine trivia book*. Most people love trivia, and many people enjoy wine. Why not marry the compelling topic of trivia along with the dynamic subject of wine? Think of the long running TV show Jeopardy. Since 1964, this television program has captivated audiences of all ages, backgrounds, and intelligence levels. Reflect on the board game Trivial Pursuit that was created in 1979 and was one of the most popular parlor games of the era. People derive satisfaction when they answer a trivia question correctly, especially when none of their peers do.

As the subject matter of wine data grows exponentially every year, many are drawn into learning more about wine-producing countries, wine regions, winery personalities, wine grapes, farming techniques, tasting events, gourmet wine dinners, etc. Serious wine books today often exceed 300-400 pages, each loaded with wine information at every level imaginable. I probably have close to 250 of those types of wine books in my own collection.

In recent years, I have observed a problem with such traditional learning methods for the newer generation. *Wine education needs to be simplified*. I know many use the Internet for wine information today, but much data is often disjointed, and in some cases, outdated and unreliable. Most books and even some publications are too detailed for wine novices, millennials, restaurant servers, retailers, wholesalers, hobbyists and even some collectors. My goal is to assist in removing frustration when learning about wine, so everybody benefits and easily builds on their existing wine foundation.

This wine trivia book is designed to be *FUN* and *EDUCATIONAL*. The format provides an alternative method of learning (not dissimilar to the flashcards used in preparation for certification examinations), thus simplifying access to wine knowledge and expertise. After composing about the first 25 questions and answers of wine trivia, I spotted a void in the format. If the questions had a true/false, fill in the blank, or one or two-word answer, I determined that having more information was necessary. I devised a bi-phasal concept of providing an *educational explanation* of the answers at the bottom of each page. I am referring to this design as a *concise wine learning tool.* None of the questions exceed a single sentence, nor do their answers coupled with an additional educational comment. My desire is that readers will be able to take a mental snapshot of the data versus the large paragraph or multipage format used in most wine educational books.

Friends and family have asked me how I determined how many questions and answers would be contained in this book. Obviously, I used thousands of sources, but one of the main parameters involved my 45+ years of copious personal notes, both handwritten and on computer. Completion to me was when my tens of thousands of individual notes were discarded, and my office became uncluttered at the same time (YAY!) One of my most challenging tasks was how to fit both questions and answers each on a single-sentence while still offering a coherent teaching opportunity.

The chapters start out with basic questions and proceed to more complicated and detailed questions. Some may say this book is too difficult to understand, but my intention is to teach utilizing ***KEY WORDS / CRUCIAL PHRASES*** that may require additional research on your part. And yes, as you grow your educational base, you will see some of the content reflects sommelier-ignited trends.

This book is divided into chapters first by countries, then by major and minor grape growing sub-regions. Does this book try to educate everybody about everything regarding wine? Absolutely not. However, if you come across an interesting topic, dig deeper on your own (invest in yourself) which will provide more information than this publication offers. All I can do is whet your appetite; the rest is up to you. Your wine growth and development are your responsibility.

Disclaimer: Whenever wine data is collected, there can be tremendously varied answers from multiple reputable sources. Wine facts and statistics change almost daily, apart from historical and perhaps geographical specifics. As a result, I have attempted to ask wine trivia questions and provide accurate educational answers that are essentially timeless. Of course, there are many exceptions that will lead you to explore further self-study. Your personal wine research may discover answers that are different than mine, but the wine industry is replete with contradictions, both subjective and objective.

Thank You.

GORDON B. SULLIVAN
President & Founder
Sullivan Wine Consulting, Inc.
Palm Beach, Florida

MY WINE JOURNEY

THE EARLY YEARS

My life began in Cambridge, Massachusetts where I was born into a close, supportive, and loving family. My father, Gordon (my all-time hero) was my inspiration for everything life had to offer. He was always in my corner, suggesting accurate guidance and counsel whenever and wherever I needed it. My mother, Ethel, was always there too, with her motherly instincts and female perspective on any problems I may have encountered. They have both passed, but they are always in my daily prayers. My three sisters, Carole, Nancy, and Joanne have provided me with similar blessings, as they always want to help and guide their favorite brother. The other huge blessing in my life has been my daughter, Joanna. She is a wonderful, loving, caring, and considerate human being.

I did not come from a wine consuming family. Back in the late 1960s and early 1970s, wine seldom made an appearance on our dinner table, just my mother's annual sip of Harvey's Bristol Cream Sherry around the holidays. My father would enjoy a cold Schlitz beer after a hot session of mowing the grass during the summer heat spikes.

My first official job at the age of 16, (I cut grass for several neighbors before that) I worked at Carlisle's (MA) only gas station (Texaco) pumping gas, (no self-service stations back then) changing tires, and performing oil changes. I remember getting my driver's license on my 16th birthday. The examiner mentioned he had never met a more relaxed driver at that age. What I didn't tell him was for well over a year I drove my father's car (with his permission) around our very sparsely populated neighborhood!

It was here that I became passionate about cars, (my first car at age 16 was a 1962 Pontiac Catalina convertible) as this gas station served as the epicenter of my teenage (and older) friends who all had customized cars. During the next summer at age 17, I worked for the Lang Volkswagen dealership in the next town Bedford MA, in the parts department and drove the tow truck.

My first job in the restaurant industry was Friday and Saturday nights during that same summer, as a busboy at the Arrowood Motor Inn, also in Bedford. Food service and customer satisfaction in the restaurant industry made a positive early impression on me.

After my early years of school, then Concord-Carlisle regional high school, I was off to Williston Academy (now Williston Northhampton) a boarding prep school and a New England tradition) in Easthampton, Massachusetts. I was the basketball team's leading scorer (17 points/game), led the team in free throw percentages, and Spring track high jumper and high hurdler. This led to a partial basketball scholarship from Susquehanna University in Pennsylvania.

Incidentally, father was employed by Millipore Filter Corporation in Bedford MA, a pioneer in air and water purification systems. They also devised wine membrane filtration systems in the 1960s used by large wineries including E. & J. Gallo Winery. Small world huh! I guess I was destined to work in the wine trade.

In the interim, my father was transferred with Millipore to Frankfurt, Germany along with the rest of my family, so I never visited Susquehanna University prior to acceptance. After working in Maine for that previous summer, and with no family around, (my 1965 VW would not have made the 7-hour drive), I took a plane from Boston to Harrisburg PA. The last 50 miles required a bus ride, hitchhiking, and walking the rest of the way to my dorm with my single suitcase containing maybe 4-5 sets of clothes, a couple pairs of shoes, and a toothbrush. Fortunately, my new roommate Jeff Greco lived a short distance away and his mother kindly supplied me with sheets, blankets, a pillow and towels. Thank you, Mrs. Greco.

I was two days late for freshman orientation, so I missed registration. I didn't get some courses I was hoping for (not that I knew the curriculum ahead of time anyway). I was envious of families dropping off other freshmen and upperclassmen with U-Hauls containing stereos, bookcases, desk lamps, alarm clocks, mini-refrigerators, school supplies and large quantities of food.

On my first day of college, I befriended Denny Eckman, (who still lives in Carlisle PA) and Steve Jackson (from Long Island) who have both remained longtime friends. Of course, I joined the basketball squad in October where I started first team varsity and lettered as a freshman. In addition to hoops in college, I was also involved in Greek life as vice president in my junior year, then president in my senior year of the Lambda Chi Alpha fraternity.

My most laborious job ever was during college where two other fraternity brothers and I unloaded railroad cars filled to the brim with lumber. Railroad cars are 2-3 times the size of standard 18-wheeler trailers. I think we unloaded a total of 3 cars over the course of several days before complete exhaustion set in, but Phil Schreyer, Bob Yankner, and I had a lot of money in our pockets. The 3 of us also teamed up to win the yearly homemade raft race down the Susquehanna River.

During the summers following prep school and throughout college, I worked in Ogunquit, a picturesque seaside village in southern Maine. The first summer, while working at Barnacle Billy's in Perkin's Cove, I lived in Wells Beach (thank you fellow Willistonian, Keith Handyside). When I turned 18 (the legal age then) I trained as a bartender at The Sandpiper, under the mentorship of great friend Jay Couser, and continued that career for the next five years in various locations.

After Wells beach, the following summers included a few rooming houses with friends in Ogunquit, and finally on Short Sands in York Beach (at a 10-room summer rental called the "ZOO" primarily housing bartenders at many local restaurants and bars) during the last 2 summers. Can you say party central?

Since tending bar was a night job, I spent a few of those summers working as an apprentice for a local electrician.

Bartending locations: 4 summers in Ogunquit, Maine at The Sandpiper and Cape Neddick Lobster Pound. During junior and senior years in college at the upscale Edison Hotel in Sunbury, Pennsylvania. After college at the Hotel LaSalle in the French speaking city of Montreal, Quebec, Canada. With great friend Jay Couser, we included frequent skiing escapades in the Laurentians mountains and including Mont-Tremblant. Contained within the hotel, my bartending position was at the Irish Lancer Bar, where I gained my passion for Irish music ballads from the nightly performers. While spending 1 winter in Hawaii, the Kona Hilton on the west coast of the Big Island was my venue. Hello to my introduction of serious numerous tropical cocktails for the vacationing tourists. I became certified in SCUBA diving in Kona, enjoying the beautiful coral reefs and fish species Hawaii has to offer.

My final bartending job was at The Breakers, Palm Beach, Florida

After my fifth and final summer in Maine, having just graduated from college with a degree in Economics, I decided to head for Florida and the great weather where I had enjoyed the beaches and parties during a couple of college spring breaks. Captain Phil Richards, the owner of the Sandpiper Bar & Restaurant in Ogunquit, owned a 50-foot Tripp-designed Columbia masthead sloop sailboat (equipped with a large spinnaker sail for reaching off the wind, and speedy downhill runs), needed another crew member to deliver the boat to Palm Beach, Florida.

Now, I never heard of Palm Beach Florida, but it sounded exotic, so I replied in the affirmative. One seasoned crew member mentioned when we finally arrived in Palm Beach, I could apply for a bartending position at The Breakers. (I never heard of that hotel either). The endless theme on the 8-track speaker system was of course "Sloop John B" by the Beach Boys, and Irish ballads.

The voyage from Maine took about two weeks in the open Atlantic Ocean; our small boat often heeled over dramatically and was violently tossed about in the large cargo shipping lanes. Our provisional stops included Newport RI, Annapolis MD, Cape Fear NC, and finally Palm Beach, FL. Believe me, this trip was not about sipping chilled martinis and enjoying Beluga caviar with a dollop of crème fraîche on whole wheat blinis on the aft deck. More accurate were the large cauldrons of chili con carne and crackers. Sailboats require midnight watches and 24/7 constant labor tasks split amongst the crew of four.

THE BREAKERS YEARS

Arriving in Palm Beach in October 1973 with only a sailor's duffel bag and perhaps a couple of hundred dollars to my name, I looked for employment and found it on the first day. After walking from the marina where the boat was docked, across the Intracoastal Waterway to The Breakers I was hired on the spot as a banquet bartender. This position was well below my bartending skill grade, but I needed a job, and thought this would get my foot in the door. I continued living on the boat for a few days until its next voyage to St. Thomas.

The Breakers is one of the finest hotels in the world, originally constructed by Henry Morrison Flagler in 1896. After a fire, it was rebuilt in 1925 in the Italian Renaissance style, inspired by architecture from the 1400s. Its grandeur is still enjoyed today by all who visit the property and enjoy its amenities.

Two years prior, in 1971, the formerly seasonal hotel opened for year-round business for the first time as the corporate convention business started taking off. From the 1920s through the 1960s, seasonal guests often brought their private staff to attend to their personal needs during their months long stay. As guest's staff lodging was no longer necessary, I was offered a former valet room at the hotel for $9 per week. I was granted a single room (I was too tall for bunk beds) complete with a small sink and telephone (local or collect calls only). Communal bathrooms and showers were at the end of the hall.

I could eat two or three buffet-style meal daily in the employee cafeteria for $1.25 per meal (the food was often leftovers from the previous night's guest banquets). After about a week, I purchased my first motorcycle, (a passion that would last more than 45 years) my sole means of transportation during this time. A fellow bartender and friend Joe Fazio and I were permitted to store our bikes overnight in a golf course maintenance barn for $10 a month. I was living large in Palm Beach, Florida.

Later in that season, my entry level bartending position lasted for just a few months as my previous high-profile bartending positions allowed my greater potential to be recognized. I was then scheduled into several of the permanent bars including the Alcazar Lounge (now the Seafood Bar) overlooking the ocean, which improved my income considerably.

Starting in 1974, employees were no longer permitted to live in the valet rooms in the hotel, so I sought housing across the Intracoastal Waterway in West Palm Beach. Cruising around (no internet yet), I found a "For Rent" sign on a private home. The owner said she would not normally rent to a biker, but she was willing to give me a trial. The 600 square foot studio was established at $150/month. That appeared to be heavy to me, so I asked if I would cut her grass would she reduced the rent. She charged me $100 per month and her landscaping look great. I spent the next 4 years living in that location, as it was about 3 miles from The Breakers.

After a season tending bar, I took notice of something that would change my career and life forever!

I observed several French-speaking employees selling wine in the main dining room, at that time called The Florentine. Toting the exceptionally large wine lists to guest tables with their tastevin cups on neck chains, wine cellar keys and custom wine openers displayed, wheeling guéridons (wine serving carts) through the dining room. Loaded with wine glasses in myriad shapes and sizes, wine cradles, decanters, candles and matches for decantation and more, these gentlemen were impressive, using their French accents and tools of the trade to maximize wine sales. I thought to myself, *"I want to do that."*

Looking back, I recall an impetus that probably directed my subliminal decision to teach myself about wine. Sophomore year summer in college, along with a few friends, we decided to travel throughout Europe. After arriving on a budget airline, we stayed in youth hostels, ate grab and go meals, used Eurail passes, purchased a 1959 Volkswagen beetle for $35 (until it died) and hitchhiked through 11 countries for almost 3 months (on extremely limited funds I may add). Observing the architecture, art museums sight-seeing, history, traditions and unfamiliar food and wine customs, etc.

was an eye-opening experience to a young American traveling abroad. I'm convinced, The Breakers became my conduit into the food and wine trade, that would last 48 years (so far).

In 1974, I requested a transfer via Beverage Manager and good friend Paul Lininger, from my bartending position into the wine department. My application was approved; however, I needed to start at the entry level of the wine department. Back then, that position was called a *glass boy* (there was no political correctness in those days). I polished and prepared the wine glasses for both The Florentine dining room and banquets for conventions, so the sommeliers were not bogged down with this tedious task.

Again, after just a few months (and coached by fellow sommelier, Jeff Kaier) I was promoted to *banquet wine steward.* Banquet dinners were generally large corporate events, often numbering 500 - 700 or more guests. We normally offered 6 - 8 wines available for purchase displayed on large banquet tables doubling as a Mise en Place with additional stemware, decanters, etc. The wine selections for the evening were strategically placed where guests entering the Venetian or Mediterranean ballrooms could easily see them and merchandised on table tents or small menu boards.

There were usually 3 – 5 of banquet wine stewards working large tables of 10. The best scenario was when one person sprang for multiple bottles for the whole table, otherwise we sold to deuces (more checks to get signed). This exercise required speed of wine service, attempting to get all wine orders prior to, or during the appetizer course, as all entrées were set at the same time. After the first bottle sale, we would become wine salesmen again, constantly cruising the room looking for that second, third, or fourth bottle sale. After dinner, the wine glasses were collected, racked, then rolled over to the dishwashing area of the main dining room. If we had discerning diners, we also had a few copies of the large Florentine wine list available. The negative here was valuable selling time lost due to the trip to the main dining room to retrieve the bottles in their bin locations, BUT they were usually much higher priced wine selections.

The next step of advancement in my wine service career afforded me the privilege of working in *The Florentine as Sommelier,* selling wine from the large wine list in a specified dining station. At the time The Breakers had 650 hotel rooms, so with double occupancy we would often serve 1,300 guests at dinner. This consisted of two seatings, 650 guests in each one. A dining plan option at the time was MAP (Modified American Plan) which included breakfast and dinner in the cost of the room. If the hotel was sold out, and it frequently was during the winter season, the scheduled five sommeliers would sell huge quantities of high-quality wine. In addition, the Chef Sommelier was always on hand to assist when we got in the weeds.

It was as sommelier that I tasted my epiphany wine: 1969 Montrachet, Domaine de la Romanée-Conti.

In 1975, at age 25, I was elevated to the position of *Chef Sommelier (Chief Wine Steward)* which I held for almost three years. (Master Sommelier Virginia Philip holds this title today; she has been at The Breakers for 21 years). My responsibilities involved adding wines to the large Florentine wine list, updating wine selections at all other food/beverage outlets and ordering and receiving wine shipments and direct import deliveries. Additional duties included re-organizing multiple storage rooms, booking wine meetings with event coordinators and setting the schedules for glass boys, banquet wine stewards and sommeliers in The Florentine. This intense schedule often had me working continuous day and night shifts.

We constantly hosted elegant wine dinners for organizations such as La Confrérie du Chevalier du Tastevin, Confrérie de la Chaîne des Rôtisseurs and The Food and Wine Society, among others. In those days I recall an event hosted by the legendary Alexis Lichine, author the most useful research book of the time: New Encyclopedia of Wines & Spirits, (and yes, the father of Sacha of Château d'Esclans' Whispering Angel fame). Incidentally, Alexis Lichine signed my copy of his book with a phrase I have never forgotten. "To Gordon, who has been the perfect link between cellar and glass, with best wishes, Alexis Lichine" This framed treasure remains in my home office to this day.

Other wine personnel included Michael Broadbent, Robert Mondavi, Rémi Krug, Claude Taittinger, and others. In addition, the Florida launch with Pierre Ernst of the Perrier-Jouët, "Fleur de Champagne" now Belle Époque bottle occurred in The Florentine dining room.

In the early to mid-1970's, The Florentine wine list was primarily French and German selections as California wines were just coming into their own after The Judgment of Paris in 1976 brought international acclaim to several top-quality California wines.

Also, In the early to mid-1970s, serious American food and beverage hotels and restaurants were often managed by classically trained German, Swiss, and Austrian professionals. The food & beverage program at The Breakers was under the leadership of Food & Beverage Director Mr. Henry Warren, Mr. Bernd Lembcke, Mr. Tom Wicky, and the Chef de Cuisine, Mr. Herman Fleckenstein from Bavaria. These four internationally acclaimed European individuals were my mentors from 1973 onward. During this time, very few, if any, dining establishments in America utilized separately staffed wine departments, with wine stewards whose sole job description was selling wine to guests during dinner. This dedication in Florida, borrowed from France, was the genius of Mr. Warren, my first wine mentor.

That stellar leadership team took The Breakers program to the next level in the 1970s and 1980s. Sadly, Mr. Warren passed in 2015 at the age of 98. Mr. Lembcke continued working at The Breakers for several years after I left. After a stint at The Cloister on Sea Island in Georgia, for the last 26 years, Bernd has held the position of Managing Director of The Mar-a-Lago Club in Palm Beach, and EVP in The Trump Organization. For 48 years now, Bernd has remained one of my closest friends and is indeed one of the most professional hospitality specialists worldwide.

In 1981—I was no longer at The Breakers but left my mark (and improved upon by Michael Weiss & Tim Ruzkowski) with an impressive wine list—Wine Spectator magazine, under the direction of Marvin R. Shanken, created an annual award for the finest wine lists in America (now the world). The Florentine Room at The Breakers was one of the 13 original **Grand Award** winners (out of 500 candidates that first year), the highest level awarded. Mr. Warren attended the first Wine Spectator Grand Award gala in New York representing The Breakers. Beginning in 1981, The Breakers has achieved that top honor every year since; what an amazing accomplishment! Today, along with

Bern's Steakhouse in Tampa, these are the only 2 restaurants worldwide that can make that claim. (Go Florida).

Although I thoroughly enjoyed all aspects of my five-year sojourn at The Breakers, including being schooled in classically trained European wine service, ultra-premium wine education, and elegantly prepared food and wine pairing exercises, I desired another wine challenge. I'd memorized The Florentine's extensive wine list of approximately 400 French selections, plus the 75 high Prädikat German wines (truly an exceptionally large wine list for the 1970s), but I wanted a more broad-based wine experience. I had no desire in relocating to Las Vegas to run another hotel/restaurant wine program. I wanted to be part of Southern Wine & Spirits.

THE SOUTHERN WINE & SPIRITS YEARS

In March 1978, I was thrilled to start the next chapter of my wine career as an employee with the family-owned and operated Southern Wine & Spirits (SWS), a distributor headquartered in Miami covering Florida as well as California and Nevada. Earlier, while at The Breakers, I was introduced to SWS's owner, Mr. Harvey Chaplin, (and later, son Wayne Chaplin), and to Mr. Mel Dick, President of the Wine Division. Based on these relationships, I purchased most of our wine list selections from SWS. Additionally, they carried the best wine portfolio in Florida, were committed to an efficient delivery system and I received first class service from my salesman, Gus Seuss and Miami insider Fred Macco. Although there were seven substantial wholesalers in the market in those days, there was only one I was interested in working for.

I was hired as a wine salesman (still no political correctness yet), and member of the ***restaurant wine division*** comprised of ten people and based out of Miami. My large number of more than 220 accounts covered a geographical area from West Palm Beach north to Vero Beach, over 90 miles up the coast. I was hired as an on-premise representative due my understanding of wine product knowledge, restaurant wine service, and my staff training abilities. I also serviced about a dozen or so independently owned retail wine and liquor stores. My first year of selling wine for SWS, I loved the job and the freedom so much, I did not even take my vacation time. The harder we worked, the more commission we were paid.

Just after being hired by SWS, I recall WEEKLY wine meetings in Miami (I lived in West Palm Beach), hosted entirely by Mel Dick, Vice President of the Wine Division. These early career meetings set the stage for me on how the wine distribution system worked. Mel is a very motivating speaker, and certainly propelled me, coupled from my Breakers background, into a very effective street sales consultant. Mel was very instrumental as my mentor, as our fine wine portfolio continued to grow.

Selling wine in the 1970s was much different than it is today. When I started, we had no cell phones, voicemail, beepers, pagers, laptops or GPS. I had to compose handwritten wine list proposals. My first car was a 40 horsepower 1964 Volkswagen beetle without air conditioning, (from The Breakers days) which was a humbling experience during that first summer of SWS employment in South Florida.

After selling the Volkswagen, I purchased a 1973 Pontiac Grand Prix with air conditioning. YAY! Before I was approved for a credit card, I remember times when I couldn't afford to fill that larger gas tank. We paid tolls on the Florida Turnpike with quarters. Rolls of dimes were needed for outside pay phones in the Florida heat and rain to call in orders or customers, part of the daily routine. I needed to work weekends for my former Breakers co-worker and friend Joe, owner of Fazio's Moving Company, to make ends meet. Another brief source of income was an elegant/ casual clothes modeling stint with a nationwide chain displaying video loops and large in-store posters. I was told however to keep my day job! LOL.

We had to learn viticulture, enology, vintages and more, by reading rather than simply relying on Google to find answers. For decades, I kept a wine book in my front passenger seat consulting it at Intracoastal bridges, railroad track signals, and traffic jams. I was addicted to gaining wine knowledge during daily down time.

During my years at The Breakers and my early years at SWS, wine drinking in America was just starting to catch on, with consumption of both imported and American wines steadily increasing every year. We were slowly shifting from beer and distilled spirits into wine. One of my early and constant personal missions was to help get the word out regarding wine education. Part of my service package to my restaurants and hotels was to provide server wine training classes to those accounts. This practice occurred because about 2 months after joining SWS, I composed my first wine list of about 20 items to a new 50 seat restaurant. After visiting the owner for several weeks hoping to get an order in addition to the weekly 3-liter jugs of Almaden. Week after week he kept explaining that they didn't sell any bottles to the tables.

Confused by lack of bottle sales, I then suggested to owner that maybe a wine education class would calm their fears of opening a wine bottle in front of guests, pronunciation of French or German wines, and understanding food/wine pairings. This idea worked, as gradually server confidence grew, and wine sales did also. From that point on, I vowed to perform multiple wine training classes with all my accounts for the next 42 years. These classes numbered in the thousands. In addition, I also provided owners and/or general managers with hundreds of 1 on 1 tutorial classes so they would be as well informed as their servers (utilizing the train the trainer concept).

Early in my career at SWS, having been groomed at The Breakers, my goal was always to make large wine lists in my accounts. The criteria needed to make business sense for them based on their cliental, they needed proper storage, and the budget to purchase the opening delivery and ongoing purchases. If owners and managers agreed to these parameters, I would propose very well constructed custom wine lists for their approval. My approach always included broad based geographical representation, a balance between mainstream and esoteric labels, diversified price points, and selections that complimented their food menu.

Another service I provided for my accounts was in the role as guest speaker in multi-course gourmet dining events. I never officially documented the number of these dinners, but I would imagine they exceeded several hundred. I am very confident that the extra effort of training classes and gourmet dinner appearances greatly contributed to my success in career wine sales. These services proved to the owners and managers that we were a team in business.

Convinced, that restaurant server wine training works, I made the determination that the public was seeking wine education as well. At the time there were no local wine classes. There were only tasting events with the local chapter of Les Amis du Vin at the Wine Cask, and the Sommeliers Guild in Fort Lauderdale. So, in 1980, my second year at SWS, and with the assistance of Mel Dick, I opened the **Sullivan Wine Institute** offering multi-session evening wine classes and wine tastings to the public, (including several trade personnel). This venture continued for about three years. I would conduct these classes at restaurants with private dining rooms or hotel meeting rooms. This also proved as a resource that cultivated attendees to get more heavily involved in the wine trade, including future employees of SWS. I concluded each seminar cluster with a wine exam, which kept focus on the material presented.

In 1981, one interesting task occurred for me regarding personalized service at a local hotel. I met the owner of the property on a Thursday, at which time he mentioned he wanted a 600-item wine list (it needed to be larger than The Breaker's List), to which I replied, "let's do this." I would be the sole composer and all the wines would be purchased through SWS. (Nice opening order). His last comment was that the proposal needed to be on his desk at noon on Monday. WHAT? I spent Friday and the weekend without sleep with plenty of high-octane coffee, and did my best from an archaic printed-out IBM multi-page inventory to deliver his request. By 12:00 PM Monday it was on his desk, albeit handwritten. (No laptops or current inventory yet). At that point he said, "good job, send me 4 bottles of each." Success!!

In 1981, while still employed with SWS, I wanted to have a more hands on approach to understanding wine production. I was set up with an apprentice program during October harvest at the **Robert Mondavi Winery** in Napa Valley. (My first trip to Napa). I spent almost 2 weeks in all aspects of the winery duties. From hand harvesting local grapes, receiving other grapes at the sugar shack using a refractometer, shoveling tank pomace, topping off oak barrels, working quality control on the bottling line, and a few days in the laboratory with Tim Mondavi. I have never forgotten any aspects of that enlightening experience.

Another example of wine education I was involved with was as the **Palm Beach Post** newspaper wine columnist from 1987 – 1991. This bi-monthly article column offered features covering all wine topics of my choosing from around the world. There were about 75 articles published, often accompanied with photographs and maps relating to the subject matter. Once again, my goal was educating others.

Palm Beach County was home to the **Florida Culinary Institute**, where I taught evening wine classes to student chefs from 1989 – 1993. Attempting to add to my own understanding of food/ wine affinities, I spent several Saturday afternoons apprenticing with executive chef Donnie Ross at Bentley's Restaurant in North Palm Beach. This provided a hands-on approach to sauces, stocks, grilling, roasting, and other food preparations. In trade, I would offer Donnie wine and food pairing ideas, and some wine bottles.

One of my most rewarding wine moments occurred in 1979 and re-surfaced in 2007 when the Wine Spectator interviewed **Chef Thomas Keller**, owner of Napa Valley's famous French Laundry restaurant. In 1979, Thomas was chef at a restaurant in Palm Beach, and I was his salesman. When the interviewer asked Thomas how he learned about wine, he explained that way back in 1979, "I got him interested in Pinot Noir, Cabernet Sauvignon, Bordeaux, and Rhône wines, and established the concept of vintages, and makers and varietals for me." When the article was published 28 years after our first meeting, I visited Thomas and asked him if he would autograph the article. He did, and it is framed and hanging in place of prominence in my home office.

I have a great story about Chef Thomas's early career. In 1979, long before he became the icon that he is today, most chefs wanted the least expensive 3-liter jugs of cooking wine. Not Thomas, who requested 750 ml. bottles of higher quality varietal wines, explaining to me that wine used in cooking was equally important as any other ingredient. I never forgot that conversation.

A pivotable point in my learning curve about ultra-premium American wines occurred for me in the late 1970's and early 1980's with the philosophy at Diamond Creek Vineyards in Napa Valley. Already with an understanding of Premier and Grand Cru vineyards in Burgundy from my years at The Breakers, labeling Cabernet Sauvignon from terroir-driven specific vineyard sites pioneered by founder Al & Boots Brounstein beginning in the late 1960's (along with Heitz Martha's Vineyard first labeled in 1966) was enlightening. Observing that Red Rock Terrace (7 acres), Gravely Meadow (5 acres), Volcanic Hill (8 acres), and Lake Vineyard, (.75 acres) offered stylistic sensory differences in both aroma and taste. Present day vineyard designations of Pinot Noir, Chardonnay, Cabernet Sauvignon among other varietals, is de rigueur in the American wine trade.

I remained a salesman (now called a sales consultant) for the next **27 years**, but dramatically reduced my area of coverage to essentially just Palm Beach County, and a few other areas of fine wine concentration.

My universe of accounts included the very exclusive island of Palm Beach, the epicenter of very high-profile restaurants, hotels, private country clubs, and yes, The Breakers. During this time, I took my wine game to the next level, studying for several years with fellow co-worker, Eric Hemer, Master Sommelier and Master of Wine (one of four worldwide). Those study sessions were good preparation for wine certifications. Eric is a passionate and patient educator. Thank you, Eric!

In 2005, while still employed with Southern Wine & Spirits, along with my business partner John Bourassa, from Jupiter Island, Florida we purchased 17 acres of vineyards off Route 29 in the Oak Knoll AVA in Napa Valley. We managed this vineyard from Florida, as we had a viticultural team in place, but we took several trips out to monitor vineyard decisions. We named the plot **Hillview Vineyard**, as it backed up to the iconic Mayacamas mountain range, and was planted with Bordeaux grape varieties. This plot was originally planted by Bruce Newlan in 1967. We owned this property until 2011, selling our fruit to several local wineries.

Also in *2005*, SWS Miami General Manager Richard Booth promoted me to *Luxury Wine Brands Manager, Platinum Team*. This position relieved me from the day-to-day duties of a sales consultant, so I could dedicate all my time to education and selling ultra-premium wines. I educated SWS employees, restaurant servers/managers, and provided individual tutoring for the on and off premise wine trade. This enabled me to increase my geographical coverage to include Key West and the upper Keys, Miami, Fort Lauderdale, Palm Beach, Naples and Tampa. My new job description included consulting to include proper wine list construction and formatting, wine list proofing, geographical balance, food/wine affinities, price point options, etc. My service package allowed many restaurants to achieve one of the three levels of the Wine Spectator awards.

Private clubs and country clubs were not eligible for the Wine Spectator awards because they are not open to the public. To remedy this, the CMAA (Club Management Association of America) created their own wine list awards with different levels of quality. I embraced this opportunity from the very first year, assisting scores of private clubs to take their wine programs to the next level. A great revenue generator for both the clubs and SWS involved doing wine education classes and tasting for the MEMBERS. After all, they are the final consumers, and with additional knowledge they often purchased higher quality wine while at dinner.

A SAMPLE OF ACCOUNTS SERVICED WHILE EMPLOYED BY SGWS

Here is a VERY limited list of the upscale properties where I composed or reformatted serious wine lists, educated staff, or conducted multi-course gourmet wine pairing dinners. I realize this is a very localized collection of restaurants, hotels and private clubs primarily located in Palm Beach County, Florida, but this was the geographical area I was responsible for. In later years with SGWS, I assisted in Ft. Lauderdale, Miami, The Keys (including Key West), Naples and Tampa. I am also listing properties that have gone out of business, or have changed ownership, but in their day, they were important players in the fine wine business.

PRIVATE CLUBS – PALM BEACH COUNTY

The Mar-a-Lago Club; Everglades Club; Bath & Tennis Club; Sailfish Club; The Beach Club; Ocean Club of Florida; Palm Beach Yacht Club; Trump National Golf Club, Jupiter; Jupiter Island Club; Jupiter Hills Club; Admiral's Cove; Frenchman's Reserve; Frenchman's Creek; Old Port Cove; Jonathan's Landing Golf Club; The Loxahatchee Club; The Dye Preserve Golf Club; Old Marsh Golf Club; Lost Tree Club; Ironhorse Country Club; The Country Club at Mirasol; Eastpointe Country Club; City Club; Old Palm Golf Club; BallenIsles Country Club; The Club at Ibis; The Bear's Club; Governor's Club; Bear Lakes Country Club; The Wellington Club; The Wanderers Club; International Polo Club, Palm Beach; Boca Raton Resort & Club; Royal Palm Yacht & Country Club; Boca West Country Club; St. Andrews Country Club; The Little Club; Woodfield Country Club; The Polo Club of Boca Raton; Boca Woods Country Club; Stonebridge Country Club; Addison Reserve Country Club; Fountains Country Club; Country Club of Florida, Indian Spring Country Club;

Wycliffe Golf & Country Club; Gleneagles Country Club; Stonebridge Country Club; Parkland Golf & Country Club.

INDEPENDENT RESTAURANTS AND CHAINS – PALM BEACH COUNTY

The Breakers; Charley's Crab (3 properties); Chesterfield Hotel; Royal Poinciana Playhouse; The Colony Hotel; Brazilian Court; Taboo; Interlude; Palm Beach Grill; Four Seasons Resort & Hotel; Okeechobee Steakhouse; Lewis Steakhouse; Okeechobee Prime Seafood; Frederic's Steakhouse; Sundy House; PGA Sheraton (now PGA National); Burt Reynold's Dinner Theater; Backstage; The Bistro; Roly's; Buonasera; Spoto's Oyster Bar (3 properties); MacArthur's Vineyard; Jupiter Beach Resort; EVO Italian; Morton's The Steakhouse (5 properties); River House; Gulfstream Hotel; The Ritz Carlton (2 properties); Colonnades Hotel; Marriott Hotels (several); Hyatt Hotels (several); The Buccaneer Restaurant; Café du Parc; Le Pavillon; Bentley's Restaurant; Pelican Café; Zuccarelli's (2 properties); Kitchen; Panama Hattie's; Waterway Café, Crab Pot, Abbey Road (4 properties); The Flame; Holiday Inn (several); Le Café; The Fish Thing; Gallery Grille; Ruth's Chris (2 properties); Capital Grille (2 properties); Lord Chumley's Pub, (2 properties); MacArthur's Vineyard; Paddy Mac's; Harpoon Louie's; Jupiter Crab Company; Paradiso; Sir Loin Pub; Hibiscus; Fathom; Shula's; The Explorers Club; Arezzo; Crab Catcher; Banana Max; Sand Dollar; Café Chardonnay; Chuck & Harold's; City Cellar; Palm Beach Kennel Club; E.R. Bradley's; DeCesare's; Le Café; Basil's Neighborhood Café; The Towers; O'Hara's; Eau Palm Beach; Café Centro; San Remo; Sandpiper Bay; Forté; This is it Pub; The Italian Village; Prime Catch; Banana Boat; The Cook and the Cork.

BEYOND PALM BEACH COUNTY

Key West & The Keys: DiGiorgio's Café Largo; Firefly; Casa Marina; Pier House; Ocean Reef Club; Bagatelle. Cheeca Lodge & Spa; Hawks Cay; Square Grouper; Roostica, The Perry Hotel; Ocean Key Resort.

Ft. Lauderdale:

Café Martorano; Café Seville; The W Hotel; 15th Street Fisheries; Thasos Restaurant.

Deerfield Beach:

Oceans 234, JB's on the Beach.

Miami:

The Forge; Loews Hotel; Red Rooster; Public Square; Ch'i; Root & Bone; Stiltsville Fish Bar; Khong River House; Rusty Pelican.

Naples:

The Club at Barefoot Beach; Royal Poinciana Golf Club.

Tampa:

Seminole Hard Rock Hotel & Casino.

THE IMPORTANCE OF OTHER LANGUAGES

Being employed in the international wine trade necessitates an understanding of imported wine labels, foreign wine growing regions, global cuisine nomenclature, gourmet terminology, and food preparation techniques, etc. I always thought it was important as an American to do my best with foreign languages, starting with my tenure at The Breakers. Having traveled extensively in Europe on wine trips and vacations, I attempted to learn pronunciation of other European languages. My first steps included the old school Berlitz tapes (conversational French, German, and Italian) in my car. There is a lot of travel downtime on the road (intracoastal boat bridges, railroad crossings, traffic jams, etc.) between sales calls.

In addition, over a period of about 4 years, I attended several evening adult education classes at local high schools for those 3 languages mentioned above. These skills were rewarded during meetings and conferences with restaurant owners and hotel food and beverage managers from European countries. The correct pronunciation of wines and regions was also very important as I've educated thousands of restaurant servers, trade personnel, and consumers. My pronunciation credibility was also strengthened in the role of guest speaker at hundreds of multi-course gourmet food/wine pairing events open to the public.

Do your best to be proficient in 1 or more other languages.

A FEW RECOGNITIONS AND PRACTICAL EXPERIENCE WHILE EMPLOYED WITH SGWS

EVENTS AND CERTIFICATIONS IN THE UNITED STATES

(Not in sequence as many overlapped)

* A two-week stint in 1981 working the harvest at Robert Mondavi Winery.

* Charter Member of the Clos du Bois Marlstone Society, (only nationwide 8 consecutive year winner).

   Had a vineyard plot labeled in my honor, and a fermentation tank labeled in my honor.

* Co-owner of 17 planted acres (Hillview Vineyard) with John Bourassa in Napa Valley: 2005 – 2011.

* Society of Wine Educators classes in enology/viticulture at University of California - Davis.

* Attended the Sterling Vineyards Vinicultural Seminar diploma class in Napa Valley.

* Attended Biodiversity University at Sokol Blosser Winery in Dundee, Willamette Valley. Oregon.

* Multi-day Viticultural and Enology seminars at Argyle Winery with Rollin Soles. Enlightening.

* Chateau Ste. Michelle, Cold Creek Club (Charter Member). Woodinville Washington.

* Beringer Vineyards. Restaurant/Hotel Salesperson of the Year. 1999.

* Renwood Winery, Brand Champion. Plymouth, California. 2006.

* Sommelier Guild, multi-year associate member in Fort Lauderdale, FL.

* Court of Master Sommeliers, Certificate Course, Chicago, 1998.

* Instructor at SWS University (Orlando) for three years on French, German, and Austrian segments.

EVENTS AND CERTIFICATIONS IN EUROPE

* Induction into the Burgundy wine society La Confrérie du Chevalier du Tastevin, December 17, 1980.

* Attended the multi-day Deinhard Wine Seminars (twice) in Koblenz, Germany.

* Numerous first-class wine trips with The Chateau & Estate Wines Company (C&E) throughout France.

* Riedel Glass Company: toured all factories in Austria & Germany hosted by Georg Riedel. Amazing.

* French Wine Society: Advanced Bourgogne Training Certificate. (8-hour class with distinction award).

* Epicurean International Association Award.

* Le Comité National des Vins de France, Certificat de Merit.

* Cercle d'Estournel Induction, Cos d'Estournel, St.-Estèphe, Bordeaux France.

* Champagne News and Information Bureau, Diploma.

* Confrérie des Amis de Barton & Guestier, Induction, Bordeaux, France.

PUBLISHING EXPERIENCE WHILE AT SGWS

* Hired as the wine columnist for the **Palm Beach Post**, publishing monthly articles from 1987 – 1991.

* Published Cognac article for **East Side Wine News.**

* Several articles for Mark Ford's **Palm Beach Wealth Builders Club** (including podcasts).

* For 10 years, I composed the bi-annual **Ultra-Premium American Wines Newsletters** for SGWS.

> *Looking back, my favorite wine moment with SWS was on September 20, 1980. It was my first wine trip to Bordeaux, France hosted by Mr. Mel Dick. We were guests of Baron Philippe de Rothschild at Château Mouton Rothschild. At lunch, our small group of ten was treated to a 6-liter bottle of 1919 Château Mouton Rothschild, an extremely rare and exceptional wine, over 40 years ago.*

THE PRESENT RETIREMENT PHASE

Fast forward to January 2020. After 42 years with Southern Glazer's Wine & Spirits (now SGWS after the merger), and five years at The Breakers, I decided to retire. This was not an easy decision, as I reflect on my career essentially as a wine pioneer with both organizations. Making great friends and business partners along the way, scores of domestic and international wine trips, world class gourmet dinners, classic rare wine tastings, and numerous awards and accomplishments made it all worthwhile with no regrets.

A TRIBUTE TO BOB CUILLO

At this point in my autobiography, I would like to offer a memorial to my decades-long, dear friend Bob Cuillo from Palm Beach. He has recently passed, but lived a long and full life. I met Bob in the early 1980s, and through various wine societies and events, we became great friends. He had a very successful career in the car dealership and warranty business, producer of several Broadway plays, restaurateur, pilot, avid wine collector and philanthropist. With his wife Gudrun, they created 2 magnificent wineries in Radda-in-Chianti, Casalvento and Livernano. I am often asked, what was my favorite wine of all time? "That's a very difficult question to answer, but I'm sure whatever that bottle was, it was shared with Bob Cuillo." Rest in Peace, Bob.

POST-RETIREMENT ACTIVITIES

The first project on my retirement bucket list was to author *Wine Q. & A*. Enjoy the journey!

I have also incorporated **Sullivan Wine Consulting, Inc.**, offering private wine education and tutoring classes, corporate events, and gourmet wine dinner speaking engagements. In addition, restaurant/hotel/private club server training classes, wine list construction and formatting changes in preparation for industry awards. Also, and to a limited degree, wine cellar consulting services.

For the last several years, I have partnered with inventor/CEO, Cheryl Gaeta, as Vice-President of research & development, and Board of Directors member, on a project called **KWÄF**. We have 11 worldwide design and utility patents. This cork-sized device is placed in the neck of a bottle, beneath a screw cap. The two options will be winery insertion at the bottling line, and an after-market version available at the retail level. This simplistic device is designed to make the wine taste as the winemaker intended, utilizing the benefits of controlled oxidation via aeration.

HOBBIES AND PASSIONS

Enology & Viticulture

A hobby of sorts, I have spent the last 2 decades or so studying fermentation science and to a lesser degree, viticulture. As a result, the last chapter of this question-and-answer book includes biochemistry, microbiology, and viticultural questions and answers. These are broken down into several headings, consolidating the topics for ease of structured learning.

Motorcycles

I have always been a motorcycle enthusiast, having owned two Hondas (my first 350 cc while at The Breakers, and a 750-four) and two Harley-Davidson's (1976 custom shovelhead, and 1993 EVO engine, soft tail custom described below) combined for over 45 years of riding. Long distance trips include back and forth from Florida to Maine twice, (including the complete multi-state, high-elevation Blue Ridge Parkway and Virginia's Skyline Drive) on one 1 trip, and the other on I-95 (boring) the second time for expediency. Also, the spectacular Rocky Mountains cruising of Colorado and Wyoming, and around San Francisco and northern California. All motorcycle trips in total, I've covered half of the states in the lower 48.

Also, living in Florida, I rode approximately ten times to Daytona Bike Week. The early years in Daytona included ideas for bike customizing, the last few were for partying, once I had my chopper set up the way I wanted. These trophy-winning radical chopper improvements included 18-inch-tall handlebars on top of 4-inch risers, forward controls 4 inches off the frame, custom wide glide forks, complete chromed engine parts, Screamin' Eagle carburation set-up, custom exhaust, old school seat, sissy bar, etc.). A well-designed radical look proportional for a guy 6 feet 5 inches tall.

Automobiles

I guess I could be labeled as an automobile motorhead of sorts as well, having owned in the vicinity of 70 vehicles. In college, I raced my 1966 Pontiac GTO (4-speed Hurst) at a drag strip in Pennsylvania. I recall the track loudspeaker announcer referring to me as the "college boy." (I'm guessing I was not the typical demographic at the drag strip that day). I did not trailer the car to the event, so I monitored the red line during shifts, as I had to drive the car back to school at the end of the races.

For over 20 years, beginning in 1996, I owned a 1988, 4-speed wide-body 911 turbo Porsche (factory model 930). This included trips to the endurance races at both Sebring and Daytona. This was ALWAYS my dream car, and on occasion I raced in the Porsche Club of America track events, and entered it in a Concours d'Élégance.

Gothic Cathedrals

My European passion for decades has always been French Gothic Cathedrals of the 12th & 13th centuries. I have toured scores of them and started a manuscript profiling the majors. During my dozens of wine trips to Europe, I would often leave my hotel about an hour before our wine touring began, and would hire a taxi to escort me around the cities to the local churches and Cathedrals, often stopping for photos.

My first exposure was an amazing 3-hour self-guided tour of Notre-Dame de Paris, my epiphany Cathedral. My very favorite is the majestic Cathédrale Notre-Dame de Reims, and followed closely by Cathédrale Notre-Dame d'Amiens. It constantly amazes me how these magnificent structures could have been constructed so long ago without modern machinery or technology.

On one occasion, while on a Rhine/Mosel wine trip to Germany, we stopped in Cologne. Of course, I had previously studied the Köln Dom and started explaining the external physical structure to other SWS members. Before long, other English-speaking tourists enlarged our group, thinking I was an official Cathedral tour guide. Little did they know!

Mettlach Beer Steins & Landscape Art.

Over the last 40 years I have collected 40 German Mettlach etched beer steins (1/2 liter up to 5.5 liter). All are antiques from the late 1800s and early 1900s. The factory burned down in 1906, so there are no records of existing stein populations. Another passionate hobby includes a large collection of nearly 60 antique European landscape oil paintings in ornate gold frames primarily from the 19th and early 20th centuries.

Other hobbies

I also collect antique wine books, scrimshaw, Porsche die-cast models, Lennox castles, American coins and jigsaw puzzles. I also have studied hundreds of traditional Irish music ballads, interior design concepts and mystery novels. Until recently, I had a unique 33 bottle sealed collection of Cognacs, some from the 1800s. These hobbies will keep me busy during retirement.

MY DAUGHTER, JOANNA

The wine trade is a very social industry, so downtime has always been especially important to me for life's balance. My top blessing along with wife Adele, has always been our daughter, Joanna. I always spent my free time with her while she was growing up. She has been my biggest joy, to say the least. Joanna did undergraduate studies majoring in psychology at Florida State University, then received her master's degree in Mental Health Counseling and Behavioral Medicine from Boston University School of Medicine. She spent the last two years as a school-based clinician working in Boston, and has recently moved to Dallas Texas, again involved in assisting the next generation as as a licensed professional pediatric mental health counselor, (MA, LPC), at Parkland Hospital. We are so proud of her.

MY CHRISTIAN WALK

Growing up in Massachusetts, Boston Irish Catholic was essentially 1 word. As a family, we worshiped in Catholic Church services and Sunday school every week in the 1950's and 1960's. Slowly, all family members drifted away from organized religion. For me, decades later, after following my loving and caring parents lead, I accepted Jesus Christ as my Lord and Savior on September 4, 1979.

That weekend, I was visiting my parents in Lexington MA. and brought a bottle of Château Margaux (one of the top 4 wines in the 1855 classification) 1975 (spectacular vintage) to share with my father. I *absolutely* saw an epiphany wine moment in his eyes, as his brilliant mind keenly observed everything I commented on. He was even astute enough to add intelligent comments of his own. WOW! Never or since, have I felt God so perfectly connect His Grace to my father and me, so early in both of our new Christian lives. I was so blessed to be granted this privilege with my earthly father before he passed. So, honored.

I was well entrenched in Florida by this time, so I bounced around to several houses of worship until I visited First Presbyterian Church in North Palm Beach. It was here that I befriended the pastor (who was my age) Walter B. "Lucky" Arnold III. Lucky is absolutely a Biblical scholar and has comforted thousands of parishioners over the decades. I took part in Lucky's first new members' class. He just retired after 40 years, which mirrored my career of 42 years at Southern Glazer's Wine and Spirits. During services, the elongated vertical east facing stained-glass window artistically displayed a tall grape vine with the mosaic Biblical passage "I am the vine, you are the branches" (John 15:5).

On a side note, the finest book I've read that blends viticulture and Biblical verses is called *Chasing Vines* by famous Biblical scholar, author and lecturer Beth Moore. If you are looking for Biblical references and God's explanations regarding the ancient life-giving attributes of the grape vine, this book is for you.

Thinking back, God has provided and protected me for decades and prayer is a very important part of my day. I've experienced ebbs and flows in my Christian walk, but since retirement over 3 years ago and COVID (although I was never infected), I started a regimen of walking 6 miles or at least 2 hours daily totally immersed in prayer. In addition to my walking prayer time, my daily quiet time includes reading the following: The Bible; *My Upmost For His Highest* (Oswald Chambers); *Draw the Circle* (Mark Batterson); *Seeds of Wisdom* (Dr. Mike Murdock) *The Illustrated Bible, Story by Story* (DK publishing). I so look forward to this time of the day. AMEN. God certainly answers prayer, and creates daily miracles.

I often think back of crewing on a small sailboat leaving Maine and docking in Palm Beach within walking distance from The Breakers, where I would start my wine career, that has lasted 48 years. Only God could have directed this pathway, as he has a master plan for each one of his children.

We must not forget God's first miracle of the transformation of water into WINE at the wedding at Cana.

CONCLUSION

For me, the compelling attraction is that wine is much more than fermented grape juice. The starting point is the complexity of the beverage. The study of wine needs to include an understanding of history, traditions, customs, travel, biochemistry, microbiology, geology, etc., etc. Enjoying wine necessitates camaraderie with others, be it family, strangers who will be your friends, or fellow professionals. These enjoyable times always involve wine's favorite partner, food. It may be appetizers on the patio, or a 10-course gourmet dinner at a 3-star restaurant. Wine makes an ordinary evening very special.

My nearly half-century career in the wine trade has constantly led me to assist others gain wine knowledge, expertise and professionalism. As the next generation matures, learning about wine needs a new format to make an impact on consumers and industry personnel. This book blends the fun of wine question and answers with a concise wine learning educational approach. I hope your future wine education will be as much fun as mine has been.

Good Luck & God Bless.

IN VINO VERITAS

PART I

NORTH AMERICA

UNITED STATES - CANADA - MEXICO

Part 1 of this book starts with North America. The first portion deals with broad questions regarding the United States. Then, the following California segments include (in order) Napa Valley, Sonoma County, Central Coast & Southern California, and inland wine growing areas. The remainder of the chapter includes Oregon, Washington State, and finishes with a few questions on Canada and Mexico.

CHAPTER 1

UNITED STATES

GENERAL QUESTIONS

1 What name did Leif Eriksson give to North America upon discovery?

2 True or False? California is considered an Old-World state because Spanish settlers planted grapes there.

3 According to historical records, where was wine first made in North America?

4 What famous 18th-19th century American planted grapevines on his Virginia estate for winemaking purposes?

5 Name the AVA on the west side of the Blue Ridge Mountains in Virginia.

6 What is considered the oldest branded wine in the United States (US)?

7 Name the first commercial winery in Napa Valley and the year it was founded.

8 Prohibition in America took place during what time span?

---

1 Vineland. (North America is home to more species of native grapes than any other continent.)
2 False. (California is a New World state in a New World country).
3 North Florida by French Huguenot settlers in the 1560s, made from native grapes.
4 Thomas Jefferson, the 3rd US President, at Monticello. There is no record stating he made wine.
5 Shenandoah Valley AVA. (Most of the other vineyards are on the east side of the Blue Ridge range.)
6 Virginia Dare, established in North Carolina in 1835 by the Garrett Brothers.
7 Charles Krug, 1861. Krug was a German immigrant. The winery was purchased in 1943 by the Mondavi family.
8 1920-1933. (The comedian W.C. Fields said, "During Prohibition, I was forced to live on food and water only".)

9 Prohibition resulted from the 19th Act of Congress known as what?

10 What was the first new winery constructed in Napa Valley after Prohibition and in what year?

11 What is the official term for a designated wine-growing region in the US?

12 What was the first AVA so designated in the US?

13 What state produces the most wine in the US?

14 What percentage of American wine is produced in California?

15 As of 2021, how many wineries are there in the US? 2,710 - 5,420 - 8,106 - 11,053 - 14,511.

16 What major wine producing state is located just south of Washington State?

17 True or False? Rosé wines from California may be made from any wine grape grown there.

18 True or False? More rosé wine is made from Cabernet Sauvignon in the US than from any other variety.

19 Who created the popular wine brand known as "Two Buck Chuck?"

20 What are the four most widely grown white wine varieties in California?

21 What are the four most widely grown red wine varieties in California?

22 Which famous wine producer is out of place here? Bronco, Constellation, Gallo, Silver Oak.

---

9 The Volstead Act. (A loophole allowed to the production of wine for sacramental and medicinal purposes.)

10 Robert Mondavi Winery, 1966. Robert left Charles Krug after a family dispute and founded his own winery.

11 American Viticultural Area (AVA.) These are approved by the US Alcohol and Tobacco Tax and Trade Bureau (TTB.)

12 Augusta, Missouri (15 square miles in size, granted in June 1980, eight months before Napa Valley).

13 California. If California were a country, it would be the 4th largest wine producing country in the world.

14 85-90%. California is first by a large margin, followed by Washington, Oregon and New York.

15 11,053. For comparison, in 1975, the number was 579.

16 Oregon, which has a cool climate influenced by the Pacific Ocean. Pinot Noir, a cool climate variety, is the most planted.

17 False. Dark skinned or dark fleshed varieties are necessary for color extraction.

18 False. Rosé is made from a numerous varieties in the US, but Cabernet Sauvignon is not among the most common.

19 Fred Franzia. The retailer Trader Joe's has sold over a billion bottles of the wine, officially labeled Charles Shaw, since 2002.

20 1: Chardonnay 2: Colombard 3: Pinot Grigio 4: Sauvignon Blanc. Colombard, widely used in generic wines, is seldom seen on a label.

21 1: Cabernet Sauvignon 2: Pinot Noir 3: Zinfandel 4: Merlot. Pinot Noir acreage increased dramatically since the movie "Sideways" in 2004.

22 Silver Oak, a medium-sized winery making 100,000 cases of wine a year. The others produce many millions of cases of wine annually.

23 True or False? California red blends may only be made from Zinfandel and Cabernet Sauvignon grapes.

24 Meiomi is a popular wine brand. What is the derivation of the name?

25 Founded in 1874, since 1948, Sutter Home Winery has been owned by what family?

26 Who started the juggernaut Kendall-Jackson Winery in 1982?

27 Name the wine brand created by Sean McKenzie and musician Dave Matthews.

28 Nicknamed the "Breadbasket of California", what large AVA is home to about 80% of grapes grown in California?

29 Many hillside Napa Valley vineyards yield 1-2 tons of grapes per acre. What is normal for the Central Valley?

30 How many wineries are operating in Virginia currently? 54 – 110 - 220 – 300 - 450.

31 Which "B" winery is not in Virginia? Breaux; Biltmore; Boxwood; Blenheim; Barboursville.

32 The Trump family owns a winery in Charlottesville, Virginia. What was the original name of the winery?

33 Approximately how many wineries are in New York (NY)? 200 – 300 – 400 – 500 - 600.

34 True or False? More than 10 wineries are currently operating on Long Island.

35 In what AVA are most of Long Island's wineries located?

36 Which of the following wineries are on the North Fork: Bedell; Channing Daughters; Duck Walk; Macari.

37 What descriptive aromatic word is often used to describe native American (vitis Labrusca) grapes like Concord?

---

23 False. (Any winery may use any red grapes to make red blends).

24 *Meiomi* means "coast" in the Native American Wappo tribal language.

25 The Trinchero Family. (The family has added scores of quality properties in recent years).

26 Jess Jackson. (An attorney, the late Jess fell in love with wine; now wife Barbara Banke is in charge).

27 The Dreaming Tree. (With a California appellation, a wide variety of wines are made, including *Crush*).

28 The Central Valley. (Extending from Sacramento & Lodi south to Fresno. ≈ 50 miles wide X ≈ 400 miles long).

29 Up to 12 tons per acre is not uncommon here where typically, quantity is prioritized over quality.

30 There are currently more than 300 wineries in Virginia.

31 Biltmore Estate Winery, located in Asheville, North Carolina.

32 Kluge Estate Winery. (My good friend Patricia Kluge created this beautiful estate before selling to Trump).

33 400. These are located primarily on Long Island and in the Finger Lakes, both of which have several AVAs.

34 True. (Currently there are close to 90).

35 The North Fork AVA. (It is more sheltered from Atlantic Ocean weather patterns and land is affordable).

36 Bedell and Macari. (The other two are in The Hamptons AVA, the South Fork of Long Island).

37 Foxy. (This describes animal or earthy aromas. *OR* was it that simply that foxes liked eating the grapes)?

38 In the 1950s, who wrote a PhD dissertation asserting that European (vitis Vinifera) grapes could thrive in upstate NY?

39 Which of the following lakes are part of the Finger Lakes? Canandaigua; Cayuga; Champlain; Erie; Seneca; Tahoe

40 What is the oldest still-operating winery in America?

41 What was the first winery to set up shop on the North Fork of Long Island?

42 Where is Benmarl Winery located?

43 True or False? Most wine is approximately 60% water.

44 The study and science of grape growing is called what?

45 The study of winemaking is called what?

46 What is the foremost higher education facility of viticulture and enology in the US?

47 What two families from Germany started their respective California wineries in 1876 and 1883?

48 True or False? Robert Mondavi started his career in Sonoma County, then moved to Napa Valley.

49 In what AVA is Jordan Vineyards and Winery located?

50 What does the word *Meritage* mean? (It rhymes with *Heritage*).

51 What varieties may be used to make a red Meritage wine?

52 What varieties are used in white Meritage wines?

53 Which winery was first to release a blended red wine labeled Meritage?

---

38 Dr. Konstantin Frank. (Born in the Ukraine, he moved to Keuka Lake in the Finger Lakes and started a winery).

39 Canandaigua, Cayuga and Seneca.

40 Brotherhood Winery in Washingtonville, New York. (Established in 1839).

41 Hargrave. (In 1973 by Louisa and Alex Hargrave, located on an old potato farm in Cutchogue).

42 In the town of Marlboro in the Hudson River AVA in New York.

43 False. (Closer to 85% water. The balance is alcohol, and chemical compounds dictating aroma and taste).

44 Viticulture. (Grape growing and vineyard care is the starting point for creating great wine).

45 Enology. (This embraces fermentation science including biochemistry and microbiology).

46 University of California, Davis. (Others include Cornell, Fresno State, Oregon State and Washington State).

47 Beringer in Napa Valley (1876) and Wente in Livermore Valley (1883).

48 False. (He started at his family's Charles Krug Winery in Napa. He founded Robert Mondavi Winery in 1966).

49 Alexander Valley in Sonoma County.

50 A made-up word blending *Merit & Heritage*, It refers to a blended red or white made from Bordeaux varieties.

51 Any of the approved Bordeaux varieties Cabernet Sauvignon, Cabernet Franc, Malbec, Merlot and Petit Verdot.

52 Sauvignon Blanc and Sémillon. (In Bordeaux, Muscadelle may also be used, but not much is grown in the US).

53 The 1985 *Meritage* by Dry Creek Vineyard in Sonoma County.

54 *Eroica* is a joint venture between Chateau Ste. Michelle and Dr. Ernst Loosen. What is the grape variety?

55 When phylloxera ravaged California vineyards in the 1980s, who suffered the most? Monterey, Napa or Sonoma?

56 True or False? The Knights Valley AVA is in the southern part of Napa Valley.

57 The North Coast AVA is made up from what 6 nested AVAs?

58 What is the smallest AVA in California?

59 What two Napa Valley wineries beat the best of France in the famous *Judgment of Paris* blind tasting in 1976?

60 What does not belong? Bacigalupi; Bancroft; Sbragia; Robert Young; Durell; Dutton.

61 True or False? Wild Horse Winery & Vineyards is based in the Wild Horse AVA.

62 True or False? It is too hot and dry to make wine in Arizona, New Mexico and Texas.

63 Name the first two modern wineries in Texas, dating to the early 1970s?

64 Approximately how many wineries are in Texas now? 100; 200; 300; 400; 500.

65 Approximately how many wineries are in New Mexico?

66 What is the best-known sparkling wine producer in New Mexico?

67 Approximately how many wineries are in Arizona currently? 45; 60; 95; 120; 135.

68 What do the 2 wineries *Sandhi* (run by Rajat Parr & Sashi Moorman) and *Dana* (run by Hi Sang Lee) have in common?

---

54 Riesling. (Eroica is the name of Beethoven's 3rd symphony).

55 Napa Valley. (Every vineyard planted on AxR1 rootstock was replanted at an approximate cost of $4-5 billion.

56 False. (Knights Valley is in Sonoma County).

57 Napa, Sonoma, Mendocino, Solano, Marin, and Lake Counties. (Many blends use grapes from several counties).

58 Cole Ranch AVA. (A quarter of a square mile and 160 planted acres within Mendocino County).

59 Stag's Leap Wine Cellars for the Cabernet Sauvignon 1973, and Chateau Montelena for the Chardonnay 1973.

60 Sbragia. (Ed Sbragia was Beringer's winemaker for decades; the others are vineyard sites).

61 False. (The winery is in Templeton in the Central Coast, and Wild Horse AVA is in Napa Valley. (Confusing).

62 False. These states have a winemaking history dating to colonial times, and many high-quality wineries today.

63 Pheasant Ridge & Llano Estacado. (Both are in the High Plains area, near the city of Lubbock, Texas).

64 500 wineries. (This number continues to grow beyond the High Plains into the Texas Hill country).

65 60. (Most at higher elevations with cool nighttime temperatures suitable for growing wine grapes).

66 Gruet Winery. (Made from the Champagne Method, production began 1984 and is linked to Champagne Gruet).

67 ≈ 120 wineries. (Arizona's 2 AVAs regions are Willcox and Sonoita).

68 Both names are from the Sanskrit language. Shandi means *Collaboration* and Dana *The Spirit of Generosity.*

69 What are the first names of these notable American women in wine (no order sequence.)

(Due to space limitations, apologies to those many notable, pioneering women in wine not mentioned here.)

____ Edwards; ____ Meredith; ____ Graf; ____ Long; ____ Sokol Blosser; ____ Cakebread.

70 ____ Turley; ____ Colgin; ____ Corison; ____ Dyer: ____ Davis; ____ Spinelli; ____ Seysses.

71 ____ Dalla Valle; ____ Viader; ____ Sterling; ____ Lail; ____ Davenport; ____ Pruss.

72 ____ Barrett; ____ Phillips; ____ Crane; ____ Klein; ____ Stackhouse;

____ Rudd; ____ Joseph.

73 ____ Crouse; ____ Van Staaveren; ____ Janssens; ____ Moller-Racke;

____ Gallo; ____ Torres; ____ Crowe

74 ____ Noble; ____ Vianna; ____ Pagano; ____ Novak; ____ Peschon; ____ Curran.

75 ____ Keplinger; ____ Nicholls; ____ Starr; ____ Myers; ____ Hepworth; ____ Joseph.

76 ____ Welch; ____ Masyczek.

69 *Merry* Edwards; *Carole* Meredith; *Mary Ann* Graf; *Zelma* Long; *Susan* Sokol Blosser; *Rosemary/Karen* Cakebread.

70 *Helen* Turley; *Ann* Colgin; *Cathy* Corison; *Dawnine* Dyer; *Jill* Davis; *Darice* Spinelli; *Diana Snowden* Seysses.

71 *Naoko* Dalla Valle; *Delia* Viader; *Joy* Sterling; *Robin* Lail; *Margaret* Davenport; *Nicki* Pruss.

72 *Heidi Peterson* Barrett; *Jean* Philips; *Eileen* Crane; *Mia* Klein; *Melissa* Stackhouse; *Samantha* Rudd; *Kathy* Joseph.

73 *Karen* Crouse; *Margo* Van Staaveren; *Geneviève* Janssens; *Anne* Moller-Racke; *Gina* Gallo; *Marimar* Torres; *Alison* Crowe.

74 *Ann* Noble; *Elizabeth* Vianna; *Janet* Pagano; *Beth* Novak; *Françoise* Peschon; *Kris* Curran.

75 *Helen* Keplinger; *Kimberlee* Nicholls; *Pam* Starr; *Janet* Myers; *Ashley* Hepworth: *Kathy* Joseph.

76 Both are *Celia*.

CALIFORNIA

NAPA VALLEY

77   In 2007 Karen Crouse was growing grapes and started making wine in 2009. Name her Winery?

78   True or False? Napa Valley AVA is the 3rd largest volume wine region in California.

79   Who was the first person to plant wine grapes in the Napa Valley?

80   Fumé Blanc from California is made using which grape?

81   Approximately how many different grapes are grown in Napa Valley AVA?

82   Decades ago, wines could carry the name *Napa Gamay* on the label. What is the official name of the grape?

83   Napa Valley AVA has how many nested AVAs contained within its boundaries?

84   Approximately what percentage of all wine produced in California comes from Napa Valley?

---

77   Mount Veeder Magic Vineyards. (Karen is certainly a voice in Napa Valley as a resident for almost 30 years)

78   False. (It is one of the smallest wine regions by volume, but by far the most famous one).

79   George Calvert Yount. (After receiving the Rancho Caymus land grant in 1836, Napa Valley became his home).

80   Sauvignon Blanc. (Robert Mondavi coined the term in 1966, changing from a sweet style to a dry style).

81   ≈ 40 grapes. (Many wineries are experimenting with new and different grapes especially with climate change).

82   Valdiguie. (Native to France, but once popular and still grown in California today).

83   16. (These are located throughout the valley on both hillsides east and west and on the valley floor).

84   4 - 5%. (Although the most famous wine region in California, it is quite small in terms of production).

85 What are the two mountain ranges that frame the Napa Valley?

86 Name the three mountain AVAs on the Mayacamas Range.

87 Name the two mountain AVAs on the Vaca Range.

88 What Native American people occupied the Napa Valley long before white settlers?

89 The Wappo called the valley Napa, meaning what?

90 What are the 2 major north-south roads in Napa Valley?

91 Who is considered the "The Dean of California Winemakers"?

92 The famous Three Palms Vineyard is owned by what winery?

93 How large is the Three Palms Vineyard?

94 Who was the founding winemaker at Duckhorn Vineyards?

95 Which winery is located on the east side of Highway 29? Inglenook; Far Niente; Whitehall Lane; Sequoia Grove; Staglin.

96 Which winery is located on the west side of Highway 29? Vineyard 29; Markham; Freemark Abbey; Ehlers Estate; Heitz.

97 Which winery is on west side of the Silverado Trail? Regusci; Clos du Val; Pine Ridge; Husic; Chimney Rock; Steltzner.

98 True or False? Chiles Valley AVA is in the Mayacamas foothills.

99 Which winery is out of place? O'Shaughnessy; Robert Craig; Outpost; J. Davies; Black Sears; La Jota; Cimarossa.

100 Which winery was founded earlier? Stag's Leap Wine Cellars or Stags' Leap Winery.

---

85 *The Mayacamas Mountains* on the west side, and the *Vaca Mountains* on the east side.

86 Mt. Veeder AVA; Spring Mountain District AVA; Diamond Mountain District AVA. (Moving from south to north).

87 Atlas Peak AVA; Howell Mountain AVA. (Moving from south to north).

88 The Wappo. (The Robert Mondavi Winery owns Wappo Hill Vineyard, on the Vaca range).

89 The term *Napa* translates to *Land of Plenty* in English.

90 *Highway 29* on the west side of the valley (more heavily traveled), and the *Silverado Trail* on the east side.

91 André Tchelistcheff. (Born in Moscow in 1901, he worked at Beaulieu Vineyard, then consulted for many).

92 Duckhorn. (At one time ownership was split between Sterling Vineyards and Dan and Margret Duckhorn).

93 83 acres. (The Selby Creek outwash created the alluvial fan and is covered with volcanic stones).

94 Tom Rinaldi. (Tom's first job was Freemark Abbey, then Duckhorn for 22 vintages. (After: Provenance & Hewitt).

95 Sequoia Grove. (Founded in 1979 under a grove of Sequoia trees in Rutherford).

96 Vineyard 29. (Wineries on the west side are still allowed to plant vineyards at higher elevations).

97 Pine Ridge. (Pine Ridge sits atop a knoll on the west side; the others approach the Vaca Range on the east).

98 False. (It is part of the Vaca Range on the east side of the valley).

99 J. Davies. (They are in the Diamond Mountain District AVA; the others are in Howell Mountain AVA).

100 Stags' Leap Winery. (In 1893, it was a retreat for guests from San Francisco and beyond).

101 Who founded Stag's Leap Wine Cellars?

102 Which winery was winemaker Mark Herold not involved in? Merus; Buccella; Kobalt; Hesten; Ovid; Harris; Story.

103 Speaking of Ovid winery, located on a 15-acre estate on Pritchard Hill, name two of the wines they make.

104 Trinchero Napa Valley makes a Cabernet Sauvignon labeled *BRV*. What do these letters signify?

105 Monticello Winery on Big Ranch Road in eastern Napa Valley is modeled after which other American structure?

106 Where has winemaker Ehren Jordan not worked? Turley Cellars; Joseph Phelps; Failla; Inniskillin; Jean-Luc Colombo.

107 What are the 2 most affordable Cabernet Sauvignon wines produced by Stag's Leap Wine Cellars?

108 Name the two more expensive Cabernet Sauvignon wines produced by Stag's Leap Wine Cellars

109 Stag's Leap Wine Cellars makes a wine called Artemis. Where does the name come from?

110 Name the 2 members of the winemaking team at Cornerstone Cellars?

111 Name the winery started by the viticulturalist that worked at Sterling; Screaming Eagle; Dalla Valle; Trefethen; etc.

112 Where did Robert Foley not work? Pride Mountain; Hourglass; Switchback Ridge; Rudd; Paloma; Heitz, Markham.

113 Who wrote the poem on the large barrel billboard viewed when entering the valley from the south?

114 What is the *other wine* produced by Opus One?

---

101 Warren Winiarski. (He started the winery in 1970 on the Silverado Trail in Napa Valley).

102 Ovid. (The winemaker at this prestigious estate is Austin Peterson. Mark worked at all of the other wineries).

103 Ovid Napa Valley; Hexameter; Loc. Cit. (Loco Citato); Syrah; Experiment. (Yearly changed red & white blends).

104 Bob, Roger, & Vera Trinchero. (Family members currently in charge, but the next generation is involved).

105 Thomas Jefferson's home. (The Corley family designed the winery after Jefferson's iconic Virginia estate).

106 Inniskillin. (Failla is the owner/winemaker's project with his wife Anne-Marie Failla based in St. Helena).

107 *Artemis*. (Napa Valley blend); & *FAY Vineyard*. (The 66 acres in were planted in 1961 by Nathan Fay).

108 *S.L.V.* (Stag's Leap Vineyard, 35 acres); & *Cask 23*. (A blend of FAY Vineyard & S.L.V. estate grapes).

109 Artemis is the Greek goddess of the hunt. (Wines Karia and Aveta also refer to Greek mythology).

110 *Charles Thomas*. (Robert Mondavi; Rudd; Quintessa, Faust). *Kari Auringer*. (Worked with 1st W/M Celia Welch).

111 Renteria Wines. (Great success story of Salvador, a hard-working Mexican farm worker from the 1960s).

112 Rudd. (Founded by the late Leslie Rudd, but Robert Foley worked at the other wineries).

113 Robert Louis Stevenson. (Author of *Silverado Squatters*, a memoir of his honeymoon to Napa Valley in 1880).

114 Overture. (This wine is a multi-vintage red blend from Napa Valley. Originally only sold at the winery).

115 After a recent winery relocation, name the winery started by Abe Schoener in Napa Valley?

116 It is unusual for 2 AVAs to overlap. Name the AVA that straddles southern Napa Valley & southern Sonoma County?

117 True or False? The Sterling Vineyards Winery is located on the valley floor in Carneros.

118 What person has been inextricably linked to Markham Vineyards for the last several decades?

119 What elaborately decorated winery in Napa Valley shows influences inspired by ancient Persia?

120 Who said, "Making good wine is a skill, making fine wine is an art""

121 Name the vineyard on Spring Mountain first planted in the 1880s, then with Pinot Noir by John Daniel Jr. in the 1950s.

122 In 1888 a northern Napa Valley winery was constructed and was called A. L. Tubbs winery. What is it called now?

123 Conn Creek Winery was founded in 1973 by Bill & Kathy Collins. What is the flagship Cabernet Sauvignon called?

124 Dr. Crane is a very famous and historic vineyard in St. Helena. Which winery occupies the original home?

125 Soil scientists categorize 12 orders of soil taxonomy worldwide. How many does Napa Valley have?

126 What year was Caymus founded and by whom?

127 Tom Eddy and his wife Kerry, founded their eponymous Calistoga winery in what year?

128 In the mid-1990s several expensive and highly collectable wines began to be known as *"Cult Wines"*. Name a few.

129 Name the famous ultra-premium red blend produced by Joseph Phelps?

115 The Scholium Project. (Abe has a Ph.D. in Greek hence the name. Modest endeavor – Simple).
116 Carneros. (Carneros AVA receives cool air and fog from San Pablo Bay, ideal for Pinot Noir and Chardonnay).
117 False. (Access to Sterling Vineyards requires a cable car ride in Calistoga).
118 Bryan Del Bondio. (Bruce Markham hired Bryan in 1978, a recent graduate of University California, Davis).
119 Darioush. (Khaledi Darioush is of Iranian descent).
120 Robert Mondavi. (He spent decades promoting the importance of food/wines/friends).
121 School House Vineyard. (Daniel obtained budwood from the Domaine de la Romanée-Conti).
122 Chateau Montelena. (This resembles a medieval castle, and features wine caves carved into the mountain).
123 Anthology. (Conn Creek is unique as they source fruit from nearly every AVA in Napa Valley).
124 Salvestrin Winery. (The vineyard was planted in 1859, and the Three D bottling is named after his 3 daughters).
125 6. (This is amazing because Napa Valley is only 29 miles long and 1-4 miles wide).
126 1972 by Charlie Wagner. (Caymus specializes in Cabernet Sauvignon and is today run by Chuck, son of Charlie.)
127 1991. (Based in Napa Valley, Tom Eddy now makes wine in several other regions as well).
128 Screaming Eagle; Harlan Estate; Bryant Family; Colgin Cellars; Araujo Estate.
129 Insignia. (In 1974, Phelps created California's first proprietary red Bordeaux-styled blend).

130 The Antinori family from Tuscany has invested in the Napa Valley. Name their first winery venture.

131 Nickel & Nickel Winery is owned by which older winery originally founded in 1885?

132 The vineyard for Far Niente Estate Chardonnay was planted with clones from what famous vineyard in Burgundy?

133 Who is the director of winemaking at Turley Wine Cellars?

134 Duckhorn Wine Company has added Calera and Kosta Browne to their portfolio. Name the other 5 "DUCK" properties?

135 Ghost Block Estate Wines was named after a famous Napa Valley pioneer. Who was it?

136 Name the owner of the famous "Sacrashe Vineyard" in Napa Valley?

137 Which is out of place? Diamond Creek Vineyards; Bryant Family; Jordan Vineyards; Cade; Dyer; St. Supéry; Laird Family.

138 In what AVA is Larry Hyde's (Hyde & Sons) Vineyard Estate located?

139 Which winery is not based in Carneros? Kent Rasmussen; Truchard; Saintsbury; Frazier; Bouchaine; Madonna; Etude.

140 A winery-based TV show that ran for 9 seasons (1981 - 1990) was called Falcon Crest. It was filmed at which winery?

141 Spring Mountain Vineyard is an 845-acre vineyard first planted in 1873. Name 2 of the 3 estates located here.

142 What Napa Valley Winery is named for the French term for maceration?

143 *Illumination* is a Sauvignon Blanc-based blend made by which winery?

144 Name the two original partners that formed Opus One, Napa Valley?

---

130 Antica. (Anti for the Antinori name, Ca for California. This is a high elevation estate on Atlas Peak).

131 Far Niente. (Gil & Beth Nickel purchased the historic property in 1979, the Nickel & Nickel winery came later).

132 Corton-Charlemagne. (These vineyard cuttings were shared with Far Niente over 30 years ago).

133 Tegan Passalacqua. (He and his team make 47 wines from over 50 vineyards, primarily old vine Zinfandel).

134 Paraduxx; Goldeneye, Migration; Decoy; Canvasback, and of course Duckhorn itself.

135 George Yount, Yountville founder. Legend says his ghost occasionally rises from his grave to admire the village).

136 Hall Vineyards. (Craig & Kathryn Hall purchased it in 1995 and is in Rutherford. Read her book: *A Perfect Score*).

137 Jordan Vineyards. (Jordan's Cabernet Sauvignon is from Alexander Valley; the others are in Napa Valley).

138 Carneros. (The 150-acre vineyard supplies fruit for their own wine as well as that of other wineries).

139 Frazier. (Frazier is located slightly northeast in Coombsville AVA).

140 Spring Mountain Vineyard. (Located in the town of St. Helena. The evening soap opera was a huge success).

141 *La Perla*. (Draper Vineyards,); *Miravalle. (257 acres); Chateau Chevalier. (120 acres).*

142 Cuvaison. (Maceration, or juice left in contact with grapeskins, adds color, tannin and more to the wine).

143 Quintessa. (A spectacular winery/vineyard in Napa Valley. *Illumination* is a blend of Napa and Sonoma fruit).

144 *Robert Mondavi* and *Baron Philippe de Rothschild*, owner of Château Mouton Rothschild, Pauillac, Bordeaux.

145 Which two winemakers shared duties for producing Opus One in the early years?

146 Franciscan Vineyards makes a Bordeaux blend called *Magnificat*. What is the significance of the name?

147 What was the first vintage of Opus One?

148 Domaine Carneros is owned by which company?

149 Henrik Poulsen is the current winemaker at Alpha Omega. Name his two winemaking consultants.

150 What is the name of the white wine blend produced at Inglenook Vineyard?

151 What winery produces Bouche d'Or? What is the bottle size in which it is packaged?

152 Hillside Select from Shafer Vineyards is one of Napa Valley's top wines. What were its previous names?

153 Shafer Vineyards makes several wines. What is out of place? Relentless, Red Shoulder Ranch, Block C, One Point Five.

154 The sophisticated Vineyard 29 has a very appropriate address in Napa Valley. What is it?

155 Which winery produces "Finch Hollow Vineyard" Chardonnay?

156 Who was the founder of the original Inglenook Vineyard in Napa Valley?

157 Tamber Bey Vineyards makes wine in Calistoga and Yountville. What is the origin of the name?

158 Which name does not belong? Heidi Barrett, Helen Turley, Genevieve Janssens, Mia Klein, Celia Masyczek.

159 What two families started Silver Oak Winery? The first winery was in Napa Valley, and later, Alexander Valley.

---

145 Tim *Mondavi* (son of Robert) and *Patrick Léon* (wine director at Château Mouton Rothschild).

146 It is named for J.S. Bach's 1723 master chorus piece for 5 voices. (Referencing the 5 grapes in the blend).

147 1979. (The original 6-bottle wooden case contained 2 bottles of the 1979 and 4 bottles of the 1980 vintages).

148 Taittinger. (This beautiful property was inspired by Taittinger's Château de la Marquetterie in Champagne).

149 *Jean Hoeflinger*. (Ex-official winemaker at Alpha Omega), and *Michel Rolland*. (International wine consultant).

150 Blancaneaux. (This wine blends traditional Rhône Valley white grapes Marsanne, Roussanne and Viognier).

151 Bouchaine. 500 ml. (Bouche d'Or is a late-harvest Chardonnay from Carneros).

152 Sunspot Vineyard, John's Block 7, Reserve Cabernet Sauvignon, then Hillside Select.

153 Block C. (This is a superior vineyard parcel at Shafer, but it is not used as a marketing name).

154 2929 Route 29. (Home to Vineyard 29 Estate Wines, Aida Estate wines, and Cru Wines).

155 Jarvis Vineyards (a Napa Valley landmark with spectacular underground aging caves).

156 Gustave Niebaum. (A Finnish sea captain, he settled in Rutherford and started a winery in 1879).

157 Barry & Carol Waitte are horse people. 2 of their horses are Tamborino & Bayamo (Deux Chevaux Vineyard).

158 They all belong. (A cast of some of the most well-established winemakers in Napa Valley and beyond).

159 *Justin Meyer*. (Franciscan Vineyards founder) and *Richard Twomey Duncan*.

160 Carl Doumani purchased the historic Stags' Leap Winery in 1971. After selling, what was his next winery called?

161 Lillian Disney (daughter of Walt) daughter Dianne, and son-in-law Ron Miller, started what winery in Napa Valley?

162 The second wine from Dominus Estate is called what?

163 Who was the original owner of the Napanook Vineyard, located in today's Yountville AVA?

164 Fast forward to 1982. Who were the next owners of Napanook?

165 *8 Years in the Desert* is a wine made by Dave Phinney. Why did he choose this name for the wine?

166 What is the hottest and wettest AVA in Napa Valley?

167 Chimney Rock Winery in Stags Leap District produces a wine called *Elevage* (red & white). What does that term mean?

168 What is the oldest continuously operated winery in Napa Valley?

169 Charles Krug Winery makes a red Bordeaux blend called what?

170 The Prisoner Wine Company: What is out of place? Thorn; Saldo; Snitch; Cuttings; Jailhouse; Erased; Blindfold; Headlock.

171 A family split occurred between Robert and Peter Mondavi in 1966. What wine re-unified their families in 2007?

172 There are 2 vineyards in Napa Valley called Eisele Vineyards. What is the difference?

173 Cakebread Cellars was started by Jack and Delores Cakebread in 1973. In which AVA is the winery located?

174 Which wine is not produced by Cakebread? Cuttings Wharf; Breadcake Estate; Suscol Springs; Dancing Bear Ranch.

---

160 Quixote. (Also in the Stags Leap District, this whimsical, eccentric winery was later sold to a Chinese company).

161 Silverado Vineyards. (Founded in 1981, winemaker Jon Emmerich has been in charge since 1990).

162 *Napanook*. (Named for the historic vineyard estate vineyard).

163 George Yount. (He planted the vineyard 1836. John Daniel Jr. owner of Inglenook, purchased it in 1946).

164 Robin Lail and Marcia Smith, daughters of John Daniel, and Christian Moueix (now the solo owner).

165 After selling *The Prisoner,* he agreed not to make a Zinfandel for 8 years. The cavalry has arrived.

166 Calistoga AVA. (It also has the largest summer diurnal shift; on extreme days, nearly 60 degrees).

167 The French term *Elevage* refers to the maturation time between fermentation and bottling.

168 Charles Krug, founded 1861. Cesare Mondavi (father of Robert and Peter) purchased the winery in 1943).

169 Generations. (The name pays homage to the Mondavi family's history).

170 Jailhouse. (Although this series has dark implications, Jailhouse is not one of their wines, YET!).

171 Ancora Una Volta, *One More Time* in Italian. (This very limited production wine was served at the South Beach Wine & Food Festival in 2007 with the brothers in attendance).

172 The Milt Eisele Vineyard is in Calistoga AVA. Volker Eisele Vineyard is in Chiles Valley AVA.

173 Rutherford AVA. (The next generation is Dennis and Bruce, continuing the dream of their parents).

174 Breadcake Estate. (This is a made-up play on words, and the others are established bottlings).

175 Which winery hired viticulturalist David Abreu to replant the old S. Anderson property in Stags Leap District AVA?

176 Clos du Val Winery was founded by John & Henrietta Goelet in 1972. Who was the first winemaker?

177 In 1979 Randy & Lisa Dunn started Dunn Vineyards. What are the two wines they make?

178 Which Napa Valley winery was founded by a gentleman who raced automobiles in Europe & Indy cars from 1983-1991?

179 Flora Springs Winery makes several wines. Which is out of place? Holy Smoke; Smooth Sailing; Wild Boar; Out of Sight.

180 Which wine is *not* part of the Orin Swift portfolio? Palermo; Scrimshaw; Machete; Mercury Head; Papillon; Abstract.

181 Can you name 3 *more* wines from the Orin Swift portfolio?

182 Who is the owner of Orin Swift, and how was the name derived?

183 Which winery owns the following vineyards? Haystack; Cloud's Nest; Central Park West; Mary's; Mario's, Vera's.

184 Z.D. is a famous winery in Napa Valley. What do the letters signify?

185 What was the original name of Trefethen winery? What year did the Trefethen family purchase it?

186 Who was the first winemaker at Spottswoode?

187 Snowden Vineyards in Napa Valley is also the owner of which Burgundy Domaine?

188 Which Napa Valley winery has created the label *Oracle*?

189 In 1943-44, Lee Stewart bought an old winery on Howell Mountain. Who was the first winemaker, in 1958?

---

175 Cliff Lede. (They named the vineyard blocks after rock songs. My Generation, Dark Side of the Moon, etc.)

176 Bernard Portet. (His father was technical director at Château Lafite).

177 Cabernet Sauvignon, Howell Mountain, & Cabernet Sauvignon, Napa Valley.

178 Lewis Cellars. (Randy Lewis received the #1 "Wine in the World" by the Wine Spectator for his 2016 vintage).

179 Smooth Sailing. (This is made-up, and the others are Cabernet Sauvignon vineyards).

180 Scrimshaw. (The art of decoratively carving whalebone and teeth).

181 Slander; Trigger Finger; Veladora; Blank Stare; Mute; China Doll; Mannequin; 8 Years in the Dessert.

182 David Swift Phinney. *Orin* is his father's middle name, and *Swift* is his mother's maiden name.

183 Trinchero Family Estates. (The historic wine family owns over 250 acres throughout Napa Valley.)

184 Gino Zepponi & Norman DeLeuze. (Started in 1969, the next generations are taking over winery operation).

185 Eschol. 1968. (This historic winery was designed by Hamden W. McIntyre in 1886).

186 Tony Soter. (Tony worked at 12 of the finest wineries in Napa, before starting Soter Vineyards in Oregon).

187 Domaine Dujac. (Jacques and wife Diana Snowden Seysses (enologist) have busy schedules).

188 Miner Family Vineyards. (This is a Bordeaux blend from the "Stagecoach Vineyard").

189 Mike Grgich. (The property, called Château Souverain, was later relocated to Sonoma County).

190 The old Napa Château Souverain winery was renamed what in the early 1970s?

191 Cain Vineyard & Winery is located where in Napa Valley?

192 Speaking of Cain, name the 3 wines they produce.

193 Describe the biggest climatic benefit that Napa Valley receives from the proximity of the Vaca Mountains.

194 Describe the biggest viticultural benefit that the Mayacamas Mountain range performs.

195 Who was the founder of B.V. (Beaulieu Vineyards), & in what year was the winery founded?

196 What does Beaulieu (Vineyards) translate from French?

197 Hanns Kornell Champagne Cellars was started in 1958 at the old 1884 Larkmead Winery. Who was the next owner?

198 Flora Springs makes two flagship wines. What are the wines, and grape compositions?

199 Donn & Molly Chappellet started their winery in Napa Valley. Where is their winery located, and when was it founded?

200 In addition to Chappellet, name two other wineries on Pritchard Hill?

201 Who was first Napa Valley winemaker to receive a perfect 100 score from Robert Parker Jr.?

202 Bruce Neyers had careers at Mayacamas and Phelps, and now Neyers. Where did his wife Barbara work in Berkeley?

203 Which winemaker consulted with Lail, Vineyard 29, Dominus, DANA, Moone-Tsai, etc. and now has his own winery?

204 What was the original name of the winery that Tim Mondavi purchased, now called Continuum?

190 Burgess Cellars. (Tom Burgess took over the property in 1972, and the next generation is now in charge).

191 In the town of St. Helena on Spring Mountain. (Started in 1980 by Jerry & Joyce Cain, specializing in Cabernet).

192 Cain Cuvée, (Blended); Cain Concept, (Benchland); & Cain Five, (The 5 Bordeaux grapes blended).

193 It shields the valley from the intense heat of the Central Valley, creating a favorable environment for premium grape varieties.

194 It shields the valley from cold marine air from the Pacific Ocean.

195 Georges de Latour, 1900. (This historic winery was one of the few to survive Prohibition).

196 Beaulieu means *Beautiful View* in French. It is aptly named.

197 The first name was Frank Rombauer, which morphed to Frank Family Vineyards.

198 *Trilogy*. (Cabernet Sauvignon, Petite Verdot, Malbec). *Soliloquy* (Sauvignon Blanc, Chardonnay, Malvasia).

199 Pritchard Hill, 1967. (Pritchard Hill is not an AVA, but it is high elevation on the Vaca Range in southern Napa).

200 Bryant Family; Colgin; Brand; Continuum; David Arthur; Ovid; Grandona; Villa del Lago, Melanson; etc.

201 Nils Venge. (For his 1985 Groth Vineyards and Winery Cabernet Sauvignon.)

202 At Alice Water's Chez Panisse. (She managed the restaurant for years).

203 Philippe Melka. (Born in Bordeaux, his first job was with Château Haut-Brion, in Pessac-Léognan).

204 Cloud View Winery. (On Pritchard Hill, the high elevation winery was owned by Leighton and Linda Taylor).

205 Which Nickel & Nickel vineyard is out of place? State Lane; Quicksilver; C.C. Ranch; Stiling; Sullinger; Branding Iron.

206 Another Cabernet Sauvignon vineyard bottled by Nickel & Nickel is Sori Bricco. Who else bottles Sori Bricco?

207 Who is the current winemaker at Dalla Valle Vineyards? Name the famous consultant also.

208 Who were the original owners of Mayacamas Vineyards?

209 Robin Lail, daughter of John Daniel Jr. owner of Inglenook in the 1940s. Name two of her wines.

210 The current Artesa Vineyards & Winery in Carneros was originally built by which wine company?

211 Which Napa based winery is the only one in California to focus exclusively on one late-harvest sweet wine?

212 Joseph Phelps Winery has made late-harvest wines for decades. Eisrébe and Delice are two labels. What is the grape?

213 In 1978 Donald Hess started the Hess Collection on what historic site?

214 Speaking of The Christian Brothers, what did longtime winemaker Brother Timothy collect?

215 Name the Napa Valley vineyard and winery started by Fritz Maytag.

216 Which wine is out of place? Violetta; Nightingale; Dolce, Single Berry Select, Delice, Sémillon de Soleil.

217 What year did Peter Newton establish Sterling Vineyards?

218 Which name is out of place? Phil Baxter; Theo Rosenbrand; Andre Tchelistcheff; Joel Aiken.

---

205 Stiling Vineyard. (It is one of their Chardonnay vineyards, and the rest are Cabernet Sauvignon vineyards).

206 Rudy Von Strasser, Diamond Mountain District AVA. (Rudy recently merged with Lava Vine in Calistoga).

207 Andy Erickson and Michel Rolland. (Two legends meld their talents to produce a world class wine).

208 Bob and Elinor Travers, 1968. (This high elevation winery is on Mt. Veeder. The new owner is Charles Banks).

209 J. Daniel Cuvée (CS), Welly (CS), Mole Hill (CS) Blueprint (CS & SB) Georgia (SB). Philippe Melka is winemaker.

210 Spain's Codorníu Raventós. (Codorníu Napa was built in 1991 to make traditional method sparkling wines).

211 Dolce. (Owned by Far Niente, the botrytis-induced grapes are grown in the Coombsville AVA).

212 Scheurebe (sourced from their "Home Ranch Vineyard" in St. Helena and bottled exclusively in 375 ml. format).

213 The Christian Brothers. (The former Christian Brother's Mont La Salle winery on Mt. Veeder.)

214 Wine openers. (His collection is on display at Greystone in St. Helena, formerly Christian Brothers Winery.)

215 York Creek Vineyards. (Fritz may be better known for Maytag appliances, Maytag cheese, and Anchor Steam).

216 Single Berry Select. (Made by Washington's Chateau Ste. Michelle under the Eroica label; the others are Napa).

217 1964. (Incidentally, Sterling was the first winery to release a 100% Merlot wine in Napa Valley).

218 Phil Baxter. (A notable winemaker from several properties, but the others all worked at Beaulieu Vineyard.)

219 Who was the first winemaker at Newton Vineyard?

220 Newton Vineyard in recent years has produced a Red Label blended program. What does this label replace?

221 The Backus Vineyard is in what Napa Valley AVA.

222 Tom & Vicki Celani own Celani Family Vineyards on the Silverado Trail. What is the flagship wine, and who is winemaker?

223 What famous winery founder calls herself "Wine Mother?" She is the *wine* mother, and her son is now the winemaker.

224 In addition to Viader, what other wines does the winery produce?

225 Who is the long-time winemaker at Schrader Cellars?

226 Name the more affordable line of Cabernet Sauvignon from Fred Schrader.

227 Who recently purchased the iconic Eisele Vineyard (previously owned by Araujo) in Calistoga?

228 Who was the founding director of Traditional Method sparkling wine producer Mumm Napa?

229 Speaking of sparkling wine, what is the name of the historic winery in Diamond Mountain District AVA?

230 What family purchased the Schramsberg property in 1965?

231 Mira winery in Yountville was the first winery in America to receive which piece of winemaking equipment.

232 What was the first U.S. wine to eclipse the $100 per bottle retail price?

---

219 Ric Forman. 1978. (Newton was founded by Peter and Su Hua Newton in 1977 after selling Sterling Vineyards).

220 Skyside. (Cabernet Sauvignon, Red Blend, and Chardonnay are made under the *Red Label* designation).

221 Oakville. (11.7 acres planted in 1975, this Cabernet Sauvignon monopole is owned by Joseph Phelps).

222 Adore. (100 % Cabernet Sauvignon. The winemaker is the passionate Mark Herold PhD).

223 Delia Viader. (She founded her winery in 1989 on Howell Mountain AVA).

224 Viader Black Label; Viader V; Dare by Viader; Homenaje by Viader; (Spanish for tribute).

225 Thomas Rivers Brown. (Working at All Seasons wine shop he befriended Fred Schrader, and the rest is history).

226 Double Diamond. (Thomas Brown is the winemaker and Oakville is the AVA, rather than a vineyard designation).

227 François Pinault (Owner of Bordeaux Grand Cru Classé Château Latour, among other estates).

228 Guy Devaux. (The ultra-premium cuvée is called DVX (DEVAUX).

229 Schramsberg. (Founded by Jacob Schram in 1862).

230 Jack & Jamie Davies. (The property has wine caves, which are a huge Napa Valley attraction).

231 Ovum. (The world's first seamless OAK egg fermentation tank made by Taransaud. Only 2 per year are made).

232 Diamond Creek's "Lake Vineyard," 1987 vintage. (Owned by Al Brounstein, in Diamond Mountain District AVA).

233 What was the first U.S. wine to eclipse the $500 per bottle retail price?

234 Harlan Estate was founded in 1984 on the western bench lands of Oakville. Who is the longtime winemaker?

235 Harlan Estate produces a second selection from the estate vineyard. What is the wine called?

236 Bond is another vineyard specific project by Bill Harlan and his team. Name 3 of the 5 single vineyard wines.

237 Which vineyard is misnamed? Gravelly Meadow, Red Rock Terrace, Volcanic Peak Vineyard, Lake Vineyard.

238 Diamond Creek Vineyards was recently sold. Who was the buyer?

239 Which winery is not linked to Marco DiGuilio? Girard; Pine Ridge; Paradigm; Lokoya; Black Coyote; Hidden Ridge.

240 Paul Steinschriber has been winemaker at Diamond Creek Vineyard for the past 29 years. What is his own label called?

241 Name the two vineyard-designated Cabernet Sauvignon wines bottled by Freemark Abbey Winery.

242 In 1981, Frog's Leap Winery was founded in Rutherford. Who is the owner/winemaker?

243 Which is out of place? Scarecrow, Schrader, Harlan Estate, Monte Bello, Abreau.

244 Which winery is not linked to Mia Klein? Palmaz; Araujo; Viader; Robert Pepi; Dalla Valle; Quintessa; Spottswoode.

245 Jayson Woodbridge owns Hundred Acre Winery. What 4 Cabernet Sauvignon wines come from his properties?

246 Which winery in Napa Valley makes Meritaggio?

---

233 Harlan Estate, 2006 vintage. (A Cabernet Sauvignon-based wine from Napa, under the direction of Bill Harlan).

234 Bob Levy. (Bob spent years at Rombauer, then with Bill Harlan at Merryvale before he founded Harlan Estate).

235 The Maiden. (The same winemaking team is in place and has a similar profile to the Grand Vin).

236 Melbury; Quella; St. Eden; Vecina; Pluribus. (The second wine from Bond's vineyard blends is Matriarch).

237 Volcanic Peak Vineyard. (It is Volcanic Hill Vineyard. All are Diamond Creek Vineyard properties).

238 The Rouzaud family of Champagne Louis Roederer fame. (They also own Roederer Estate in Mendocino County.)

239 Paradigm. (This is under the direction of Heidi Barrett, and the others (and more) are Marco DiGuilio).

240 Watermark. (In 2004, and he started bottling Cabernet Sauvignon from Napa Valley and Mt. Veeder AVAs).

241 Bosché Vineyard, Sycamore Vineyard. (Both historic vineyards are in Rutherford).

242 John Williams. (John worked at Stag's Leap Wine Cellars prior to founding Frog's Leap Winery).

243 Monte Bello. (Monte Bello is from the Santa Cruz Mountain estate and the others are from Napa Valley).

244 Quintessa. (This is the property owned by the Huneeus family, but Mia worked at all of the others).

245 Ark Vineyard; Kayli Morgan Vineyard; Few and Far between Vineyard; (And *Wraith* is a blend of the 3).

246 David Arthur. (The wine is a red Bordeaux blend plus Sangiovese, the famous Italian variety).

247 Name the 13-acre vineyard on Diamond Mountain owned by Peter Thompson?

248 Name the winery in Napa Valley owned by Fritz Hatton making wines *On the White Keys, Variation One,* & *H Block.*

249 Which winery is Celia Masyczek not linked to? Staglin; Husic; Cornerstone; Rocca Family; Frank Family; Silverado.

250 Who was the first winemaker at Revana Family Vineyard in St. Helena?

251 The most expensive wine from Napa Valley is Screaming Eagle. Who was the founder, and in what year?

252 What is the other less expensive red wine produced by Screaming Eagle?

253 Which restaurant is out of place? Bistro Don Giovanni; John Ash; French Laundry; Bottega; Mustards; La Toque; Press.

254 Name the two families responsible for the HdV wines?

255 In 2007 Heidi Peterson Barrett and John Schwartz started a high elevation project in Napa Valley. What is the winery?

256 Name the 3 *Justice* labels by Bounty Hunter (new owner Alejandro Bulgheroni), and Andy Beckstoffer and Tim Milos?

257 What was the first private label Cabernet Sauvignon label sold at Thomas Keller's French Laundry restaurant?

258 Vineyard 7 & 8 is on Spring Mountain and was started in 1999 by Launny Steffens. What do the 7 & 8 numbers signify?

259 What family owns Whitehall Lane Winery in Rutherford?

---

247 Andrew Geoffrey. (This Cabernet Sauvignon vineyard is named after Peter's two sons).

248 Arietta. (Musical based labels include Beethoven's last piano sonata, Opus III. Fritz is a famous wine auctioneer).

249 Frank Family. (Part of the Rombauer empire, but the others were linked to Celia.

250 Heidi Barrett. (The original plot was 9 acres started in 1997, and Jim Barbour was the viticulturalist).

251 Jean Phillips. Founded in Oakville in 1986, first vintage 1992. (Heidi Barrett was first winemaker).

252 Second Flight. (This Merlot based wine is the sister to Screaming Eagle. They also now make a Sauvignon Blanc).

253 John Ash. (This is located in Sonoma County; the others are in Napa Valley).

254 Aubert de Villaine of DRC & Larry Hyde (Carneros grape grower). HdV stands for Hyde de Villaine.

255 Au Sommet. (This ultra-premium Cabernet Sauvignon is from a high-altitude vineyard (2,100 feet) on Atlas Peak).

256 *Blind* (Cabernet Sauvignon, To Kalon); *Frontier* (red blend, Dr. Crane); *Poetic* (red blend, To Kalon).

257 Modicum. (Created in 2000 by Laura Cunningham & Sommelier Bobby Stuckey, from a vineyard above Auberge).

258 Launny worked in finance, (numeric industry). 7 is good luck in our culture, and 8 prosperity in eastern cultures.

259 The Leonardini family. (Tom, Sr; Tom II; Katie). It was purchased in 1993 from businessman Hideaki Ando.

260 What four Jackson Family Napa wineries does Chris Carpenter make wine for?

261 What is unique about the four Cabernet Sauvignon bottlings from Lokoya?

262 What is the name of the Carneros vineyard founded by artist Rene di Rosa in the 1960s?

263 *To Kalon* is a famous vineyard in Oakville adjacent to the Robert Mondavi Winery. What does the name mean?

264 Maybach Family Vineyards, in Oakville, has historic German roots. What is the more recent German connection?

265 Who originally planted the To Kalon vineyard, and in what year?

266 Who are the current majority owners of To Kalon Vineyard?

267 Who was the first winemaker at Dominus Estate?

268 Philip Togni, the acclaimed winery owner/winemaker, arrived in Napa Valley in 1959. Where did he work in Bordeaux?

269 Continuing with Philip Togni, in addition to his Napa Valley Cabernet Sauvignon, what other 2 wines does he make?

270 The Tesseron family of Château Pontet-Canet in Pauillac took over a winery in Napa Valley. What is it called?

271 Staglin Family Vineyard was founded in 1985 in Rutherford. In addition to Staglin, name other labels they produce.

272 Name the recently created winery that occupies space on Bella Oaks Lane where the Rhodes family started.

273 Martha's Vineyard Cabernet Sauvignon from Heitz Cellar often yields aromatics of which unique compound?

---

260 Cardinale, La Jota, Lokoya, Mt. Brave. (Chris is a high elevation specialist in red wine production).

261 Each bottling is from four mountain peaks in Napa Valley: Mt. Veeder; Spring Mtn; Diamond Mtn; Howell Mtn.

262 Winery Lake Vineyard. (Sterling Vineyards makes single vineyard Pinot Noir and Chardonnay from here).

263 A Place of Highest Beauty. (from the Greek language).

264 Maybach automobiles. (The ultra-premium joint venture between Mercedes-Benz and Daimler AG).

265 Hamilton Crabb, 1868. (He once called the site *Hermosa*).

266 Robert Mondavi Winery and grape grower Andy Beckstoffer.

267 Chris Phelps. (Chris's tenure at Dominus began in 1984 and he remained through 1996).

268 Philip studied under Émile Peynaud at University of Bordeaux & was Régisseur at Château Lascombes, Margaux.

269 Tanbark Hill Vineyard, Cabernet Sauvignon, (more accessible) & Ca' Togni (Constantia inspired red dessert wine).

270 PYM RAE. (Middle names of Robin William's children, who started Villa Sorriso (Smiles) on Mt. Veeder).

271 Salus; Stagliano; Ineo; Booth Bella Oaks.

272 Bella Union Winery. (From Far Niente/Nickel & Nickel a Cabernet Sauvignon & Sauvignon Blanc).

273 Eucalyptus. (The Eucalyptus tree lined vineyard drips pungent volatile oils that adhere to the grape skins).

274 What was the label difference between the 1973 & 1974 vintages of Martha's Vineyard?

275 Who was the first woman to own and operate a winery in California?

276 Which wine is not produced by Colgin Cellars? Cariad; Colgate; Herb Lamb; Tychson; IX Vineyard.

277 What is the name of the Napa Valley blended Cabernet Sauvignon made by DANA estates?

278 DANA estates took over from which family winery that was established in 1976?

279 Legendary winemaker/winery owner John Kongsgaard has had an illustrious career. Name his top Chardonnay bottling?

280 What architect designed Far Niente, Inglenook, Trefethen, Del Dotto, BV, Montelena, & Greystone?

281 Who owns PlumpJack Winery?

282 Ladera Winery located on Howell Mountain had two prior names. What were they?

274 The 1973 had the traditional brown hued label, and the 1974 had a colorful winery label.

275 Hannah Weinberger of Napa Valley (1882. She is also recognized as the first commercial woman winemaker in California). Josephine Tychson of Napa's Freemark Abbey is #2 (1886).

276 Colgate. (This is toothpaste, and the others are vineyard designations or cuvées).

277 ONDA. (Sourced from Helms, Hershey, Lotus, & Crystal Springs vineyards).

278 Livingston Moffett. (Prior to the Livingston's tenure, the vineyard was planted in 1883 by H.W. Helms).

279 The Judge. (The Judge is named after his father, a Napa Superior Court judge. My epiphany Napa Chardonnay).

280 Hamden W. McIntyre. (Did much of his designing in the 1880s and employed gravity flow physics).

281 California Governor Gavin Newsom, Gordon Getty, and general manager John Conover. (Purchased in 1995).

282 Originally the Nouveau Médoc Vineyard (1886) renamed Château Woltner in 1985.

CALIFORNIA

SONOMA COUNTY

283 What does the native American term Sonoma mean?

284 Which is larger, Sonoma County or Napa Valley?

285 Who is considered the "Father of the California Wine Industry"?

286 True or False? Sonoma County is located south of San Francisco.

287 Sonoma County AVA has 17 nested AVA's. Name 3 of the 5 AVAs with the word Sonoma in their titles?

288 True or False? Kunde Family Winery is a recent upstart winery managing 25 acres in Sonoma Valley.

289 During the 1960's TV advertisers coined the phrase "That little old winemaker, me." Which winery sponsored the ad?

290 Where did the name Italian Swiss Colony come from?

---

283 There are a few derivations, one is *Valley of the Moon*, and another is *Abandoned Camping Place*.

284 Sonoma County is more than twice the size of Napa Valley.

285 Agoston Haraszthy. (In 1857, the native Hungarian founded Buena Vista Winery in Sonoma Valley).

286 False. (Sonoma County is north of San Francisco).

287 Sonoma County, Sonoma Coast, Sonoma Mountain, Sonoma Valley, Northern Sonoma.

288 False. (Founded in 1904, Kunde farms the largest contiguous vineyard in Sonoma Valley).

289 Italian Swiss Colony. (In the 1990s, Beringer brought the property and renamed it Cellar 8 @ Asti winery).

290 Started in 1881 by a group of Italians and Swiss immigrants.

291 Who owns Camp Meeting Ridge Vineyard on the Sonoma Coast?

292 Richard Arrowood and wife Alis have recently sold Amapola Creek Vineyards & Winery. Who is the new owner?

293 Name two wineries that bottle Bismark Mountain Vineyard grapes?

294 Marcy Keefer's vineyard is in which AVA?

295 Merry Edwards Winery in the Russian River Valley was recently sold. Who was the buyer?

296 What is the name of Chateau St. Jean's Bordeaux blend?

297 What type of wine is the Sterling family's Iron Horse Vineyards known for?

298 In the 19th century, the Martinelli family started farming land in Sonoma. In 1993, who was the new winemaker?

299 Name the veteran Jordan Vineyards & Winery winemaker who retired in 2019.

300 Richard Arrowood was the first winemaker at what winery?

301 Kenwood makes wine from a vineyard named for what famous author?

302 Rodney Strong Vineyards makes three top quality vineyard-designated Cabernet Sauvignons. Name them.

303 The current Blue Rock Vineyard estate was purchased by Cheryl & Kenny Kahn in 1987. What was the original name?

304 Ferrari-Carano in Sonoma County produces two red blends. What are they called?

305 The stunningly appointed Ferrari-Carano winery was recently sold. Who is the new owner?

306 Cecil DeLoach established his winery in 1973. Who did he sell it to in 2003?

307 Name the first winery constructed in the Dry Creek Valley AVA?

---

291 Walt and Joan Flowers. (Growing genuinely cold climate Pinot Noir and Chardonnay).

292 B. Wise Vineyards. (Brian Wise is a neighbor in Sonoma Valley, and has a similar winegrowing philosophy).

293 Hanna Winery & Ram's Gate. (This vineyard is in the newly appointed Moon Mountain District AVA).

294 Green Valley AVA. (Nested within Russian River Valley AVA).

295 The Rouzeau family. (Champagne Louis Roederer, Roederer Estate in Anderson Valley).

296 Cinq Cépages. (In French, "5 grapes" defining the traditional Bordeaux red grape mix).

297 High quality sparkling wines. (Joy Sterling put Green Valley, within Russian River Valley, on the map).

298 Helen Turley. (Their neighbor and owner of Marcassin Vineyard).

299 Rob Davis. (Beginning in 1976 (first vintage), Rob worked 43 harvests. Maggie Kruse is the new winemaker).

300 Chateau St. Jean. (He was there from 1974 -1985, then founded Arrowood and Amapola Creek).

301 Jack London. (Planted to Cabernet Sauvignon, Merlot, and Zinfandel on Sonoma Mountain).

302 Alexander's Crown; Rockaway; Brothers. (All vineyards are in the Alexander Valley AVA).

303 Villa Maria Winery. (Started in the 1880s, prohibition halted business until the Kahn's bought the ghost winery).

304 *Trésor* (Treasure, their Bordeaux blend); *Siena* (True to their Italian heritage, it is a Sangiovese based wine).

305 Foley Family Wines. (Businessman Bill Foley recently added to his large portfolio of wineries).

306 Jean-Charles Boisset. (Boisset owns other properties including Raymond Vineyards and Buena Vista Winery).

307 Dry Creek Vineyard. (In 1982 by MIT grad David Stare; a true Sonoma Country pioneer).

308 In the 1980s, what three words created California's longest winery bumper sticker?

309 True or False? Jordan Vineyards sources Chardonnay and Cabernet from the same AVA.

310 Which winemaker was a bicycle racer, bagpiper on the Queen Mary, aids researcher, Winemaker of the Year, 2010?

311 After starting the winery in 1978, name 3 vineyard designated/cuvées Chardonnays made by Kistler Vineyards?

312 Which Sonoma County Chardonnay icon started the Occidental Pinot Noir project?

313 What winery did Don Patz & James Hall work at prior to setting up their winery in Sonoma?

314 Sir Peter Michael makes several wines. What is out of place? Le Pavots; L'Après Midi; Au Revoir; Belle Côte, Aux Paradis.

315 Adam & Dianna Lee started Siduri Wines in 1994. What does the name signify?

316 Who is the owner of Adobe Road Winery and a legendary world class race car driver and car owner?

317 Extra credit regarding Adobe Road Winery. What image is incorporated in the mountain range on the front label?

318 Far Niente started a Pinot Noir project in The Russian River Valley. What is the name?

319 Mark Aubert is a very accomplished winemaker. Which vineyard does not belong? CIX, Lauren, Powder Keg, Eastside.

320 Mark Aubert makes a Chardonnay & Pinot Noir from the *UV-SL Vineyard*. What do these letters signify?

321 Which winery based in Healdsburg has the mission statement, *Truth, Justice, & Cabernet*?

322 What is the name of the gentleman that started Sonoma-Cutrer in 1972?

---

308 Gundlach Bundschu Gewürztraminer. (Family owned since 1858 in the Sonoma Valley).

309 False. (Cabernet Sauvignon from Alexander Valley AVA, Chardonnay from Russian River Valley AVA).

310 Greg La Follette. (Simi; Hartford Court; La Crema; Flowers; Tandem; now Alquimista Cellars; La Follette Wines).

311 Vine Hill; McCrea; Hyde; Hudson; Durell; Dutton; Trenton Roadhouse; Cuvée Cathleen, etc.

312 Steve Kistler. (After decades of making Chardonnay, Steve now has a dedicated Pinot Noir endeavor).

313 Flora Springs, Napa Valley. (They are now producing several Chardonnay and Pinot Noir vineyard designations).

314 Au Revoir. (Just in case people have forgotten how to say good-bye in French).

315 In Babylonian, *Goddess of Wine*.

316 Kevin Buckler. (The Racer's Group (Porsche) and Aston Martin USA racing director).

317 A Porsche 911 silhouette is embedded at the top of the mountain.

318 EnRoute. (This is a blend from three vineyard sites in the Russian River Valley).

319 Powder Keg. (He does however bottle a Powder House Vineyard Chardonnay).

320 *UV*. (Ulises Valdez, the famed vineyard manager for years), *SL*. (Stoetz Lane, where Ulises lives).

321 Judge Palmer. (Although based in Sonoma, owner Palmer Emmitt produces some majestic Napa Cabernets).

322 Brice Jones. (After selling this primarily Chardonnay label, he created his *Emeritus* Pinot Noir project).

323 True or False? Williams Selyem makes super premium Cabernet Sauvignon in Sonoma County.

324 Who was the founder of Hanzell Vineyards in Sonoma Valley?

325 Joseph Phelps is based in Napa Valley. What is the Chardonnay and Pinot Noir project from Sonoma Coast called?

326 Richard Arrowood started at Chateau St. Jean in 1974. He labeled a Riesling TBA in 1976. What did these letters mean?

327 Dan Goldfield is partner/winemaker with grape grower Steve Dutton at Dutton-Goldfield. What year did they team up?

328 Name three *vineyard designated* Pinot Noirs produced by Dutton-Goldfield Winery.

329 Which is not made by Kosta-Browne? Gap's Crown; Kanzler; Sangiacomo; Keefer; Garys'; Rosella's; Pisoni; Cerise.

330 Which is not made by Williams Selyem? Foss; Morning Dew; Calegari; Ferrington; Fiddlestix; Weir; Hirsch; Heintz.

331 What are the three labels produced by Vérité (Truth)?

332 Which restaurant is not in Sonoma? Salt & Stone; The Charter Oak; Madrona Manor; Café La Haye; Layla; Valette.

333 Which lodging is not in Sonoma? Harmon Guest House; Vinters Resort; Hôtel La Mars; Solage; MacArthur Place.

---

323 False. (They make super premium Pinot Noir in Sonoma County).

324 James Zellerbach. (Founded in 1953, he made Burgundian-styled Chardonnay and Pinot Noir).

325 Freestone. (Phelps prefers the cool Sonoma Coast over Carneros for these cool climate varieties).

326 Totally Botrytis Affected. (He could not use Trockenbeerenauslese (TBA), so he crafted his own term).

327 1998. (Together they produce Pinot Noir, Chardonnay and Zinfandel mostly from the Russian River Valley AVA).

328 Dutton Ranch; Cherry Ridge; Fox Den; Emerald Ridge; Azaya Ranch; Freestone; McDougall; Devil's Gulch.

329 Sangiacomo. (An exceptionally large collection of vineyards, but not part of the Kosta-Browne portfolio).

330 Fiddlestix Vineyard. (This property is in the Sta. Rita Hills in Santa Barbara County far from Sonoma County).

331 La Joie (Joy); La Muse (Inspiration); Le Désir (Desire). (All are Bordeaux blends).

332 The Charter Oak. (This restaurant is in St. Helena in Napa Valley).

333 Solage. (This resort is on the Silverado Trail in Napa Valley).

CALIFORNIA

OTHER NORTHERN CALIFORNIA WINE REGIONS

334 In what AVA is Maggy Hawk Vineyard (known for Pinot Noir named after famous racehorses) located?

335 What is the highest point in Lake County?

336 What is the Indian translation of Konocti?

337 What is the Duckhorn-owned winery in Anderson Valley?

338 Which is not a Goldeneye bottling? Ten Degrees; Gowan Creek; Confluence; Anderson Special Cuvée; Narrows.

339 In what AVA would you find Ferrington Vineyard and Morning Dew Ranch Vineyard?

340 Who was the original owner of Guenoc Estate (and horse farm) in the 1800s?

341 Name the gentleman that owned Guenoc Winery (Lake County) in the mid-1970s, and in 1980 released his first wine.

---

334 Anderson Valley, Mendocino. (This winery is owned by Barbara Banke of Jackson Family. Barbara loves horses).

335 Mount Konocti. (An ancient volcano adjacent to the natural (not created by a dam) Clear Lake.

336 Mountain Woman. (This 4,300 feet high dormant volcano last erupted about 11,000 years ago).

337 Goldeneye. (Goldeneye specializes in Pinot Noir and also bottles a Pinot Noir Rosé).

338 Anderson Special Cuvée. (This is a made-up name. The others are official vineyards or plots).

339 Anderson Valley. (Both Pinot Noir and bottled by William Selyem as vineyard designated wines).

340 British-American actress/socialite Lillie Langtry.

341 Orville Magoon. (A very accomplished civil engineer and passionate winery owner).

342 Montevina (Spanish for mountain vine), wines are still made in Amador County. What is the winery's new name?

343 What is unique about the Mendocino Ridge AVA?

344 Which winery is out of place? Lazy Creek; Navarro; Paul Dolan; Pacific Star; Obsidian Ridge; Husch

345 Name four popular grapes grown in The McDowell Valley AVA within Mendocino County.

346 What is the name of the large, mountainous AVA located east of Sacramento and west of Lake Tahoe?

347 Amador County AVA is in the western Sierra Foothills ≈ 100 miles east Of San Francisco. Name two AVAs here.

348 Which winery does not belong? Deaver, Renwood, High Valley, Renaissance.

349 Parducci Wine Cellars is in which AVA?

350 Roederer Estate, Anderson Valley, is owned by Champagne Louis Roederer. What is their top American cuvée called?

342 Terra d'Oro. (Zinfandel is their specialty, especially that made from 130-year-old vines from Deaver Ranch).

343 It is only planted above 1,200 feet and when the fog rolls in it looks like islands in the sky from above.

344 Obsidian Ridge. (That is in Lake County AVA, and the others are in Mendocino AVA).

345 Grenache; Syrah; Marsanne; Viognier (and of course, Zinfandel).

346 Sierra Foothills. (The heart of Gold Rush country. Gold was discovered here in 1848 and the rush was on).

347 Shenandoah Valley & Fiddletown. (Both are in the northern part of the county near the town of Plymouth).

348 High Valley. (High Valley is in Lake County AVA, and the others are in the Sierra Foothills AVA).

349 Mendocino County AVA. (Working with his father, John Parducci started this winery in 1932).

350 L'Ermitage. (Available in white and rosé versions).

CALIFORNIA

CENTRAL COAST & SOUTHERN CALIFORNIA

351 Paso Robles AVA is nested within what larger AVA?

352 True or False? Paso Robles AVA is larger than all of Sonoma County's AVAs.

353 What was the terroir-driven reason that Josh Jensen, founder of Calera was attracted to Mt. Harlan in 1975?

354 Which vineyard designation does Calera *not* make? Selleck; Magnum; Ryan; Reed; Mills; Muns.

355 In the movie *Sideways*, what wine did Miles drank at the fast-food restaurant at the end of the movie?

356 Arroyo Seco is a sub-AVA of Monterey. What is the definition of Arroyo Secco?

357 What was the first American winery to produce Pinot Noir?

---

351 Central Coast AVA. (This large AVA extends from San Francisco Bay to Santa Barbara County).

352 True. (Paso Robles is larger than all of Sonoma County and Napa Valley combined).

353 Limestone soil like Burgundy, France. (The Oxford educated Jensen found it in the Gavilan mountain range).

354 Magnum. (Josh was a fan of Ferraris & private investigator TV shows, so no Magnum, but Selleck is a vineyard).

355 1961 Château Cheval Blanc, St.-Émilion. (Ironically, almost half of the blend is Merlot, which Miles detested).

356 Dry Riverbed. (The AVA was awarded in 1983. Wente's Riva Ranch vineyard is located here).

357 Mirassou Winery. (One of California's oldest wineries founded in 1854 in the Santa Clara Valley).

358 What actor, star of the 1960s TV show Daniel Boone, founded his own winery in California?

359 Jonata Winery is in Ballard Canyon AVA. Which wine do they *not* make? El Alma; Fenix; Todos; Flor; Ballard Cuvée.

360 Michael David winery in Lodi makes unique wines. What does not fit? Inkblot; Earthquake; Circus Clown; Freakshow.

361 Which is not a Monterey sub-AVA? Hames Valley; San Bernabe; San Lucas; Carmel Valley; Santa Lucia Highlands.

362 The Hahn family started their winery in 1979. Name three of their six vineyards in Monterey County.

363 Name the largest single vineyard in the US?

364 Who owns the San Bernabe Vineyard?

365 In 1980, developer Jack Nevin founded a winery in San Luis Obispo that specialized in Chardonnay. Name the winery.

366 Which vineyard is *not* in Edna Valley AVA? Talley; High Rock Formation; Alban; Tolosa; Paragon; Chamisal.

367 Within the Monterey AVA, what is unique about the topography of the Chalone AVA?

368 Who was the gentleman that re-established Chalone Vineyards in 1965?

369 What notorious event in the world of wine helped cement Chalone's reputation as a top-quality winery?

370 In 1975, Andrew & Laurel Quady founded their eponymous winery in Madera. Name their famous dessert wines.

371 Name the current leader of the Gallo family wine empire.

---

358 Fess Parker. (1987 in Santa Ynez Valley AVA. Featured in the movie *Sideways*).

359 Ballard Cuvée. (A made-up name but talented winemaker Matt Dees produces all the other wines).

360 Circus Clown. (Although Freakshow has circus themed names, Circus Clown is not one of them).

361 They are all sub-AVA's of Monterey AVA. (More include: Arroyo Seco; Chalone; San Antonio Valley).

362 Lone Oak; Smith; Hook; & Doctor's in the Santa Lucia Highlands, Ste. Nicolas & Ste. Phillippe in Arroyo Seco).

363 San Bernabe Vineyard. (The planted vineyard is ≈ 8,500 acres in size and has its own AVA).

364 The Indelicato Family. (Owners of Delicato Winery founded by Gasparé Indelicato in 1912).

365 Edna Valley Vineyard. (The vineyards were originally planted in the 1800s).

366 High Rock Formation Vineyard. (This is a made-up name; the others are real vineyards).

367 High elevation. (1,800 – 2,200' in the Gavilan range. Original plantings in 1919 by Frenchman Maurice Tamm).

368 Richard Graff. (Although Philip Togni made the 1960 vintage, Dick Graff was the owner).

369 The Chardonnay was part of the now famous Judgment of Paris blind tasting in 1976. It placed 3rd).

370 *Essensia* (made from Orange Muscat) and *Elysium* (made from Black Muscat).

371 Gina Gallo. (Granddaughter of co-founder Julio, she has greatly expanded the Gallo reach).

372 The Bien Nacido Vineyard is in which AVA?

373 In 1987, Justin Vineyards & Winery created a red Bordeaux blend called what?

374 What year did Dick Sanford (Sanford Winery & Vineyards) start his winery? What AVA is it in?

375 What is the name of Dick Sanford's winery that he started after he sold Sanford Winery & Vineyards?

376 Sanford Winery & Vineyards made two top rated vineyard designated Pinot Noirs for years. What are they?

377 What is the smallest AVA in Santa Barbara?

378 Margerum Wine Company is a second career for Doug Margerum. What was the name of his famous restaurant prior?

379 Name the line of wines introduced by Charles Woodson and sourced from Paso Robles and Monterey County.

380 What is the oldest winery in downtown Los Angeles, and is still in operation?

381 The Sandhi wine project was started by which famous California sommelier?

382 What three properties are part of Rajat Parr's wine club offerings?

383 Which is not part of Domaine de la Côte. Bloom's Field; La Côte; Hautes de Nuits; Memorious; Sous le Chêne.

384 What phenomenon allows cool climate grapes to be grown in a normally warm climate like Santa Barbara?

385 Who was the founder and winemaker of Au Bon Climat?

372 Santa Maria Valley AVA. (Spanish for *Born Well*, this vineyard sells grapes to many high-profile producers).

373 Isosceles. (This Paso Robles producer was a pioneer in the Central Coast AVA with this flagship wine).

374 1971, Sta. Rita Hills. (Dick Sanford was a pioneer in the Santa Barbara AVA, now in the sub-AVA Sta. Rita Hills).

375 Alma Rosa. (This was founded in 2005, but he sold it to Bob & Barb Zorich in 2014. Sta. Rita Hills vineyards).

376 *Sanford & Benedict* Vineyard & *La Rinconada* Vineyard. (Both are in Sta. Rita Hills AVA).

377 Happy Canyon AVA. (Within the larger Santa Ynez Valley, less than 500 acres are planted).

378 The Wine Cask. (The family restaurant started in 1981, and in 1994 it got The Grand Award from the Spectator).

379 Intercept. (The perfect name for his wines as he had 65 career interceptions over 18 seasons in the NFL).

380 San Antonio Winery. (Founded 1917 by the Riboli family. They own 2 other wineries in Ontario & Paso Robles).

381 Rajat Parr. (Santa Barbara & Sta. Rita Hills. Raj is also involved with Evening Land Winery in Oregon).

382 Domaine de la Côte; Sandhi; & Evening Land. (Raj likes the vineyards of southern California & Oregon).

383 Hautes de Nuits. (A French play on words, but the others are his limited production Sta. Rita Hills vineyards).

384 There are wind gap breaks in the coastal mountain range creating transverse valleys for cold and fog.

385 The venerable Jim Clendenen founded his winery in 1982. (Sadly Jim passes in 2021).

386 Speaking of Jim Clendenen, name his white wine blend with historical significance back to Burgundy?

387 Which winery shared space with Jim Clendenen at Au Bon Climat from the beginning?

388 Wild Horse Winery & Vineyards produces a Pinot Noir with a clever eponymous label. What is it?

389 True or False? Santa Barbara AVA contains the sub-AVA of Santa Inez Valley.

390 Name the mountain vineyard in Ballard Canyon AVA farmed by Beckman Vineyards.

391 Which winery bottles labels from Sleepy Hollow Vineyards and Diamond T Vineyards?

392 Tablas Creek Winery in Paso Robles was started by which two wine families?

393 SIDEWAYS (2004) was a movie set in Santa Barbara wine country. What restaurant was often visited by Miles et al?

394 Which is out of place: Isosceles, Justification, Lithology, Savant?

395 Melville Winery in the Sta. Rita Hills bottles a Chardonnay with the term INOX listed on the label. What does this mean?

396 True or False? Fiddlehead Cellars bottles a Pinot Noir from the Fiddlestix Vineyard.

397 The iconic Ridge Vineyards was founded in which AVA?

398 Speaking of Ridge Vineyards, who was the decades long winemaker just recently retired?

399 Name another winery in The Santa Cruz Mountain AVA founded in 1964 shortly after Ridge Vineyards.

400 The Clos Pepe Vineyard is in what AVA? Who was the vineyard manager?

401 Where is Callaway Vineyards & Winery located?

---

386 Hildegard, wife of Charlemagne. (Pinot Gris, Pinot Blanc and Aligoté were once planted in Corton-Charlemagne).

387 Qupé. (Bob Lindquist began his adventure in 1982 and recently sold to Vintage Wine Estates).

388 Cheval Sauvage. (The French term for Wild Horse. The grapes are from the Santa Maria Valley).

389 True. (The Santa Barbara AVA also contains the Santa Maria Valley AVA and Sta. Rita Hills AVA).

390 Purisima Mountain. (A biodynamic vineyard with 125 acres planted to several Rhône varieties).

391 Talbott Vineyards. (Monterey).

392 The Perrin Family (Of Château de Beaucastel in the Rhône Valley, and Robert Hass, founder of Vineyard Brands).

393 The Hitching Post, Buellton. (Partners Gray Hartley and Frank Ostini started Hitching Post Winery in 1979).

394 Lithology. (This is produced by Alejandro Bulgheroni, and the others are bottled by Justin Vineyards).

395 Inox is French for stainless steel. (In other words, no oak barrels here).

396 True. (Kathy Joseph has owned this vineyard plot in the Sta. Rita Hills since 1996).

397 Santa Cruz Mountains AVA. (Ridge is home to the iconic Monte Bello vineyard).

398 Paul Draper. (Paul became winemaker in 1969 and is now Chairman of the Board).

399 David Bruce Winery. (His Chardonnay was part of the famous Judgment of Paris blind tasting in 1976).

400 Sta. Rita Hills AVA. (Wes Hagen was the very intellectual viticulturalist, and now works for J. Wilkes winery).

401 Temecula Valley. (Founder Ely Callaway started in textiles, moved into wine, then Callaway Golf (Big Bertha).

402 What year did the varietal name "Chardonnay" first appear on a California wine label?

403 Belle Glos makes a vineyard designated Pinot Noir from the Clark & Telephone Vineyard. What AVA contains it?

404 What are the four labels from The Sea Smoke Vineyards in the Sta. Rita Hills?

405 Who was the founder of Sine Qua Non winery in Ventura county sourcing fruit mostly from Santa Barbara County?

406 Sine Qua Non. What is the definition?

407 Who are the two gentlemen that own Garys' Vineyard in the Santa Lucia Highlands?

408 Who was one of the original Rhône Rangers featured on the cover of The Wine Spectator in 1989?

409 Randall Grahm made a southern Rhône-style wine modeled after the Brunier's family flagship. What was the wine?

402 1936. (From Wente Bros. Winery in Livermore Valley).
403 Santa Maria Valley AVA. (Santa Maria Valley AVA is in southern California, within Santa Barbara County AVA).
404 Pinot Noir, (2) *Southing*, (south facing vineyards), *Ten*, (10 clones); *Chardonnay, Sea Spray* (sparkling).
405 Manfred Krankl. (Founded in 1994, the Austrian born owner specialized in Rhône varieties).
406 Latin: *without which nothing....* (Something that is indispensable or essential).
407 Gary Pisoni and Gary Franscioni. (Several wineries purchase Pinot Noir & Syrah from their 51 acre plot).
408 Randall Grahm. (Founder of Bonny Doon Vineyard, creating Rhône-style wines like *Le Cigare Volant*).
409 Old Telegram. (This was a play on words named after Domaine du Vieux Télegraph, Châteauneuf-du-Pape).

OREGON

GENERAL QUESTIONS

410 Which mountain looms large above the vineyards of northern Oregon?

411 What is the largest and most popular AVA wine region in Oregon?

412 Today, Chardonnay thrives in the Willamette Valley. Why was Chardonnay problematic in the early days?

413 What 2 mountain ranges frame the Willamette Valley?

414 What is the predominant grape planted in the Willamette Valley?

415 What ancient catastrophic event reshaped much of Oregon's land mass?

416 What was the first commercial vineyard/winery planted in Oregon?

417 There is a winery in Yamhill-Carlton AVA that is named after the post Missoula flood formations called what?

---

410 Mt Hood. (The perpetually snow-capped mountain rises to 11,250 feet above sea level).

411 The Willamette Valley. (Located in the northern part of the state, just south of Portland).

412 Primarily, Chardonnay clones brought from California didn't work well with the Willamette soil/climate.

413 The Coastal Range on the west, and the Cascade Range on the east.

414 Pinot Noir. (83% of the state's planting of the grape comes from the Willamette Valley).

415 The Missoula Floods. (Occurred numerous times, most recently is from the last ice age. ≈ 15,000 years ago).

416 Hillcrest Vineyard. (Founded by Davis graduate Richard Sommers in 1961 in southern Oregon Umpqua Valley).

417 Gran Moraine. (The valleys are called *moraines* and has repositioned sediment from the floods).

418 Who was the founder Beaux Frères Winery? Also, name the famous brother-in-law partner?

419 In addition to Beaux Frères Winery, what other three projects are the Etzel family and partners involved in?

420 Name three AVAs in Southern Oregon.

421 What is a new AVA in the Willamette Valley that allows for west-east cooler temperatures and fog?

422 After the Van Duzer Corridor AVA was established, which two new Willamette Valley AVAs were added in 2020?

423 Maison Joseph Drouhin is a famous Burgundy négociant/estate landowner. What is their Oregon property called?

424 Domaine Drouhin Oregon (DDO) has been making world class Pinot Noir since 1987. What is their affordable line?

425 The famous Shea Vineyard is in which AVA?

426 Which two dynamic wine personalities own Evening Land Winery that contains the Seven Springs Vineyard?

427 Maison Louis Jadot of Burgundy started a winery in the Willamette Valley. What is the winery's name?

428 Who wrote the book "At Home in the Vineyard"?

429 Cristom Winery makes several vineyard bottlings. Which is out of place? Joanna, Louise, Emilia, Jessie, Eileen, Marjorie.

430 The venerable Master Sommelier Larry Stone started a winery in Eola-Amity Hills. What name was chosen?

431 What was the first winery built in the Chehalem Mountains area?

---

418 Michael Etzel, Robert Parker. (A genuinely great producer of Pinot Noir from Newberg in Ribbon Ridge AVA).

419 Domaine Roy & Fils, Sequitur and Coattails.

420 Rogue Valley, Umpqua Valley, Applegate, Red Hill Douglas County, Elkton.

421 Van Duzer Corridor AVA. (This east-west valley links to the Pacific Ocean, bringing cooling air and fog inland).

422 Laurelwood District & Tualatin Hills AVA. (Both are in the northwest corner of the Willamette Valley).

423 Domain Drouhin Oregon. (Founded in 1987 in the Dundee Hills, is managed by Véronique Drouhin-Boss).

424 Véronique Drouhin-Boss and her team have created the *Roserock* (soil color) series from Eola-Amity Hills.

425 Yamhill-Carlton. (A sub-AVA of the Willamette Valley).

426 Rajat Parr (World-class Sommelier & James Beard award winning author) and Sashi Moorman (winemaker).

427 Resonnance. (This is a Pinot Noir estate in the Yamhill-Carlton AVA and started in 2013).

428 Susan Sokol-Blosser. (The book details her amazing journey of perseverance in a male dominated industry).

429 Joanna. (My daughter's name, the other names are historical from winegrower/owner Tom Gerrie's family).

430 Lingua Franca. (*Speak frankly* in the universal language of bringing diverse people together for the good of all).

431 Adelsheim Vineyards. (David & Ginny Adelsheim purchased acreage in 1971 and started the winery in 1978).

432 The late Gary Andrus (RIP 2009) started Pine Ridge (1978) in Napa Valley. What two Oregon projects did he start?

433 Who was the founder-winemaker of Argyle Winery in the Dundee Hills?

434 Ken Wright Cellars began in 1994 in the town of Carlton in the Willamette Valley. How many Pinot Noirs does he bottle?

435 Speaking of Ken Wright Cellars, each of his Pinot Noirs have unique and exciting wine labels. Who is the dynamic artist?

436 Located at 45 degrees latitude, the Willamette Valley corresponds to what wine region in France?

437 What Oregon winery is the largest producer of Pinot Gris in the state?

438 Dr. Revana, owner of the Revana Winery in Napa Valley, has started a winery in Oregon named what?

439 Name the three of the seven AVAs of the Willamette Valley.

(Clones are genetic sub-types of a grape variety that allow options: color; intensity; tannin; yields; alcohol; etc.).

440 Name two of the numerical Dijon clones of Pinot Noir used in Oregon viticulture.

441 What AVA is directly south of Walla Walla Valley, extending into Oregon?

442 The Willakenzie Estate name references what two things?

443 Which AVA does not belong? Eola-Amity Hills, Applegate, Umpqua, Rogue.

444 Who is out of place? Tom Mortimer; Ken Wright; Meredith Smith; Mike Etzel; Rollin Soles.

445 Who is affectionally known as *Papa Pinot*?

446 Finish the official title of A to Z _____.

---

432 Archery Summit in 1993 and Gypsy Dancer in 2002. (And Christine Lorrane Cellars in New Zealand).

433 Rollin Soles, 1987. (Now co-owns with spouse Corby ROCO Winery in Newberg).

434 13. (The fruit is hand sorted, small batch open top fermentation, and complete minimalist approach).

435 David Berkvam. (A talented local artist, Ken and wife Karen fell in love with his work at a Portland show).

436 Burgundy. (Not coincidentally, both regions produce world-class Pinot Noir and Chardonnay.)

437 King Estate. (Located southeast of Eugene in southern Oregon. Founded in 1991).

438 Alexana. (This winery is named after his daughter Alexandra. His passion is Pinot Noir).

439 Dundee Hills, Yamhill-Carlton, Eola-Amity Hills, McMinnville, Chehalem Mountains, Ribbon Ridge, Van Duzer.

440 113; 114; 115; 667; 777; 828, etc.

441 The Rocks District of Milton-Freewater AVA. (Perhaps the lengthiest name for an AVA in the US)?

442 Willakenzie is a local *soil type* named for two local rivers, the Willamette and McKenzie.

443 Eola-Amity Hills. (An AVA in northern Oregon (Willamette Valley), and the others are from southern Oregon).

444 Meredith Smith. (She is the winemaker at Ste. Chapelle in Idaho, the others are from the Willamette Valley).

445 David Lett, Eyrie Vineyards. (David & Dianna started their winery in 1965 in Dundee. He passed in 2008).

446 Wineworks. (Founded in 2002 by winery veterans Deb & Bill Hatcher, Sam Tannahill and Cheryl Francis).

447 Which winery bottles a Nuthouse & Spirithouse label? They include Pinot Noir, Chardonnay, and Riesling.

448 Which is out of place? Bergström; Domaine Serene; Adelsheim; Leonetti Cellar; Brick House; Archery Summit; Ponzi.

447 Argyle. (Located in the Dundee Hills, these labels are reflective of their farming history).

448 Leonetti. (Leonetti is based in Walla Walla Valley AVA in Washington, the others are from Oregon).

WASHINGTON STATE

GENERAL QUESTIONS

449 True or False? Washington ranks #3 in American wine production behind California and New York.

450 Approximately how many wineries are in Washington State? 245, 460, 728, 1,000, 1,350.

451 How many AVAs are in Washington?

452 What were the first 3 AVA designated in Washington State?

453 Columbia Valley AVA is located on which side of the Cascade mountain range?

454 True or False? Wineries on the east side of the Cascade mountain range never need to irrigate the vineyards.

455 True or False? The Columbia Valley AVA is the 3rd largest wine growing region in Washington.

456 What is the most recent AVA named in Washington State?

---

449 False. (Washington is the # 2 volume behind California).

450 In 2021, the number slightly exceeded 1,000.

451 20.

452 (The first was *Yakima Valley AVA* in 1983, followed by *Columbia Valley AVA* & *Walla Walla Valley AVA* in 1984).

453 East. (The Cascades act as a rain shadow keeping all the wet weather in the west, and arid on the east).

454 False. (Almost everybody needs to irrigate as annual rainfall is 6-8 inches. The Columbia River is the reservoir).

455 False. (The largest by far, composed of 11,000,000 total acres, with about 60,000 acres planted).

456 Rocky Reach AVA granted in 2022.

457 What are the other three AVAs that overlap Washington and Oregon?

458 Name the largest winery in Washington State.

459 What is the name of the joint venture winery between Chateau Ste. Michelle and Piero Antinori in Washington?

460 Which does not belong? Andrew Will, Beaux Frères, Betz Family, Quilceda Creek, Buty; Cayuse.

461 Which winery bottles the following? Harrison Hill; Chaleur Estate; Grand Ciel; Four Flags; Métier; D2.

462 Where does the Red Mountain AVA get its name from?

463 Canvasback Winery is owned by which larger winery?

464 The ultra-premium Klipsun Vineyard on Red Mountain was just sold by Patricia and David Gelles. Who was the buyer?

465 Where did the name Klipsun come from?

466 What does not belong? Yakima Valley, Horse Heaven Hills, Dundee Hills, Naches Heights, Snipes Mountain.

467 Eroica (Riesling) is named after what?

468 Who was the first person to plant Riesling in Washington State?

469 What is the winery project started by Chateau Ste Michelle's Alan Shoup and several international winemakers?

470 Which is out of place? L'Ecole No. 41; Leonetti; Quilceda Creek; Argyle; Col Solare; Kiona Vineyards.

471 Name the winery in Walla Walla Valley that makes Perigee and Apogee wines?

---

457 Columbia Valley, Columbia Gorge, and Walla Walla Valley.

458 Chateau Ste. Michelle. (The winery's roots date back to the repeal of Prohibition).

459 Col Solare. (Italian for *Shining Hill*, this Cabernet Sauvignon is produced from the Red Mountain AVA.)

460 Beaux Frères. (This winery is from The Willamette Valley in Oregon, and the others based in Washington).

461 DeLille Cellars. (Based in Woodinville, the project was started by Charles Lill and Chris Upchurch in 1992).

462 Often one can see reddish colored grass in the spring.

463 Duckhorn. (Canvasback is in the Red Mountain AVA, within the larger Columbia Valley AVA in Washington State).

464 Terlato Wines International. (The 120-acre property, established in 1984, is planted to seven varieties).

465 In the native Chinook dialect, it translates to sunset.

466 Dundee Hills. (Dundee Hills is an AVA in Oregon, and the others are AVAs in Washington).

467 Beethoven's Third Symphony. (Joint venture from Chateau Ste. Michelle / German winemaker Ernst Loosen).

468 W.B. Bridgman. (In 1917 he planted the grapes on what is now Snipes Mountain AVA).

469 Long Shadows. (Poet's Leap, Feather, Pedestal, Pirouette, Sequel, Saggi, Chester-Kidder).

470 Argyle. (Argyle is in the Willamette Valley in Oregon and the others are based in Washington).

471 L'Ecole No. 41. (*Perigee* is from Seven Hills Vineyard, and *Apogee* is from Pepper Bridge Vineyard).

472 Which winery was founded in 1978 by Alex & Jeanette Golitzen? (Son Paul has achieved six 100-point Cabernets).

473 Gary & Nancy Figgins started Leonetti Cellar in 1977. Where did the name Leonetti come from?

474 Northstar Winery is in Walla Walla Valley had their first vintage in 1994. Who was the first winemaker?

475 Which is not made by Charles Smith? Velvet Devil; Boom Boom; Eve; The Raveonettes; Kung Fu Girl; Band of Roses.

472 Quilceda Creek. (This top Cabernet producer sources from Champoux; Palengat; Lake Wallula, etc.,).
473 Walla Walla Valley's 1st winery was originally owned by Francesco & Rosa Leonetti, Gary's grandparents.
474 Jed Steele. (Current winemaker is Dave Merfield, and Jed still consults).
475 The Raveonettes. (This was a Danish duo rock band managed by Charles Smith, and the others are his wines).

CHAPTER 2

CANADA

GENERAL QUESTIONS

476 Name the two major wine growing provinces of Canada?

477 Is wine made in any other Canadian provinces?

478 True or False? All Canadian wines are made from European vine species.

479 There are approximately how many Canadian wineries? 200; 400; 600; 800; 1,000.

480 What do the letters VQA mean and signify regarding Canadian wines?

481 Name British Columbia's largest and most famous wine region?

482 Name the largest and most popular wine region in Ontario?

483 True or False? Canadian Ice Wine production is 3rd in volume behind Germany & Austria.

484 True or False? Riesling is the primary grape used for Canada's Ice Wine production.

---

476 *British Columbia* in the western part of the country and *Ontario* in the eastern part of the country.

477 Yes. 7 out of the 10 provinces make wine commercially.

478 False. (Recent plantings have been European varieties, but many are hybrids & vitis Labrusca (American species).

479 ≈ 800. (In recent years, the number of commercial wineries has grown dramatically).

480 Vintners Quality Alliance. (It signifies that the wine is purely Canadian wine, no blends from other countries).

481 Okanagan Valley. (This north-south valley is ≈ 150 miles long and is home to over 300 wineries).

482 Niagara Peninsula. (This region is larger than the Okanagan Valley by almost twice the planted acreage).

483 False. (Canada produces more Ice Wine than the rest of the world combined. Germany is # 2 in volume).

484 False. (The French hybrid grape *Vidal Blanc* is the most common grape used in Ice Wine production).

485 Briefly describe the steps in producing a Canadian Ice Wine. (PS. They must have a specific grape listed on the label).

486 Which is not a winery in the Okanagan Valley? Cedar Creek; Sandhill; Gehringer; Gray Monk; Fielding; Blue Mountain.

487 Which is not a winery in the Niagara Peninsula? Cave Spring; Lailey; Château des Charmes; Sumac Ridge; Creekside.

488 Where is the famous Inniskillin winery located?

489 Which winery in Canada was the first to commercially produce an Icewine?

485 Frozen grapes are handpicked; grapes are pressed while frozen; only the most sugar-rich juice is exuded.
486 Fielding. (This winery is based in the Niagara Peninsula, and the others are from the Okanagan Valley).
487 Sumac Ridge. (This winery is based in the Okanagan Valley; the others are from the Niagara Peninsula).
488 Inniskillin has properties in both the Niagara Peninsula and the Okanagan Valley.
489 Hillebrand. (Their 1st vintage was 1983, and they are in the Niagara Peninsula).

CHAPTER 3

MEXICO

GENERAL QUESTIONS

490 True or False? The history of Mexican wine dates to the mid-1800s following the lead of California.

491 Name the largest wine growing area in Mexico.

492 Approximately how many wineries are in Baja California? 50; 100; 150; 200; 250.

493 Name the most famous wine region within Baja California.

494 What Pacific Ocean influence brings cold air into the Valle de Guadalupe?

495 In addition to the Humboldt Current, what other geographical feature mitigates the heat of Mexico?

496 Name the oldest winery in the New World, which happens to be in Mexico.

497 Name the dominant wine producer in Baja California.

---

490 False. (Wine grapes were first planted in Mexico in the 1500s, nearly 200 years before California).

491 Baja California. (This area represents nearly 90% of all wine produced in Mexico).

492 ≈ 150 wineries. (Many produce vitis Vinifera, many also distill wine to produce brandy).

493 Valle de Guadalupe. (The valley is often referred to as Mexico's Napa Valley).

494 The Humboldt Current. (Mexico's climate is generally warm, and grapes benefit from the cooling effect).

495 Elevation. (The current trend is to plant grapes on hillsides at higher elevations).

496 Casa Madero. (Founded in 1597, it is still in business).

497 L. A. Cetto. (Founded in 1928, they own vineyards in many subregions, all producing large volumes of wine).

498 L. A. Cetto grows many grapes, but what is their most famous grape variety, exported worldwide?

499 What well-known Spanish company that invested in Mexico's Brandy business.

500 Name the other Spanish wine company that replaced Domecq in Mexico.

501 True or False? If grape blends are listed on a label, they must designate the highest to lowest percentages in order.

502 Which is not a winery from Mexico? Casa Madero; San Luis Potosi; Vinisterra; Viñedos Malagon; Monte Xanic.

498 Nebbiolo. (The famous grape of Barolo, brought to Mexico by Italian immigrants).

499 Domecq. (They brought their Spanish Brandy expertise to Mexico).

500 González Byass. (Owners of Tio Pepe Fino Sherry, El Presidente Mexican Brandy, etc.).

501 False. (Although some do that, it is not an official regulation).

502 San Luis Potosi. (This is a geographical wine producing area near Mexico City, and the others are wineries).

PART II

EUROPE

(FRANCE - ITALY - GERMANY - AUSTRIA - SPAIN - PORTUGAL)

CHAPTER 4

FRANCE

France is a remarkably diverse country with a long and storied history of grape growing and winemaking as well as distilled spirits. Each wine region will have its own set of wine trivia questions and the corresponding educational answers. The first set of questions we be general in nature, followed by a more in-depth study.

Note: France's highest quality wines and spirits are made under an official "named place" system called Appellation d'Origine Protégée (AOP.) This term has recently replaced the older term, Appellation d'Origine Contrôlée (AOC.) You will still find both terms being used by French wine producers.

WINE PRODUCING REGIONS

Champagne: *General questions, including a section on bottle sizes, and Champagne bubble properties.*

Bordeaux: *General questions followed by Left Bank, Right Bank and Whites Wines (sweet and dry).*

Burgundy: *Starting with a few general questions, followed by:*

La Côte d'Or: *Côte de Nuits, Côte de Beaune, (red and white), and an extra credit segment.*

Chablis

Côte Chalonnaise, Mâconnais, Beaujolais.

Northern Rhône Valley

Southern Rhône Valley

The Loire Valley

Alsace

Languedoc and Roussillon

The Remaining French Wine Regions

Spirits Producing Regions

Cognac

Armagnac

FRANCE

FRANCE

GENERAL QUESTIONS

1   What do you call a person who is passionate about all things French, including wine?

2   The French Revolution occurred in 1789, creating what new situation for many of the vineyards?

3   After the French Revolution, what other change occurred relating to inheritance laws and fragmentation of ownership?

4   What year was the AOC instituted?

5   What wine region was the first official AOC so designated in France in 1936?

6   Currently, how many wine AOPs are there in France?

7   What is the smallest AOP in France?

8   True or False? French grapevines for the most part, are planted more southerly than Spain's vineyards.

---

1   Francophile. (These people often put French wines above all else).
2   The Revolution took vineyards away from royalty and religious orders, selling them affordably to the people.
3   The Napoleonic Code of 1804. (Prior, the oldest son inherited everything, now equally divided among all heirs).
4   Discussions started in 1935, but 1936 is considered the official start year.
5   Châteauneuf-du-Pape. (AOC regulations were modeled upon those already in place in Châteauneuf-du-Pape).
6   360. (Although this number changes 360 (±) is consensual, including the 11 major wine growing areas).
7   La Romanée. (This 2-acre estate is in the Burgundy region. More information in the Burgundy chapter).
8   False. (Latitudinally, almost the entire country of France is located north of Spain).

9   Which region is more northerly, Bordeaux or Burgundy?

10 Which wine region is larger in acreage and wine volume, Burgundy or Bordeaux?

11 What term refers to a producer that purchases wine from growers and matures and bottles it under their own label?

12 What French term is a service that brokers wine between growers and négociants?

13 What term is used in Burgundy (and other regions) for families that make wine from their own vineyards?

14 What French term is used defining "bringing up" the wine, referring primarily to time spent aging in barrel?

15 What French term is used for a vineyard that has a walled parameter?

16 True or False? Rouge and Blanc in French refers to styles of Champagne.

17 What wine district is the city of Strasbourg located in?

18 What is the closest wine region to Paris?

19 What is the French word for wine?

20 What is the French term for grape variety/varieties?

21 The term *hectare* is used in France (and throughout Europe). What is a hectare?

22 True or False? Beaujolais wine is produced in almost every country in Europe.

23 What broad category of wine is often consumed in the French Riviera during the summer vacations?

24 Champagne bubbles are created from which three gases?

---

9   Burgundy. (Burgundy is north and east of Bordeaux, and in the central/eastern part of the country).

10 Bordeaux is larger by far with ≈ 300k acres planted versus ≈ 70k acres planted in Burgundy.

11 Négociant. (This meets their own needs as well as provides income for growers that don't make their own wine).

12 Courtiers. (Essentially the middleman that sets up pricing and often the logistics of wines being picked-up).

13 Domaine. (Normally small individually owned vineyards.)

14 Élevage. (Used in several regions of France, but commonly used on négociant labels in Burgundy).

15 Clos. (Often a historic walled enclosure. Commonly used in Burgundy and Champagne).

16 False. (Rouge and blanc are French for red and white.)

17 Alsace. (Alsace is in northeast France. The Rhine river forms the border between France and Germany).

18 Champagne. (The Champagne region is about 90 miles northeast of Paris).

19 Vin. (A white wine is called vin blanc, red wine is vin rouge, and a rosé wine is vin rosé. Vins is plural).

20 Cépage(s). (A grape may be singled out, but Cépages could be used defining the % of specific grapes in blends).

21 A metric unit of land measurement. (1 hectare = 2.47 acres).

22 False. (It is distinctly French, specifically from the Beaujolais region in the southern part of Burgundy).

23 Rosé. (Most from the Côte de Provence AOC and made from both red and white grapes).

24 Carbon dioxide is the *only* gas.

25 Name the term the French use for traditional method sparkling wine made outside of the Champagne region?

26 True or False? Bordeaux produces more white wine than red wines.

27 True or False? Pouilly-Fuissé and Pouilly-Fumé are the *same wines* from two different villages in France.

28 What is the French spelling for Burgundy?

29 True or False? True Chablis may be produced in California.

30 Many regions of France use the term Château on their labels. Does the term define production styles or tasting notes?

31 True or False? A French wine that is *vintage dated* refers to the year in which the grapes were harvested.

32 In Burgundy, which category denotes higher quality, Premier Cru or Grand Cru?

33 How does the confusing term *Cru* translate from French to English?

34 What microscopic aphid devastated the vineyards of France (and most of Europe) in the mid-to-late-1800s?

35 Which is out of place? Burgundy, Bordeaux, Loire Valley, Normandy, Rhône Valley, Champagne, Alsace.

36 What is the French term for winemaker?

37 After the fall of the Roman Empire in the 5th century, who started controlling the vineyards in France?

---

25 Crémant. (Crémant de Bourgogne, Crémant d'Alsace and Crémant de Limoux, etc.).

26 False. (There is much more red wine produced, although white, rosé and sparkling wines are made as well).

27 False. (Pouilly-Fuissé is from Burgundy (Chardonnay), and Pouilly-Fumé is from Loire Valley (Sauvignon Blanc).

28 Bourgogne. (The entry level wines from the area are simply called Bourgogne blanc and Bourgogne rouge).

29 False. (Chablis is a protected Burgundian sub-appellation for white wine made exclusively from Chardonnay).

30 Neither. (Château is defined as mansion or a simple home owned by the family living on the wine estate).

31 True. (The term "non-vintage" refers to a wine made from two or more vintage years).

32 Grand Cru. (Both terms indicate officially classified vineyards, but Grand Cru are the greatest of these).

33 Cru roughly translates to "superior growing site". (It can refer to villages or vineyards in France).

34 Phylloxera. (This pest was accidentally imported from the US. It feeds on the roots, eventually killing the vine).

35 Normandy. (Normandy is notable for Calvados, a spirit. The rest are primarily winegrowing regions.)

36 (*Vigneron*-pronounced veen-yer-ahn.)

37 The Catholic Church. (The Benedictine and Cistercian orders were very diligent in documenting vine/wine data).

38 What is one explanation as to why the standard wine bottles is 750 ml., or three-quarters of a liter?

39 The French phrase "*La vie est trop courte pour boire du mauvais vin.*" translates to what in English?

---

38 When wine bottles were handmade, this was roughly the size that a glassblower could create in 1 breath.
39 "Life is too short to drink bad wine."

FRANCE

CHAMPAGNE

40 True or False? The word *Champagne* is legally allowed on any bottle that contains bubbles produced worldwide.

41 Is the region of Champagne in northern or southern France?

42 At what latitudinal line is Champagne located?

43 True or False? Champagne is located approximately 130 miles northwest of Paris.

44 True or False? The finest Champagne producers all use irrigation and mechanical harvesting to get the best results.

45 What are the 3 major wine growing districts of the Champagne region?

46 In what two towns/cities are many of the most famous Champagne "houses" located?

47 True or False? Only white grapes are used in the production of Champagne.

48 What are the three major grapes used for champagne production?

---

40 False. (Champagne is a protected appellation of origin in France).

41 Northern France. (The cool climate is ideal for growing Chardonnay and Pinot Noir, the primary grapes used).

42 49th N. (It is sometimes difficult to ripen grapes this far north, although climate change is pushing the boundary).

43 False. (The region is about 90 miles northeast of Paris).

44 False. (Neither of these techniques are allowed by local regulations).

45 Vallée de la Marne (Central), Côte des Blancs (South) and Montagne de Reims (North).

46 Épernay (in the Vallée de la Marne) and Reims (in the Montagne de Reims).

47 False. (Of the three primary varieties, two are red grapes).

48 *Pinot Noir, Meunier*, both red grapes, and *Chardonnay*, a white grape).

49 Approximately what are the percentages of the three grapes planted in the Champagne region?

50 In a few words, describe what each grape adds to the wine: Pinot Noir; Meunier; Chardonnay.

51 In addition to the three primary varieties, what are the four additional permitted varieties?

52 What grapes are allowed to make a Blanc de Blancs (white wine from white grapes) style Champagne?

53 There are several soil compositions in the region. Name the major type.

54 Approximately how many acres make up the Champagne region?

55 The late Jurassic (152-157 million years ago) → Kimmeridgian soil (Chablis, Sancerre) etc. Which Champagne area has it?

56 Approximately how many major Champagne houses exist in the region? 125; 208, 295, 350, 460.

57 In sequence of volume of production, list the top four Champagne producers.

58 What term is used for *still wines* produced in the region?

59 True or False? Côteaux Champenois is exclusively a white wine.

60 What is the name of Bollinger's Côteaux Champenois?

61 What phrase is out of place? Primary fermentation, prestige cuvée, secondary fermentation, riddling, disgorging.

62 What is the difference between *vintage* Champagne and *non-vintage* Champagne?

63 What was the original name of Champagne Deutz, founded in 1838 in the village of Aÿ?

64 What are 2 techniques are used to produce Rosé Champagne?

---

49 Pinot Noir ≈ 40%; Meunier ≈ 32%; Chardonnay ≈ 28%.

50 *Pinot Noir*: Body; Structure; Power. *Meunier*: Fruitiness; Suppleness. *Chardonnay*: Finesse; Elegance; Delicacy.

51 Arbane, Petit Meslier, Pinot Blanc, and Fromenteau (Pinot Gris).

52 Chardonnay, Arbane, Petit Meslier, Pinot Blanc and Fromenteau are all allowed.

53 Limestone. (This is a blend of chalk and marl (calcium carbonite and clay/silt) is about 75% of the mix).

54 Approximately 84,000 acres. (The majority is owned by growers who sell grapes to producers).

55 The Côte des Bar in the Aube. (This chalk/marl/limestone is the primary soil in bedrock of the vineyards).

56 ≈ 350. (This number may sound high, however there are approximately 4,700 small producers).

57 Moët & Chandon; Veuve Clicquot; Nicolas Feuillatte; G.H. Mumm.

58 Côteaux Champenois. (These wines are very dry and high in acid).

59 False. (By far, more red wine is produced. White and rosé are also produced, but in tiny quantities).

60 La Côte aux Enfants. (This is a still red wine and is vintage dated, from a 10-acre plot in the village of Aÿ).

61 Prestige Cuvée. (This is a *luxury style*, while the others relate to production steps).

62 Vintage is made from a single harvest year, non-vintage is a blend of two or more years, creating consistency.

63 Deutz & Geldermann. (In 1983 the house was acquired by the Rouzaud family, owners of Louis Roederer).

64 Skin contact with dark skinned grapes or blending still red and white wine until the desired color is achieved.

——————   FRANCE   ——————

65 True or False? Stainless-steel tanks are the only medium used for primary fermentation.

66 What is the French term for the Champagne *cellar master* in charge of the entire production team?

67 What years defined the life span of Dom Pierre Pérignon?

68 In what location did Dom Pérignon practice his craft?

69 What term identifies the *indentation* at the bottom of the Champagne bottles?

70 What is the French term for the wire cage that holds the wine cork in place?

71 What is the French term for the metal disc anchored to the top of the cork by the Muselet?

72 What do you call these people that collect plaque de muselet souvenirs?

73 What word is used for Champagne's effervescence once it is in the glass.

74 In the cellar, what is the French term for the daily turning/angling of the bottles, funneling the yeast towards the neck?

75 What is the French term for the A-framed shaped riddling racks?

76 How many Champagne bottles can a good *Remueur* (bottle turner) rotate in a day?

77 What is the French term for the automated riddling machine?

78 How many bottles may be stacked in a gyropalette?

79 Submerging the bottles in very cold salty water does what to the yeast deposit in the neck of the bottle?

80 What is the name of the clarifying process that expels the frozen yeast from the bottle?

65 False. (Oak barrels and glass/resin lined concrete tanks are used by some producers).

66 Chef de Cave. (This talented person oversees all phases of winemaking, blending, and aging).

67 1639 – 1715. (His statue adorns the courtyard at Moët & Chandon in Épernay).

68 Abbaye Saint-Pierre d'Hautvillers. (Formally a Benedictine monastery in the Marne départment).

69 Kick or Punt. (This configuration adds strength to the base of the bottle to handle up to 90 pounds of pressure).

70 Muselet. (Muzzle in English, this cage prevents the cork from exploding into the ionosphere).

71 Plaque de Muselet. (Normally the producer's logo, or a special cuvée graphically displayed on this disc).

72 Placomusophiles. (I guess there is a name for every type of collector).

73 Mousse. (The bubble activity (mousse) is ferocious from bottle to glass, then the mousse activity dissipates).

74 *Remuage.* (Riddling in English), is the late-stage task of turning the bottles daily within the riddling racks.

75 Pupitre. (These wooden racks normally hold 120 bottles).

76 ≈ 40,000 bottles. (Turning the bottle 1/8 to 1/4 turn and using gravity to bring the yeast to the top of the bottle).

77 Gyropalette. (This modern technology has mostly replaced tedious hand-riddling).

78 504. (This machine accomplishes the task in one week versus six weeks for hand-riddling).

79 It freezes the yeast deposit (making the next step in the process possible.)

80 Disgorging. (Dégorgement). This step utilizes the CO_2 pressure in the bottle to eject the frozen yeast plug).

81 List three of the seven established terms that define the *driest* levels of Champagne.

82 List the remaining four of the seven established terms that defines sweeter levels of Champagne.

83 Who many grams per liter of sugar are allowed in a Sec (Dry); Demi-Sec; and Doux?

84 Perrier-Jouët makes a cuvée called Nuit Blanche. How does this flavor profile differ from La Belle Époque?

85 Name three ways that blending plays an especially important role in Champagne production.

86 What is the newer term meaning the same thing as Méthode Champenoise (Champagne Method)?

87 What term is used for Champagne houses that may own some vineyards, but also purchase grapes from farmers).

88 What is the French term for a grower/producer in the Champagne region?

89 What casual term did importer Terry Theise coin for Récoltant-Manipulant producers?

90 Name 2 Récoltant-Manipulant producers that were introduced to the US over the years by Terry Theise.

91 Referring to the merits of R-M Champagne, who said "Blending blurs distinction, and erases diversity"?

92 Name the largest Coopérative-Manipulant (C-M) (meaning Cooperative Producer) in Champagne?

93 Which does not belong? G.H. Mumm; Perrier-Jouët; Louis Roederer; Veuve Clicquot; Ruinart; Krug; Taittinger.

94 What does not belong? Cristal, Belle Époque, Cuvée Monsieur Napoléon, Cuvée Sir Winston Churchill, Palmes d'Or.

---

81 Brut Nature; Extra Brut; Brut. (Brut indicates a dry style but may contain up to 12 grams/liter or 1.2% sugar).

82 Extra Dry; Sec (Dry); Demi-Sec; Doux. (These are based on higher residual sugar content).

83 < 17-32 g/l.; < 32-50g/l.; 50 plus g/l. (These are often served with a dessert course if you can even find them).

84 Nuits Blanche fits into the *SEC* category of higher levels of RS, as the dosage is ≈ 20 g/liter.

85 Different varieties are blended, villages/vineyards are blended, and vintages are blended.

86 Méthode Traditionnelle (Traditional Method.) (In EU regulations, *Tradition* replaces *Champenoise*).

87 Négociant-Manipulant (N-M). (They negotiate prices with grape growers and make wine under their own label.)

88 Récoltant-Manipulant. (R-M). (A producer that makes their own Champagne from their own vineyards).

89 Farmer Fizz. (Also known as Grower Champagne).

90 Chartogne-Taillet; A Margaine; René Geoffroy; Vilmart; Gaston-Chiquet; Pierre Gimonnet; Pierre Péters, etc.

91 Rajat Parr. (The rauthor of: *Secrets of the Sommeliers* and *The Sommelier's Atlas of Taste*).

92 Nicolas Feuillatte. (Based in Chouilly, outside Épernay, this organization works with 5,000 growers).

93 Perrier-Jouët. (Based in the Épernay, (Côte des Blancs), the others are in Reims (Montagne de Reims)).

94 Cuvée Monsieur Napoléon. (This is a made-up name, and the others are prestige cuvées).

95   Which name is out of place? Perrier-Jouët; Pierre Gimonnet; Moët & Chandon; Veuve-Clicquot; Pommery.

96   Which does not belong? Egly-Ouriet; Cédric Bouchard; Frère Jacques; Jacques Selosse; Jérôme Prévost; Paul Bara.

97   Name 3 Champagne houses with Heidsieck in their names.

98   Name 3 Champagne houses with Perrier in their names.

99   What term is used in Rosé production when skins are left in the tank and the pink wine is removed?

100 Name Philipponnat's most famous specific vineyard site?

101 Which Champagne house produces N.P.U. (Ne Plus Ultra). 1990 was the first vintage.

102 Which Champagne producer is older? Perrier-Jouët or Moët & Chandon?

103 Many mis-pronounce Moët & Chandon & Perrier-Jouët. What are the correct pronunciations?

104 What is the French term for the ring of bubbles at the top of the Champagne glass?

105 In addition to the three major Champagne wine growing districts, what are the two lesser-known areas?

106 What term is out of place? Liqueur de Tirage; Aÿ; Autolysis; Pupitres; Sur-Lie; Dégorgement; Remuage; Vin Clair.

107 Champagne producer L. Aubry makes a cuvée using all 7 of the original grapes. Name the wine?

108 Bollinger Champagne makes a blend labeled R.D. What does R.D. stand for?

109 What is one reason that Champagne producers keep the juice in contact with the lees in the bottle for so long?

---

95 Pierre Gimonnet. (He is a small grower-producer (R-M), and the others are large négociants (N-M).

96 Frère Jacques. (This is a famous French nursery rhyme; the others are exceptional R-M producers).

97 Charles Heidsieck; Heidsieck & Co. - Monopole; Piper-Heidsieck.

98 Joseph Perrier; Laurent-Perrier; Perrier-Jouët.

99 Saignée. (French term meaning *to bleed*, as in bleeding the pink wine off the skins.)

100 Clos des Goisses. (Just over 14 acres in size, this wine was first released in 1935).

101 Bruno Paillard. ("There Is Nothing Beyond." 4 Grand Cru villages; 12 years aging in the cellar).

102 Moët & Chandon. (Founded in 1743 by Claude Moët; Perrier-Jouët was founded in 1811).

103 Mo-ETT ay Shahn-don; Per-ee-AY Joo-ETT. (The T in each name is pronounced)

104 Collerette or Collar. (These bubbles remain intact until they eventually burst).

105 Côte de Sézanne and Côte des Bar, aka the Aube. (These areas are located south of the main regions).

106 Aÿ. (Aÿ is a Grand Cru village in the Vallée de la Marne. The other words relate to Champagne production).

107 Le Nombre d'Or. (They also make a Blanc des Blancs from the 3 white grapes called Le Nombre d'Or, *Sablé*).

108 Recently Disgorged. (Récemment Dégorgé in French. After extended aging a youthful freshness is created).

109 Decades on the lees prevents oxidation, so recently disgorged Champagnes remain stylistically more youthful.

110 Founded in the village of Aÿ in 1829, Bollinger makes a Blanc de Noirs Champagne named what?

111 Name the two "Clos" bottlings from Krug Champagne.

112 How large is the Clos du Mesnil vineyard? How large is the Clos d'Ambonnay vineyard?

113 Which Champagne producer bottles Volupé, Expression, Empreinte and Les Houtrants?

114 What was the first vintage of Dom Pérignon?

115 What was the first vintage of Dom Pérignon Rosé?

116 In 2000, Richard Geoffroy, Chef du Cave of Dom Pérignon, created a series of much older vintage blends called what?

117 Taking Oenothèque up a level, what was Geoffroy's next step showing "time is not linear" same vintage bottling project?

118 What does the Dom Pérignon Plénitude (P2 & P3) project define? Plénitude refers to a *Plateau* of evolutionary change.

119 Who is the Chef de Caves at Dom Pérignon that replaced the 28-year veteran Richard Geoffroy?

120 What is the *average* Champagne bubble size? 1/100 mm; ½ mm; 1 cm, 5 cm.

121 Approximately how many bubbles are in a bottle of high-quality Champagne?

122 Who was the artist that created Champagne Perrier-Jouët's iconic Belle Époque (flower) bottle?

123 Cuvée Sir Winston Churchill is the Prestige Cuvée of what Champagne house? What was the first vintage?

---

110 Vieilles Vignes Françaises. (This from a tiny vineyard planted to very old, un-grafted pre-phylloxera vines.)

111 *Clos du Mesnil* (First vintage 1979, 100% Chardonnay), *Clos d'Ambonnay* (First vintage 1995, 100% Pinot Noir).

112 Clos du Mesnil is ≈ 4.5 acres; Clos d'Ambonnay is ≈ 1.67 acres.

113 René Geoffrey. (Based in the western Grande Vallée, primarily in Cumières and in Aÿ).

114 1921. (Dom Pérignon is arguably the most famous of all Prestige Cuvée Champagnes).

115 1959. (This was commercially released in 1962).

116 Oenothèque. (All recently disgorged and showed their unique aging capabilities).

117 Plénitudes. (P1: Current vintage Dom Pérignon; P2: additional aging; P3: aged ≈ 25 years complex/integration).

118 Normal aging of yeast contact (P1), P2 & P3 incorporate maturation elevations of mouthfeel, aromas, and color.

119 Vincent Chaperon. (Vincent worked with Richard for 13 years, so his talents extend the tradition).

120 ½ millimeter is probably closet. (The bubble size changes at various stages, especially closer to the surface).

121 50 Million. (Although tests vary, according to Bill Lembeck (Beekmanwine.com) ≈ 50 million is the calculation).

122 Émile Gallé. (This art-nouveau glassmaker's first label was in 1902, but then discontinued until 1964 vintage).

123 Champagne Pol Roger. 1975. (Released in 1984, marking the 10th anniversary of the death of Churchill-1965).

124 Louis Roederer created a luxury Champagne in 1876 called what, and for which Russian Czar?

125 What was unique about the "Cristal" Champagne bottle itself? (It was probably the first Prestige Cuvée).

126 Which Champagne house produces *Le Clos Saint-Hilaire*?

127 *Liqueur de Tirage* initiates what step in Champagne production?

128 What French term is used after primary fermentation has occurred, and the Liqueur de Tirage is added?

129 During the lees aging process in the bottle, what is the minimum aging time for the *non-vintage* category?

130 During the lees aging process in the bottle, what is the minimum aging time for the *vintage* category?

131 Name the two other historic additions that were once allowed at the Liqueur de Tirage step of production?

132 To create the standard 6 atmospheres of pressure, how many grams of sugar are required in the *liqueur de tirage*?

133 *Liquer d'expédition* is a term that completes what step in Champagne production?

134 What is the term used to describe the breaking down of dead yeast cells during the bottle aging process?

135 Name 3 of the 6 Grand Cru Villages in the Côte des Blancs (Chardonnay villages).

136 What is the most widely planted grape in the Côte des Bars?

137 What was the name of the now-defunct system that ranked Grand and 1er Cru villages on a scale of 80-100%?

---

124 Cristal. Czar Alexander II. (Alexander II was considered a *good* Czar and lived in the late 18th – early 19th century).

125 Made from clear glass so nothing (poison?) could be hidden, and no punt, so explosives could not be hidden.

126 Billecart-Salmon. (Named after the patron saint from the local church in Mareuil-sur-Aÿ. First vintage was 1995).

127 (This is the yeast/sugar combination that is the catalyst creating CO_2 as a captured by-product).

128 *Prise de Mousse*. (Literally, *Foam Creation*. This step may last years as the bottle is aging on its side).

129 15 months. (Although many producers allow more aging time to develop additional complexity).

130 3 years. (Again, many producers provide additional aging as *vintage* is riskier and is higher priced).

131 *Bentonite. (Clay)*. (Prevented yeast from sticking to the side of the bottle). *Cognac*. (If alcohol level was too low).

132 24 grams. (4 grams of sugar (and yeast) create 1 atmosphere of pressure. 4 x 6 = 24 grams).

133 (After dégorgement, a small quantity of wine and sugar called *dosage*, creates the final sugar level).

134 Yeast Autolysis. (Autolysis creates the aromatics of yeast, toasty, biscuit, brioche, etc.).

135 Les Mesnil-sur-Oger; Oger; Avize; Cramant; Chouilly, Oiry.

136 Pinot Noir. (Approximately 85%).

137 The Échelle des Crus 1911-2010 (The higher the ranking, the more growers were paid for their grapes.)

138 How many Grand Cru villages are there in the Champagne region?

139 How many planted acres are contained within the 17 Grand Cru villages?

140 How many Premier Cru villages are there in the Champagne region?

141 How many planted acres are contained within the 41 Premier Cru villages?

142 The remaining villages were ranked from 80% – 89% and referred to as simply *Cru* villages. How many villages here?

143 What is the oldest *winery* in the Champagne region?

144 What is the oldest Champagne house originally making Champagne as we know it today?

145 Which village does not belong? Oiry; Le Mesnil-sur-Oger; Oger; Cuis; Avize; Chouilly; Cramant.

146 Which producer is out of place? Diebolt-Vallois; Duval-Leroy; Marc Hébrart; Larmandier-Bernier; Jacques Selosse.

147 Name the wine made by the legendary Anselme Selosse that uses a *Solera* system like Jerez?

148 Name the Cuvée de Prestige from Veuve-Clicquot in Reims.

149 Name the Cuvée de Prestige produced by Laurent-Perrier?

150 Name the Champagne producer that uniquely makes only one wine, located in the Côte des Blancs.

151 The famous Champagne Ayala was sold in 2005 to whom?

152 Regarding the village of Chouilly, state the unique circumstances of the Chardonnay and Pinot Noir plantings?

153 The reverse Grand Cru / Premier Cru grape classification occurs in which village?

138 17. (The 17 Grand Cru villages were all ranked at the 100% level).

139 ≈ 7,500 acres. (This equates to ≈ 8.6% of all planted vineyards).

140 41. (These villages were ranked between 90% - 99%).

141 ≈ 18,000 acres. (This equates to ≈ 22% of all planted vineyards).

142 In the remaining ≈ 260 villages, farmers were paid between 80% - 89% of the Grand Cru village's prices.

143 Gosset. (Currently owned by the Renaud Cointreau family; founded in 1584, but no bubbles back then).

144 Ruinart. (Founded in 1729, and still in production today).

145 Cuis. (This a Premier Cru village in the Côte des Blancs and the others are Grand Cru villages in Côte des Blancs).

146 Marc Hébrart. (He is based in the Grande Vallée, and the others are in the Côte des Blancs).

147 Substance. (Sourced from two vineyards in Grand Cru village Avize, comprised of every vintage back to 1986).

148 La Grande Dame. (Named for Barbe-Nicole Ponsardin Clicquot who took over after her husband died in 1805).

149 Grand Siècle. (Great Century. The company was founded in 1812, and this cuvée was first release was 1959).

150 Salon. (The fruit source is Les Mesnil-sur-Oger, and is only made from single great vintages, starting in 1905).

151 Bollinger. (Both houses are in Aÿ, and Bollinger is updating the Ayala property, founded in 1860).

152 Chouilly is a Grand Cru village for Chardonnay, and a Premier Cru village for Pinot Noir.

153 Tours-sur Marne. (Grand Cru village for Pinot Noir, and Premier Cru village for Chardonnay).

154 Which does not belong? Charles Dufour; Bérêche et Fils; Drappier; Dosnon; Fleury; Vouette & Sorbée.

155 Founded in 1971, the term *Special Club* was created, and in 1999 was renamed what?

156 Which does not belong? Gaston Chiquet; Paul Bara; Billecart-Salmon; Pierre Gimonnet; Marc Hébrart; A. Margaine.

157 Name the book written by an expert who has tasted and documented more than 8,000 Champagnes.

---

154 Bérêche et Fils. (They are in the Montagne de Reims, and the others are in the Côte des Bars).

155 Club Trésor de Champagne. (There are 28 members of R-M producers judging each other's wines).

156 Billecart-Salmon. (The others are members of the Club Trésor (Special Club) organization).

157 A Scent of Champagne. (Written by Richard Juhlin and contains much more information than tasting notes).

FRANCE

CHAMPAGNE BOTTLE SIZES

These names often reflect Biblical figures including rulers, kings, and emperors.

158 What two bottle sizes are smaller than the standard bottle (750 ml. or 75 cl.).

159 Name the next two sizes larger than the standard 750 ml. bottle in Champagne terms?

160 What does the word *Magnum* mean from a historical translation?

161 Name the next four sizes larger than the Jeroboam.

162 Nebuchadnezzar is a very large Champagne bottle. It is the equivalent of how many standard bottles?

163 Name the three sizes of Champagne bottles above Nebuchadnezzar.

164 And name the last two Champagne bottle sizes greater than the Sovereign.

165 Winston Churchill was a Champagne enthusiast, and many quotes are attributed to him, including the following.

---

158 *Piccolo.* (Also known as a *split* or *quarter bottle*, 187 ml.). *Demi.* (Also known as a half-bottle, 375 ml.).

159 *Magnum.* (Double bottle, 1.5 liter). *Jeroboam.* (3.0 liter or equivalent to 4 standard bottles in one).

160 The definition is *large or great* in Latin.

161 *Rehoboam* (4.5 liters); *Methuselah* (6 liters); *Salmanazar* (9 liters); *Balthazar* (12 liters.)

162 20 standard bottles. (15 liters.)

163 *Melchior* (18 liters); *Solomon* (21 liters); *Sovereign* (25 liters).

164 *Primat* (27 liters); *Malchizedek* (30 liters, equivalent to 40 standard bottles).

165 During WWII: "Remember Gentlemen, it's not just France we're fighting for, it's Champagne."
Regarding Champagne: "In victory, I deserve it. In defeat, I need it."
"The magnum is the perfect sized bottle of Champagne for two people, if only one is drinking!"

CHAMPAGNE BUBBLE PROPERTIES AND FLUID DYNAMICS

166 What is the French word for the sound made when a Champagne cork is extracted?

167 Champagne bottles contain around 6 atmospheres of pressure. What is the underwater equivalent?

168 Early mathematical calculations (yeast/sugar ratios) for tensile bottle strength was determined by which law of physics?

169 Name a reason that bubbles get *larger in size* as they ascend towards the top of the glass.

170 You may observe the bubble pathways are either organized or chaotic. What term defines bubble streams as chaotic?

171 Bubbles may have their shapes deformed as they rise in the glass. What is this a result of?

172 What term is used defining if the bubble stream uses a zig-zag pattern, or has a uniform consistent pathway?

173 What would the term *bubble containment* mean prior to bubble explosion?

174 Only a portion of the bubble extends into the liquid barrier. What is this phase called?

175 After the bubble bursts, what two observations follow?

176 What is the law of physics that keeps bubbles stable and not visible in the sealed bottle?

---

166 *Soupir* (sigh). A gentle whisper versus the celebratory pop often heard at celebratory occasions.

167 50 meters under water. (Not to be confused with PSI (pounds per square inch), which is 90 PSI).

168 Boyle's Law. (How gasses behave regarding volume and pressure in a container).

169 Excess CO_2 penetrates the existing bubble wall and through absorption adds volume to the air pocket.

170 Wake Instabilities. (Larger bubbles overpower the streams created by the smaller bubbles).

171 Speed of bubble ascension is coupled with liquid pressure creating distortion and yielding a zig-zag pathway.

172 Oscillation. (Both bubble trails have their causes and impacts, and all glasses show both trajectories).

173 The bubbles at the top are held under a film of liquid, with capillary forces stronger than the buoyancy factor.

174 The Bubble Cap. (This phase lasts until the surface area tension is overpowered by the bubble kinetics).

175 The burst creates a crackling sound, and a cloud of tiny droplets appear. (Effervescence).

176 Henry's Law of Thermodynamic Equilibrium. (Once opened, CO_2 and bubbles egress → instability → froth).

FRANCE

MY THOUGHTS ON CHAMPAGNE STEMWARE

In the past, Champagne and other sparkling wines were served in a glass called a coupe. These shallow, wide-mouthed glasses were traditional, but not practical. Imagine a server walking around with a tray of coupes at a reception, spilling more wine onto the tray than was left in the glasses, not to mention the speed of bubble dissipation, i.e. the wine went flat quickly.

Starting in the 1970s, Champagne became more expensive, and this called for a better glass. Enter the flute. This narrow, long, cylindrical glass was perfect for visually following the kinetic oscillation pathways of the CO_2 bubbles. However, the very narrow chimney diameter limited the scope of aromatics to yeast and bread dough. "The Sense of Place" aromatics remained non-existent. When using a flute, you are not allowing the Rolls Royce out of the showroom!

The recent movement for Champagne and other premium sparkling wines being served in a white wine glass makes sense. Champagne is first a wine, and secondly a wine that contains bubbles. These bubbles, among other attributes, act as a transport system for aromas. Would you prefer your premium Champagne served in a traditional flute, or in a trending white wine glass? By swirling the wine in the glass (yes, bubble dissipation occurs) you may pick up the nuances and subtleties of terroir not noticeable in a flute.

The Riedel Crystal glassware company has been making various Champagne glasses for years, but current CEO Maximilian Riedel has perfected a Champagne wine glass exclusively for Dom Pérignon that embraces extensively researched swirling bowl metrics with a chimney diameter that focuses and intensifies a multitude of aromas.

More wine stemware comments:

Years ago, I had an amazing opportunity to travel with Maximilian's father Georg Riedel to all his glass factories in Austria and Germany. This visit widened my eyes to the importance of engineered wine stemware. For the past two decades, I incorporate into all my lectures the three-pronged approach to enjoying wine. The viticulturalist must pass on quality grapes to the enologist. Once these two feats are accomplshed, the proper wine glass completes the circle for maximum pleasure.

FRANCE

BORDEAUX - GENERAL QUESTIONS

177 Where within France is the Bordeaux wine region located?

178 How did the region of Bordeaux historically get its name?

179 How many AOP regions are contained within Bordeaux?

180 True or False? The Bordeaux region makes only red wines.

181 Name 3 of the 5 primary red wine varieties allowed in Bordeaux AOPs.

182 Name 2 of the 3 primary white grapes allowed in Bordeaux AOPs.

183 There is a large AOP between the Garonne and Dordogne rivers. What is the name of this AOP?

184 One often observes the term *Château* when discussing Bordeaux wines. What does it normally infer?

185 What is the most widely planted red grape in the Bordeaux wine region?

---

177 The southwestern part of the country. (The city of Bordeaux is the 9th largest city in France).

178 Au Bord de L'eau. *Along the Water's Edge.* (Between the Atlantic Ocean and the Gironde River).

179 Currently, ≈ 60. (Numbers vary as there has been some consolidation and new AOPs in recent years).

180 False. (Although about 85% is red, white (dry & sweet) pink, and sparkling wines are also produced).

181 Cabernet Sauvignon, Cabernet Franc, Merlot, Malbec, and Petite Verdot. (Hint: C.C.M.M.P.)

182 Sauvignon Blanc, Sémillon, Muscadelle. (These 3 grapes are often blended in varying percentages).

183 Entre-duex-Mers [Between two seas (waters). White wines only]..

184 It defines the estate vineyards, the winery, the aging cellars, and often the homestead of the owner.

185 Merlot. (Approximately 70% of all red wine varieties planted).

186 In English, what word does *Merlot* translate to?

187 What are the names of the three major rivers in Bordeaux?

188 What Bordeaux château is the largest in acreage? What is the smallest in acreage?

189 An antiquated term but still in use today, what word was used by the English for Bordeaux wine?

190 How many acres are under vine in the Bordeaux AOP?

191 Is the city of Bordeaux located north or south of the Haut-Médoc AOP?

192 The sparkling wine produced in Bordeaux is labeled by which generic term?

193 What year did Eleanor of Aquitaine of France marry King Henry II of England? Bordeaux was her dowry.

194 When was the Bordeaux region returned to the French?

195 Which *Disney* movie features the 1961 Château Latour and the 1947 Château Cheval Blanc on display?

186 Little Blackbird. (Probably alluding to the color of the grape skin).

187 Gironde, Garonne, and Dordogne. (They all merge and empty into the Atlantic Ocean).

188 Largest: *Château La Borne*. (≈ 800 acres, generic Bordeaux). Smallest: *Château Linot*. (< 2 acres, St.-Estèphe).

189 Claret. (The T is pronounced but was taken from the French word *Clairet* (meaning light in color).

190 Approximately 300,000 acres.

191 South. (The AOPs of Sauternes, Pessac-Léognan and Graves are located south of the city).

192 Crémant de Bordeaux. (Secondary fermentation occurs in the bottle, just like Champagne).

193 1152. (As a result, Bordeaux became part of England, reinforcing the still current British commercial connection).

194 After the Hundred Years War ended in 1453, which in turn led to the War of the Roses just two years later.

195 Ratatouille. (The 2007 animated movie follows Remy, a French country rat seeking a Parisian cooking career).

FRANCE

BORDEAUX – THE MÉDOC AND GRAVES-(AKA THE LEFT BANK)

196 True or False? The French understood how to drain the marshland of the Médoc to plant grapes in the 1700s.

197 True or False? The Gironde River separates the Left Bank from the North Bank of Bordeaux.

198 Name the four village (commune) appellations in the Haut-Médoc where most of the classified châteaux are located.

199 Name two additional village appellations in the Haut-Médoc.

200 What is the last village in the Haut-Médoc AOC before the Médoc AOP begins?

201 What is arguably the most prestigious château in the village of Saint-Seurin-de-Cadourne?

202 What year was the famous Bordeaux Wine Official Classification created?

203 How many Châteaux are currently ranked in the Médoc Classification of Bordeaux?

---

196 False. (It was the Dutch that understood drainage, due to low lying Holland's water problems).

197 False. (The Left Bank is correct, but the other side is referred to the Right Bank, not the north bank).

198 St.-Estèphe; Pauillac; Saint-Julien, Margaux. (Each of these villages is home to dozens of classified châteaux).

199 Listrac and Moulis. (These further inland from the Gironde River than the previously stated four villages).

200 Saint-Seurin-de-Cadourne. (Northwest of this village begins the Médoc AOP).

201 Château Sociando-Mallet. (The Cru Bourgeois classified estate, purchased in 1969 by the late Jean Gautreau).

202 1855. (The wineries represented commanded the highest prices and enjoyed long business histories).

203 61. (There are 5 levels that were ranked from 1st to 5th growths.)

—————— FRANCE ——————

204 Which vintage on the Left Bank was not as good as the others? 1982; 1986; 1988; 1989, 1990; 1992.

205 Did the Bordeaux Wine Official Classification incorporate all the regions of Bordeaux?

206 What was the name of the Château from Graves that was included?

207 Which château is not a Cru Bourgeois? Haut-Marbuzet; Kirwan; Les Ormes-de-Pez; Pontensac; Phélan-Ségur; Siran.

208 What Château in St.-Estèphe AOP is adorned with a Chinese pagoda motif?

209 Château Calon Ségur (3rd Growth) in St.-Estèphe has a heart shaped graphic on the label. What does this signify?

210 What commune boasts of containing 3 of the top 5 Premier Grand Cru Classé wines?

211 Which commune is home to Château: Lagrange; Langoa-Barton; St.-Pierre; Branaire-Ducru; and Gruaud-Larose?

212 In the 1930s, Baron Philippe de Rothschild released Bordeaux's first branded wine. What was it called.

213 Name the two estates in the Pauillac AOC with *Pichon* in their name.

214 Which family owns Château Pontet-Canet (5th Growth, Pauillac?)

215 What year was Château Mouton purchased by the Rothschild family?

216 Why was Château Mouton Rothschild classified as a 2nd Growth at the time of the Classification of 1855?

217 What year was the first "artist label" released by Château Mouton Rothschild? Who was the artist?

---

204 1992. (Off-vintages in any wine region are normally decided by lack of sun, excessive rain, frost, and hail).

205 No. (Just the Haut-Médoc and one famous estate in Graves).

206 Château Haut-Brion. (Graves was the original name of the region, and since 1987 Pessac-Léognan AOP is used).

207 Château Kirwan. (This château is classified as 3rd growth Margaux, and the others are Cru Bourgeois).

208 Cos d'Estournel. (Ranked as a Second Growth along with Château Montrose in the St.-Estèphe AOP).

209 In the 1800s the Marquis de Ségur also owned Châteaux Lafite and Latour, but his *heart* was at Calon.

210 Pauillac AOC. (Home to Château Lafite Rothschild, Château Mouton Rothschild and Château Latour).

211 Saint-Julien. (Saint-Julien is home to 11 of the classified Châteaux, five of which are Second Growths).

212 Mouton-Cadet. (The year was 1930, and Cadet translates to *junior*, or the "little brother of Mouton").

213 Pichon-Longueville Comtesse de Lalande and Pichon-Longueville Baron de Longueville.

214 The Tesseron Family. (Also, owners of Château Lafon-Rochet, 4th Growth St.-Estèphe).

215 1853. (Two years before the classification of 1855).

216 Both winery and vineyards were in disrepair and could not be updated before 1855.

217 1924. Jean Carlu. (This practice proved to be too liberal for many and wasn't repeated until decades later).

218 What year was the second artist label released by Château Mouton Rothschild? Who was the artist?

219 Who was the artist commissioned for the 1958 Château Mouton Rothschild label?

220 Who was the artist commissioned for the 1970 Château Mouton Rothschild label?

221 In what year was Mouton Rothschild elevated from 2nd to 1st Growth? Which artist designed the label?

222 What is the reason for Châteaux to produce what are referred to as *Second Labels*?

223 Which second label does not belong? La Dame de Montrose, Les Forts de Latour, Lafite de Mouton, Lacoste-Borie.

224 What is the only Haut-Médoc AOP commune that has at least one château in *each* of the 5 classification levels?

225 The most recent purchase of Château Margaux occurred in 1978 by which supermarket empire family?

226 At one point, Château Lascombes and Château Prieuré-Lichine were owned by the same man. Who was he?

227 What are the names for the red and white second labels from Château Margaux?

228 Which château is out of place? Lascombes; Brane-Cantenac; Phelan-Ségur; Rauzan-Ségla; Palmer; Kirwan

229 In 2004, which château created the *Historical 19th Century Cuvée*?

---

218 1945; Philippe Jullian. (Baron Philippe was a POW during WWII, so the 1945 was a "V" label. *Victory in Europe*).
219 Salvador Dali. (The master of surrealism, the *sheep* on the label had the innocent charm of a child's drawing).
220 Marc Chagall. (Incidentally, he created three stained glass window panels for the Reims (Champagne) cathedral).
221 1973. Pablo Picasso. (Each year Baron Philippe commissioned a different artist to create the label).
222 Second labels are made from a second selection of wines after the blend for the *Grand Vin* is created.
223 Lafite de Mouton. (This name is made up, and the others are second labels of famous Châteaux).
224 Margaux AOP. (From Château Margaux as a First Growth, down to two positioned as 5th Growths).
225 Mentzelopoulos. (Daughter Corinne took over after her father André's death in 2003).
226 Alexis Lichine. (My first textbook mentor after attempting to read his Encyclopedia of Wine & Spirits in 1974).
227 Pavillon Rouge du Château Margaux and Pavillon Blanc du Château Margaux.
228 Château Phelan-Ségur. (This Château is in St.-Estèphe AOP, and the others are in Margaux AOP).
229 Château Palmer. (The blend was 85% estate fruit, and 15% Syrah from Hermitage. 100 cases produced).

230 The village of Margaux is contained within the commune of Margaux AOP. What village is just southeast?

231 What is the southernmost Cru Classé château observed when entering the Haut-Médoc AOC from the south?

232 True or False? Ducru-Beaucaillou, Beychevelle and Léoville-las-Cases are among the top estates in St.-Julien AOP.

233 How many Premier Grand Cru Classé are in St.-Julien AOP?

234 What is the second wine of Château Léoville-las-Cases in St.-Julien?

235 Which château is out of place? Cos Labory, La Tour Carnet, Camensac, Cantemerle, Lynch-Bages.

236 Since 1999, who owns Château La Tour Carnet?

237 In what year was the Pessac-Léognan appellation created?

238 What is the new name for the second wine Château Bahans Haut-Brion from Château Haut-Brion?

239 What château is the oldest named estate in Bordeaux?

240 Who currently owns Château Pape-Clément, now part of the Pessac-Léognan AOP?

241 Although backed by the local growers' organization, which gentleman stood at the forefront creating Pessac-Léognan?

---

230 Cantenac. (A few châteaux incorporate the village in their name. Cantenac-Brown, Brane-Cantenac).

231 Château La Lagune. (The next Cru Classé north from Château La Lagune is Château Cantemerle).

232 True. (Others include Château Talbot; Léoville-Barton; Léoville-Poyferre; Gruaud-Larose; Gloria, etc.).

233 None. (However, the commune is home to 11 classified châteaux and famous names in Bordeaux).

234 Le Petit Lion du Marquis de Las Cases. (In 2007 a change from Clos du Marquis, now a separate vineyard).

235 Château La Tour Carnet. (It is a fourth growth, and the other 4 are fifth growths).

236 Bernard Magrez. (Bernard also owns Châteaux Pape-Clement, Fombrauge, Clos Haut-Peyraguey, etc.).

237 1987. (The northern area of Pessac-Léognan has the greatest concentration of top châteaux in the Graves).

238 Le Clarence de Haut-Brion. (After Clarence Dillon, the American financier who purchased Haut-Brion in 1935).

239 Château Pape-Clément. (Established in the early 1300s in the Graves region).

240 Bernard Magrez. (Wine entrepreneur owning several wine estates in several countries).

241 André Lurton. (Owner of Châteaux La Louvière, Couhins-Lurton, de Rochemorin, de Cruzeaux, etc.)

FRANCE

BORDEAUX – RIGHT BANK

242 In what year were the wines of Saint-Émilion classified for the first time?

243 How many wine estates are within the Pomerol classification system?

244 True or False? Like many châteaux on the Left Bank, Cabernet Sauvignon is the predominant variety in Pomerol.

245 Which commune is out of place? Pauillac, Pomerol, St.-Estèphe, St.-Julien, Margaux.

246 Name the 4 satellites villages north of Saint-Émilion AOP.

247 What is the largest estate in Pomerol?

248 Who is the owner of Château Valandraud? He was one of the original *garagiste* producers.

249 Who owns Château L' Évangile in Pomerol?

250 How large is the famous Pomerol estate Le Pin?

251 How did Le Pin get its name, and who is the current owner?

---

242 1955. (100 years after the Haut-Médoc classification).

243 None. (Pomerol does not have a classification).

244 False. (The predominant grape is Merlot. These wines typically drink earlier than those of the Left Bank).

245 Pomerol. (Pomerol is a Right Bank commune, and the others are Left Bank communes).

246 Saint-Georges-Saint-Émilion; Montagne-Saint-Émilion; Puisseguin-Saint-Émilion; Lussac-Saint-Émilion.

247 Château de Sales. (Owned by the same family for over 500 years, there are 116 acres planted.)

248 Jean-Luc Thunevin. (In 1989, he and his wife Murielle Andraud purchased 1.5 acres in St.-Émilion).

249 Domaines Barons de Rothschild. (Also, owners of Lafite-Rothschild, Duhart-Milon and Rieussec).

250 5 acres. (Although small, there are several famous smaller estates in France).

251 Le Pin is the single pine tree on property. The Thienpont family released the 1st vintage in 1979.

252 Château Angélus is one of the top estates in St.-Émilion. What were the two previous names of the winery?

253 Which Château does not belong? Petite-Village; Figeac; La Conseillante; Clos l'Eglise; Pétrus.

254 Which Château does not belong? La Mondotte; Tertre Roteboeuf; Troplong Mondot; Vieux Château Certan.

255 What family currently owns Château Pétrus in Pomerol?

256 Who is the famous Bordeaux-based oenologist that consults to wineries in 13 countries? What is his family château?

252 Château L'Angélus (before 1990); Château Mazerat (Pre-1909). Owned by Hubert Boüard de Laforest.
253 Château Figeac. (It is in the commune of St.-Émilion, and the others are from the commune of Pomerol).
254 Vieux Château Certain. (This estate is in Pomerol, and the others are in St.-Émilion).
255 Originally Jean-Pierre Moueix, now the son and family of Jean-François Moueix, head of Groupe Duclot).
256 Michel Rolland; Château Le Bon Pasteur. (The flying winemaker makes his home in Libourne, Pomerol).

FRANCE

BORDEAUX WHITE WINES - (SWEET & DRY)

257 What are two of the most famous sweet white wine AOP communes in Bordeaux?

258 Which was the first Château in the Médoc to make to make a white wine? What year?

259 Speaking of whites from the Médoc, what is the name of Château Mouton Rothschild's white?

260 What Château entry does not belong? Bouscaut, Carbonnieux, Haut-Bailly, Smith Haut-Lafitte.

261 Harvesting botrytized grapes is labor intensive. In 1999, Château Suduiraut needed how may days? 10; 18; 27; 31; 42.

262 Name the *dry white wine* produced by Château d'Yquem from Sauternes?

263 What was the first vintage of "Y"?

264 What family owned Château d'Yquem for over 400 years?

---

257 Sauternes and Barsac. (Similar but lesser known are Cadillac, Cerons, Loupiac, and Ste.-Croix-du-Mont).

258 Château Loudenne. 1880. (Additional châteaux making white wine include Talbot, Margaux and Lynch-Bages).

259 Aile d'Argent. (First released in 1991, following the release of Blanc de Lynch-Bages in 1990).

260 Haut-Bailly. (It makes only red wines now, while the others make red and white wines also).

261 42 days. (Repetitive passes along the rows of vines is one contributor for high bottle prices of Sauternes).

262 "Y." (In French, pronounced *egrec*, yet the label must carry Bordeaux Supérieur, rather than Sauternes).

263 1959. (The Sauternais take the first letter for dry wines. "S" de Suduiraut; "R" de Rieussec; "G" de Guiraud, etc.).

264 Le Comte Alexandre de Lur Saluces. (Generally considered the greatest sweet white wine in the world).

265 Who owns Château d'Yquem now?

266 What Château does not belong? Lafaurie-Peyraguey; Doisy-Vedrines, Haut-Bages Libéral; Coutet, Climens.

265 Bernard Arnault owner of LVMH. (Legal battles in 1996-1999 came to an end with the purchase).

266 Haut-Bages Libéral. (This Château is in Pauillac, others are sweet white wines from Sauternes/Barsac).

FRANCE

BURGUNDY – GENERAL QUESTIONS

267 Where in France is the region of Burgundy located?

268 True or False? Since it is called Burgundy, this wine region produces only red wines.

269 What is the primary grape used to produce red Burgundy wine?

270 What is the primary grape used to produce white, Burgundy wine?

271 Burgundy has what type of climate?

267 East / central France. (Cool continental climate perfect for Chardonnay and Pinot Noir).

268 False. (Burgundy also makes white and sparkling wine).

269 Pinot Noir. (Gamay Noir is the primary grape in Beaujolais, the southernmost region in Burgundy).

270 Chardonnay. (Aligoté is a secondary white wine variety).

271 Continental. (Cool to cold climate with early ripening capabilities).

—————— FRANCE ——————

FRANCE

BURGUNDY - LA CÔTE D'OR

272 What is the finest, highest quality sub-region of Burgundy proper called?

273 What is the derivation of the term Côte d'Or?

274 What are the two famous sub-regions of La Côte d'Or called?

275 Most think the Nuits of Côte de Nuits or Nuits-St. Georges refers to night. What is the true derivation of the name?

276 Although similar in length, which is longer, the Côte de Beaune or the Côte de Nuits?

277 La Côte d'Or is essentially an east facing slope. Between top slope, mid-slope, or lower slope, which is premium?

278 What are the four ascending appellations of Burgundy wines? List them in quality from entry level to specific vineyards.

279 In 2017 a new category was created allowing producers to blend villages from La Côte d'Or. Name the classification?

---

272 La Côte d'Or. (This ultra-premium region produces the finest of all Burgundy wines).

273 Slope of Gold. (Canopy autumn colors; the "gold"; equivalent prices for the wines; vineyards facing Orient (east).

274 The *Côte de Nuits* (to the north), and the *Côte de Beaune* (to the south).

275 Nuts or walnuts. (Latin *natium*, (ancient plantings) morphed to Nuits. In French *noyer/noix* is nuts or walnuts).

276 The Côte de Beaune is ≈ 18 miles north to south, and the Côte de Nuits is ≈ 13 miles in length north to south.

277 Mid-slope. (The top is windier, the lower has too much soil accumulation; the mid-slope is just right).

278 Regional; Villages; Premier Cru; Grand Cru.

279 Bourgogne Côte d'Or. (For red or white wine and must be sourced from La Côte d'Or).

280 To the west of the major Côte d'Or villages, there are two large non-village AOC's called what?

281 Percentage wise, how much red wine is made versus white wine in the Côte de Nuits and Côte de Beaune?

282 Are there more Premier Cru or Grand Cru vineyards in the Côte d'Or?

283 Two nomenclatures appear on Premier Cru wines. What is the difference between Premier Cru & 1ER Cru?

284 What is the main auto route that runs through La Côte d'Or?

285 What is the French term for a named Burgundy vineyard site that is not classified Premier Cru status?

286 In Burgundy (and other parts of France) one often encounters the term Monopole. What is the definition?

287 There is a wine term that blends minimum 1/3 Pinot Noir, and 2/3 Gamay. What is the term?

288 What does the French term *Table de Tri* mean?

289 What is the definition of a Régisseur?

290 Who was the individual who ordered the Gamay grape to be banished from La Côte d'Or?

291 Who was responsible for constructing the *Hospice de Beaune*?

292 Who is the largest landowner of Premier and Grand Cru vineyards in the Côte d'Or?

293 Which Domaine is the largest owner of Grand Cru vineyards in Burgundy?

294 Name three prestige Burgundy estates owned by Jean-Charles Boisset?

295 Which two companies were the *First Négociants* in Burgundy?

280 Côte de Beaune-Villages and Côte de Nuits Villages; umbrella appellations each with several villages.
281 Côte de Nuits ≈ 97% red, 3% white; Côte de Beaune ≈ 70% red, 30% white.
282 Many more Premier Cru (≈ 635*) versus 32* Grand Cru vineyard sites (*calculations of classifications vary).
283 No difference. (1ER means Premier in French, Or 1st (First) in in English).
284 RN 74. (Incidentally, the Michael Mina group has a restaurant named RN 74 in Seattle).
285 Lieu-Dit. (Plural lieux-dits). The term *Climat* is also used as a named specific vineyard site.
286 Monopoly. (The specific vineyard is owned or controlled by a single family, winery, or wine company).
287 Bourgogne Passe-tout-grains. (Typically, Pinot Noir from Côte d'Or, and Gamay from Mâconnais).
288 The sorting tables. (After harvest, grapes are inspected on a type of conveyor, and rejects grapes if unfit).
289 The general manager of a Domaine, and if it is a small estate, he/she may also be the winemaker.
290 Philip the Bold in 1395. (One of the Dukes of Burgundy who lived from 1363 – 1404).
291 Philip the Good. (Another Duke of Burgundy, he created the hospital for the indigent in 1443).
292 Bouchard Père & Fils. (Their Premier Cru vineyards ≈ 182 acres, and Grand Cru vineyards ≈ 30 acres).
293 Domaine Louis Latour. (They own ≈ 70 acres of Grand Cru vineyards and are based in Aloxe-Corton).
294 Domaine de la Vougeraie; Bouchard Aîné & Fils; Jean-Claude Boisset; J. Moreau et Fils.
295 Champy, founded in 1720, and Bouchard Père & Fils, founded in 1731. (Both are based in Beaune).

——————— FRANCE ———————

296 What is the French term for *punching down* the grape cap for tannin and color extraction during fermentation?

297 What is the French term for *pumping-over* the solid grape cap for tannin and color extraction?

298 What is the French term for *rack and return*?

296 Pigeage. (A gentle procedure for extraction often performed from a catwalk above the open tank).

297 Rémontage. (Pumping over involves pumps (not natural) placing the wine above the cap using buoyancy).

298 Délestage. (Wine is pumped to a tank under the cap on the bottom and skins rise, aiding extraction.)

FRANCE

BURGUNDY - CÔTE DE NUITS – RED WINES

299 Name one Grand Cru vineyard in the village of Fixin and one Grand Cru vineyard in the village of Marsannay.

300 Name a famous domaine making wine in Marsannay AOP?

301 Name the Premier Cru monopole within the Fixin AOP?

302 True or False? Gevrey-Chambertin is the largest AOP in the Côte de Nuits.

303 The village of Gevrey-Chambertin contains how many Grand Cru vineyards?

304 Name the largest Grand Cru in Gevrey-Chambertin.

305 Mazoyères-Chambertin (Grand Cru) may also be labeled as another Grand Cru by what name?

306 True or False? Chambertin-Clos de Bèze Grand Cru may also be labeled as Chambertin, another Grand Cru.

---

299 Located in the northern part of Côte de Nuits, neither village has any Grand Cru vineyards.

300 Bruno Clair; Sylvain Pataille; Jean Fournier; Joseph Roty; Coillot; Bart, etc.

301 Clos Napoléon. (This 4.5-acre plot was purchased in 1950 by Pierre Gelin and is still owned by the family).

302 True. (A total of 1,075 acres of vineyard area).

303 9. (Out of a total of 24 Grand Cru in the Côte de Nuits).

304 Charmes-Chambertin. (At 46 acres, including Mazoyères-Chambertin, Grand Cru. See next question).

305 Charmes-Chambertin. (Translated as *charm or allure*, the elegant term is softer than Mazoyères).

306 True. (Although the reverse is not).

307 Which vineyard is out of place? Charmes, Chapelle, Clos St.-Jacques, Griotte, Clos de Bèze, Ruchottes.

308 Ruchottes-Chambertin, Grand Cru (≈ 8 acres) has a monopole climat contained within the vineyard called what?

309 Thus far, we have mentioned 7 of the 9 Grand Cru in Gevrey-Chambertin. What two have we not mentioned?

310 Which Domaine owns *Clos de la Bussière* in Morey-Saint-Denis?

311 Name the largest Grand Cru vineyard in the Côte de Nuits.

312 Why is the Clos de Vougeot vineyard so fragmented with 80 different owners?

313 True or False? All parcel owners in the Clos de Vougeot produce about 200 cases of wine annually.

314 What does the term *vieilles vignes* signify on a Burgundy label?

315 What Lieu-Dit within the Clos de Vougeot is pronounced the same as a neighboring village, but spelled differently?

316 Clos de Vougeot is home to which International Burgundy Society? Events are held in the *elaborate monastery building.*

317 What does the name of this wine society, Confrérie des Chevaliers du Tastevin, mean in English?

318 Madame Lalou Bize-Leroy owns what two Domaines in Burgundy?

319 Which Grand Cru does not belong? La Grande Rue, Musigny, La Romanée, Romanée St.-Vivant.

320 Which village contains more Grand Cru vineyards, Chambolle-Musigny or Morey-Saint-Denis?

---

307 Clos St.-Jacques. (It is a Premier Cru in Gevrey-Chambertin, the others are Grand Crus in Gevrey-Chambertin).

308 Clos des Ruchottes. (This 3-acre monopole is owned by Domaine Armand Rousseau).

309 Mazis-Chambertin (22 acres), & Latricières-Chambertin (18 acres).

310 Domaine Georges Roumier. (This 6.4-acre plot is a Premier Cru monopole vineyard).

311 Clos de Vougeot. (Only Corton, Grand Cru in the Côte de Beaune is larger).

312 After French law changed, all children inherited equally, and ownership multiplied over generations.

313 False. (200 cases is the average, nearly 1/3 of the owners produce less than 75 cases annually).

314 Old Vines. (Although an unofficial term, older vines often yield more concentrated grapes, and better wine).

315 En Musigni. (Made by Domaine Gros Frère et Soeur. The parcel is near the village of Musigny).

316 Confrérie des Chevaliers du Tastevin. (I was proudly inducted on December 17, 1980).

317 Brotherhood of the Knights of the Tasting Cup.

318 Domaine Leroy & Domaine d'Auvernay. (Very high-quality estates of Premier Cru & Grand Cru vineyards).

319 Musigny. (It is a Grand Cru in Chambolle-Musigny, and the others are Grand Crus in Vosne-Romanée).

320 Morey-Saint-Denis contains five, and Chambolle-Musigny two (Bonnes-Mares straddles both villages).

321 What is arguably the most famous Premier Cru vineyard in Chambolle-Musigny?

322 What year did the village of Gevrey-en-Montagne change its name to Gevrey-Chambertin?

323 What year was the village Vosne hyphenated to create Vosne-Romanée?

324 What year was village Chambolle hyphenated to create Chambolle-Musigny?

325 What year was the village Morey hyphenated to create Morey-Saint-Denis?

326 What is the only Grand Cru monopole in Morey-Saint-Denis AOC? Who owns the property?

327 LVMH recently purchased which famous Grand Cru estate in Morey-Saint-Denis?

328 Speaking of Bernard Arnault, what other properties do LVMH represent?

329 What is out of place? Le Clos Blanc; Les Cras, Les Petite Vougeots, Clos de Vougeot; Clos de la Perrière.

330 What Premier Cru is out of place? Les Cazetiers; Les Beaux-Monts; Les Suchots; Aux Malconsorts; Les Petits Monts.

331 What is the *smallest* Grand Cru vineyard in Vosne-Romanée AOC?

332 Who owns, La Grande Rue, Grand Cru monopole in Vosne-Romanée?

333 Who owns Romanée-Conti, Grand Cru monopole in Vosne-Romanée?

334 The two Grand Crus in Flagey-Echézeaux AOC are named what?

335 Which Grand Cru does not belong? Romanée-Conti, Le Chambertin, La Tache, La Grande Rue, La Romanée.

---

321 Les Amoureuses. (This 13+ acre vineyard is bottled by de Vogüé, Roumier, Frédéric Mugnier, Groffier, etc.).

322 1847. (This name change brought credibility to Gevrey thanks to its most famous Grand Cru, Chambertin).

323 1866. (This name change brought credibility to Vosne, from its three Grand Cru vineyards named Romanée).

324 1878. (This name change brought credibility to Chambolle from its most famous Grand Cru vineyard, Musigny).

325 1927. (This name change brought credibility to Morey from its most Grand Cru vineyard, Saint-Denis).

326 Clos de Tart. (François Pinault's, Groupe Artémis purchased it from the Mommessin family in October 2017).

327 Clos des Lambrays. (Chairman/CEO Bernard Arnault is now neighbor to François Pinault's Clos de Tart).

328 Château Cheval Blanc, Château d'Yquem, 60% Colgin Cellars. (Plus: Moët, Krug, Ruinart, Clicquot, etc.).

329 Clos de Vougeot. (This is a Grand Cru vineyard, and the others are Premier Crus in the village of Vougeot).

330 Les Cazetiers. (This is a Premier Cru in Gevrey-Chambertin; the others are Premier Crus in Vosne-Romanée).

331 La Romanée. (Owned by Domaine François Lamarche. The monopole is just two acres in size).

332 Comte Liger-Belair. (La Grande Rue is ≈ 4 acres).

333 Domaine de la Romanée-Conti. (Romanée-Conti is ≈ 4.4 acres).

334 *Grands-Echézeaux* (22 acres) and *Echézeaux* (86 acres).

335 Le Chambertin. (That is a Grand Cru with many owners, and the others are monopoles (single ownership).

336 What Abbey in Nuits -St.-Georges was built in 1098?

337 How many Grand Crus are contained in the village of Nuits-St.-Georges?

336 Abbé Cîteaux. (Built by the Cistercian order, the monks were remarkably effective vineyard record keepers).
337 No Grand Crus, but there are 30 Premier Crus.

FRANCE

BURGUNDY - CÔTE DE BEAUNE – RED WINES

338 Fill in the blank for the geographical village name Aloxe- _____.

339 The Grand Cru vineyard of Le Corton lies in what three villages?

340 What Grand Cru vineyard has the Domaine de la Romanée-Conti recently added to their portfolio from the Côte de Beaune?

341 Why are the village names of Meursault, Pommard and Volnay not hyphenated like Puligny-Montrachet?

342 How many Grand Cru vineyards are in Pommard?

343 Name one Premier Cru vineyard in the village of Pommard.

344 Which of these villages contain at least one Grand Cru vineyard? Meursault; St.-Romain; Volnay; Beaune.

345 Which is the largest Grand Cru for red wine in Burgundy?

---

338 Corton. (This commune is in the northern part of the Côte de Beaune).

339 Aloxe-Corton, Pernand-Vergelesses and Ladoix-Serrigny.

340 Le Corton. (Parcels from Prince Florent de Merode, including Les Bressandes, Les Renardes, and Le Clos du Roi).

341 They do not contain a Grand Cru vineyard (like Puligny-Montrachet, Chassagne-Montrachet and Aloxe-Corton.)

342 None. (However, there are 28 Premier Cru vineyards in the village).

343 Les Rugiens; Les Epenots; Les Arvelets; Les Fremières, Les Charmots; Les Bertins; Les Clos Micot; etc.).

344 None of those villages contain a Grand Cru vineyard.

345 Le Corton. Covering ≈ 400 acres. (With many designated climats; Corton Clos du Roi, Corton-Bressandes, etc.)

346 Approximately how many producers make wine from the Grand Cru Corton?

347 How many Grand Cru vineyards are in the village of Beaune?

348 How many Premier Cru vineyards are in the village of Beaune?

349 When you see Savigny-lès-Beaune and Chorey-lès-Beaune, what does the *lès* signify?

350 Name the Bouchard Père & Fils Premier Cru vineyard monopole for red wine in Beaune.

351 What Premier Cru vineyard contains the parcel *Vigne de l'Enfant Jésus* (vines of baby Jesus)?

352 Which is not a climat of Grand Cru Le Corton? Bressandes; Marconnets; Clos du Roi; Pougets; Renardes.

353 Which négociant does not belong? Louis Jadot; Louis Latour; Bouchard Père et Fils; Faiveley.

354 What village does not belong? Monthélie; Auxey-Duresses; St.-Aubin; Fixin; Ladoix-Serrigny.

355 Which village does not belong? St.-Aubin; St.-Romain; Chorey-lès-Beaune, Marsannay, Savigny-lès-Beaune.

356 Which village is out of place? Flagey-Echézeaux; Marsannay, Pernand-Vergelesses; Corgoloin; Comblancien.

357 Which village is out of place? Gevrey-Chambertin, Vosne-Romanée, Pommard, Nuits-St.-Georges, Chambolle-Musigny.

358 Which is not a Premier Cru vineyard in Volnay? Taillepieds; Blagny; Clos des Ducs; Clos des Chênes; En Chevret.

359 Which village, Pommard or Volnay, is considered to make wine which is more delicate than that of the other?

---

346 200. (Again, this is the largest Grand Cru in the Côte d'Or).

347 None. (It is however the epicenter for commerce and headquarters for several négocians and domaines).

348 42. (Beaune is the third largest wine commune behind Gevrey-Chambertin and Meursault).

349 Near. (The villages of Savigny & Chorey are near in proximity to the well-known village of Beaune).

350 Clos de la Mousse (This 8.3-acre plot has produced since 1872).

351 Beaune-Grèves. (This is a Premier Cru proprietary/exclusivity of the house of Bouchard Père & Fils).

352 Marconnets. (This is a Premier Cru vineyard in Beaune).

353 Faiveley. (Located in Nuits-St.-Georges, the others in Beaune).

354 Fixin. (Located in the Côte de Nuits, the others in the Côte de Beaune).

355 Marsannay. (Located in the north end of the Côte de Nuits, the others in the Côte de Beaune).

356 Pernand-Vergelesses. (Located in the Côte de Beaune, others in the Côte de Nuits).

357 Pommard. (In the Côte de Beaune, the others in the Côte de Nuits).

358 Blagny. (This is a *hamlet* above Meursault and Puligny-Montrachet).

359 Volnay. (This is true in parcels of vineyard where there is a significant difference in soil).

FRANCE

BURGUNDY – WHITE WINES

360 Who is the only producer in the Côte de Nuits that can produce a Grand Cru white wine?

361 Which Grand Cru is out of place? Le Montrachet, Bâtard-Montrachet, Corton-Charlemagne, Chevalier-Montrachet.

362 Corton-Charlemagne production is what percentage of all Grand Cru White Burgundy?

363 What two villages are allowed to produce Corton-Charlemagne, Grand Cru?

364 Referring to the question above, what third village *may* be added to produce Corton-Charlemagne?

365 The DRC has leased a 7-acre parcel of Grand Cru Corton-Charlemagne. Which estate leased the land?

366 Approximately how many bottles of Corton-Charlemagne Grand Cru are produced per year?

---

360 Comte Georges de Vogüé. (During replanting from 1993 to 2015 it was Bourgogne Blanc, now Musigny Blanc).

361 Corton-Charlemagne. (A Grand Cru from northern Côte de Beaune, and the others from further south).

362 ≈ 60%. (This vineyard is ≈ 130 acres, larger than the other white Grand Crus combined).

363 Aloxe-Corton and Pernand-Vergelesses. (From Le Charlemagne & En Charlemagne parcels).

364 Ladoix-Serrigny. (Controversial, as this village may produce Corton rouge, but is a minor source for Chardonnay).

365 Domaine Bonneau du Martray. (This is arguably is finest estate on the hill of Corton).

366 ≈ 300,000 bottles. (There are about 50 producers of Corton-Charlemagne).

367 Which is out of place? Puligny-Montrachet, Chassagne-Montrachet, Criots-Bâtard-Montrachet, Meursault.

368 Name the Bouchard Père & Fils Premier Cru vineyard monopole for white wine from Beaune.

369 Which is not a Premier Cru in Puligny-Montrachet? Les Pucelles; Les Folatières; Morgeot; Champs Canet; Cailleret.

370 True or False? The village of Meursault in the Côte de Beaune produces only white wines.

371 Between the villages of Puligny-Montrachet, Chassagne-Montrachet, and Meursault, which one makes the most wine?

372 Which Domaine produces Meursault, Clos Richemont?

373 Who is the importer of Domaine Jean-François Coche-Dury, an iconic producer based in Meursault?

374 True or False? The village of Chassagne-Montrachet in the Côte de Beaune produces only white wines.

375 Name the top white Grand Cru vineyard in Burgundy?

376 Le Montrachet is divided between which two villages in the Côte de Beaune.

377 Who is the largest landowner of Le Montrachet? (Scroll down to the extra credit section for the definition).

378 Name the négociant who is responsible for distributing Marquis de Laguiche wines worldwide?

379 Of the 4 Grand Cru white Burgundies hyphenated with the name Montrachet, which is the largest?

380 What is the only white Grand Cru totally contained in the village of Chassagne-Montrachet?

---

367 Criots-Bâtard-Montrachet. (A Grand Cru vineyard in the Côte de Beaune, the others are village names).

368 Clos Saint-Landry. (This plot is less than 5 acres. Owned by Bouchard since 1791).

369 Morgeot. (A Premier Cru in Chassagne-Montrachet).

370 False. (Meursault produces ≈ 33% of *all* white wine in the Côte d'Or, but ≈ 36 % of Meursault is red wine).

371 Meursault. (There are ≈ 100 Domaine bottlers in Meursault with no Grand Crus, but 18 Premier Crus).

372 Domaine Darnat. (This is a Premier Cru monopole owned by the Darnat family).

373 Kermit Lynch. (When this top importer requested a meeting, it was only when J-F completed his vineyard tasks).

374 False. (Approximately 40% of the wine from the village is red, however, white grapes create more revenue).

375 Le Montrachet. (At just under 20 acres in size, many call this the finest white wine vineyard in the world).

376 Puligny-Montrachet and Chassagne-Montrachet. (The vineyard is almost equally divided between them).

377 Marquis de Laguiche. (This family has owned their 5+ acres since 1363. The entire plot is in Puligny-Montrachet).

378 Joseph Drouhin. (Since 1947 Drouhin also distributes the other Laguiche wines).

379 Bâtard-Montrachet is ≈ 28 acres.

380 Criots-Bâtard-Montrachet. (This is < 4 acres in size and does not overlap into Puligny-Montrachet).

381 Of the 4 Grand Cru white Burgundies hyphenated with the name Montrachet, which is the smallest?

382 What Grand Cru in the Côte de Beaune is located on a slight slope above Le Montrachet?

383 Both Louis Latour and Louis Jadot bottle a special cuvée from a plot in Chevalier-Montrachet called what?

384 Which Grand Cru Montrachet is missing? Bâtard-Montrachet; Chevalier-Montrachet; Criots-Bâtard-Montrachet.

381 Criots-Bâtard-Montrachet is ≈ 3.87 acres.

382 Chevalier-Montrachet. (This plot is 18.45 acres and is consistent every year due to small yields).

383 Les Demoiselles. (This plot of just over 2.5 acres is in Le Cailleret, now considered part of Chevalier-Montrachet).

384 Bienvenues-Bâtard-Montrachet. (This 9-acre Grand Cru is in the village of Puligny-Montrachet).

FRANCE

BURGUNDY – EXTRA CREDIT

385 Which is not an AOC in the northern Cote de Nuits? Fixin; Aux Fauques; Comblanchien; Brochon; Premeaux; Corgoloin.

386 Name the American author and Burgundy importer that brought Domaine Ponsot & Marquis d'Angerville to the US?

387 Chardonnay and Pinot Noir are the primary grapes grown in La Cote d'Or. Name another white and two more reds.

388 What French term is a form of sharecropping where the vigneron gets paid with wine from the vineyard owner?

389 Name the Premier Cru vineyard next to Grand Cru Richebourg in the village of Vosne-Romanée.

390 In addition to Henri Jayer's family heirs, who else has recently bottled Cros Parantoux, Premier Cru?

391 Name the *only* Premier Cru monopole vineyard in Vosne-Romanée and owned by Domaine Michel Gros.

---

385 Aux Fauques. (This is a specific vineyard site in Comblanchien).

386 Frank Schoonmaker. (In the mid-1930s he pioneered importing growers versus négociants).

387 *White*: Pinot Blanc. *Reds*: Pinot Beurot and Pinot Liébault.

388 Métayage. (The payment is in the form of the same wine, but with a different label preventing confusion).

389 Cros Parantoux. (This 2.4-acre vineyard was in a state of disrepair when purchased by Henri Jayer in 1951).

390 Domaine Méo-Camuzet and Domaine Emmanuel Rouget.

391 Clos des Réas. (In business for 150 years in Vosne, the family considers this the crown jewel).

392 Le Musigny Grand Cru is made up of three Lieux-Dits primarily owned by Comte Georges de Vogüé. Name them.

393 Within the village of Nuits-St.-Georges, name three monopole Premier Cru climats and their owners?

394 What was the original name for Domaine Dujac, based in Morey-Saint-Denis?

395 In what year was the Domaine de la Romanée-Conti (DRC) incorporated?

396 The DRC owns some of the finest vineyards in Burgundy. One is Grand Cru La Tâche. How was the name derived?

397 In 1929, the DRC bottled a Premier Cru vineyard in Vosne-Romanée. What is the name of the wine?

398 Starting in 1999 (but not in every vintage) the DRC has produced a Premier Cru red bottling. What is the name?

399 Name the 2.5-acre 1er Cru vineyard planted to white grapes above the Clos de la Roche vineyard in Morey-St.-Denis.

400 Corton-Charlemagne is divided into Le Charlemagne and En Charlemagne. Name the village each belongs to.

401 The two Grand Cru labels of Montrachet and Le Montrachet denote something specific. What is the difference?

ABOVE: *It must be noted that not all owners/producers follow the village parameters for labeling their Montrachet.*

402 Bouchard Père & Fils bottled a separate climat contained within Grand Cru Chevalier-Montrachet. Name the parcel.

403 Name the famous barrel maker (tonnellerie) based in St.-Romain.

---

392 Les Grands Musigny, Les Petits Musigny and La Combe d'Orveau. (Jacques Prieur also owns the latter parcel).

393 Clos des Porrets (Henri Gouges); Clos de la Maréchale (J.F. Mugnier); Le Clos de Thorey (Antonin Rodet).

394 Domaine Graillet. (Jacques Seysses purchased it in 1967, now run by son Jeremy and his wife Diana Snowden).

395 1911. (The history goes back to 1631, then Duvault-Blochet family in 1869, to Aubert de Villaine since 1953).

396 A *tâcheron* is a vigneron who gets paid for all annual *tasks* (la tâche) in the vineyard, rather than hourly pay.

397 Les Gaudichots. (This is in fact a vineyard, however after 1932 most of this parcel was absorbed within La Tâche).

398 Vosne-Romanée Premier Cru, Cuvée Duvault-Blochet. (Named after the 19th century Domaine founder).

399 Clos des Mont Luisants. (Planted with *Aligoté*, this vineyard is a monopole of the Ponsot family).

400 Le Charlemagne is within Aloxe-Corton, and En Charlemagne is within Pernand-Vergelesses.

401 *Montrachet.* (≈ 11 acres) is in Puligny-Montrachet, *Le Montrachet.* (≈ 10 acres) is in Chassagne-Montrachet.

402 La Cabotte. (This translates as a small stone structure for rest and shelter from the rain).

403 François Frères. (American Burgundy importer Becky Wasserman worked here before selling grower Burgundy).

404 What village contains the 1er Cru Les Murgers des Dents de Chien?

405 Château de Pommard owns the large monopole called Clos Marey-Monge. Name the seven terroir driven parcels.

404 Saint-Aubin. (Producers: Larue, J-C Bachelet, Hubert Lamy, H. Prudhon, Coffinet-Duvernay).
405 Simone, Nicolas-Joseph, Grands Esprits, Chantrerie, 75 Rangs, Micault, and Émilie

FRANCE

CHABLIS

406 Is Chablis AOC located north or south of La Côte d'Or?

407 What is the approximate distance from Chablis to Beaujolais?

408 What is the only grape permitted for wine made in the Chablis AOP?

409 How would you describe the climate of Chablis?

410 Which département is Chablis AOP located in?

411 What river runs through the Chablis region?

412 Name the four AOPs of Chablis in ascending level of quality.

413 How many vineyards are classified as Chablis Grand Cru?

414 How many vineyards are classified as Chablis Premier Cru?

415 Can you name a few of the Chablis Premier Cru vineyards?

---

406 North. (About 100 miles north of the city of Beaune).

407 Depending on your start/finish line, the distance is ≈ 200 miles.

408 Chardonnay. (Traditionally Chablis has little to new oak character, unlike many La Côte d'Or white wines).

409 Cool continental. (Climate hazards include Spring frosts and Summer hailstorms).

410 The Yonne. (This is the name of the département but is also the name of the river).

411 Serein River. (This river is ≈ 117 miles long and bisects the Chablis wine growing region).

412 Petit Chablis, Chablis, Chablis Premier Cru and Chablis Grand Cru.

413 There are seven Grand Cru vineyards. (Les Clos is the largest and produces the most wine).

414 41. (However, more obscure vineyards are allowed to use one of 17 better-known names).

415 Fourchaume, Vaillons, Mont de Milieu, Montmains and Montée de Tonnerre are among the better known.

416 How many acres of vines are planted in Chablis?

417 What is the name of the famous soil type found in the best appellations in Chablis?

418 What is the primary soil type found in the lesser quality sites in Chablis?

419 Are bottle-fermented sparkling wines produced in the Chablis region allowed to use the Chablis AOP?

420 Maison/Domaine Louis Latour owns the only sparkling wine producer located in Chablis. What is the name?

421 Name two Chablis Grand Cru vineyards that begin with the letter "V".

422 Now, name other five Grand Cru Chablis parcels.

423 What is the largest of all the Chablis Grand Cru parcels?

424 Domaine William Fèvre makes a wine from a specific climat in Grand Cru Bougros called what?

425 Name the most famous and the largest wine cooperative in Chablis.

426 The famous négociant J. Moreau & Fils founded in 1814 is still in business. What two companies are offshoots?

427 Name two of the most reputable producers in Chablis? (The list below is extremely limited, many more exist).

---

416 11,900 acres. (Mostly at the Chablis AOP level).

417 Kimmeridgian. (A chalky limestone/clay named for Kimmeridge, a village in southern England.)

418 Portlandian. (Portlandian soil is ≈ 120/130 million years old, and Kimmeridgian is ≈ 140/150 million years old).

419 No, this wine is made under the Crémant de Bourgogne AOP. (Crémant indicates traditional method French sparkling wine produced in a region outside Champagne).

420 Simonnet-Febvre. (They produce Crémant de Bourgogne in both white and rosé versions).

421 Valmur and Vaudésir. (These 2 Grand Cru parcels are higher up the slope and separated by Les Grenouilles).

422 Blanchots, Bougros, Les Clos, Grenouilles and Les Preuses.

423 Les Clos. (This parcel is ≈ 67 acres composed of firmly packed white Kimmeridgian clay/limestone).

424 Chablis Bougros, "Côte Bouguerots." (This 5-acre parcel is at the foot of the hill, with full southern exposure).

425 La Chablisienne. (Founded in 1923, they control ≈ 25% of total Chablis production at all classification levels).

426 Domaine Christian Moreau and Domaine Louis Moreau.

427 François Raveneau, Domaine René & Vincent Dauvissat, Domaine William Fèvre, Domaine Billaud-Simon.

FRANCE

BURGUNDY – (CÔTE CHALONNAISE – MÂCONNAIS – BEAUJOLAIS)

428 Heading south from La Côte d'Or, what is the name of the next Burgundian wine region?

429 What are the five AOPs in the Côte Chalonnaise region?

430 Name the Montagny Premier Cru produced by Louis Latour.

431 Which producer is the largest in Côte Chalonnaise?

432 What AOP in Côte Chalonnaise has the most planted acres?

433 Name the white wine grape often associated with Bouzeron?

434 Name the most famous producer in Bouzeron?

435 Heading south from Côte Chalonnaise, what is the name of the next Burgundian wine region?

436 Name 3 AOP regions in the Mâconnais.

---

428 Côte Chalonnaise AOP. (Red wines made from Pinot Noir, white wines from Chardonnay and Aligoté).

429 Rully, Mercurey, Givry, Montagny and Bouzeron.

430 La Grande Roche. (A proprietary blend from several Premier Cru vineyards).

431 Cave de Buxy. (This is a co-operative winery producing about 2/3 of all wine from Montagny).

432 Mercurey. (≈ 1,600 acres of which about 80% is red. There are 32 Premier Cru vineyards).

433 Aligoté. (This grape is an alternative to Chardonnay, with less intensity).

434 Domaine A & P de Villaine. (Aubert de Villaine of Domaine de la Romanée-Conti).

435 The Mâconnais. (90% of production is white wine from Chardonnay).

436 Pouilly-Fuissé; Pouilly-Vinzelles; Mâcon-Villages; Mâcon-Lugny; St.-Véran; Viré-Clessé and more.

437 True or False? The Mâcon-Villages AOP produces mostly red wines and a small quantity of white wines.

438 What year was St.-Véran granted AOC/AOP status?

439 Although a small percentage of plantings, name the two red wine grapes allowed in Mâconnais?

440 Château de Fuissé is a leading producer in Pouilly-Fuissé AOP. Name two of their special bottlings?

441 What five villages are allowed to use the Pouilly-Fuissé AOP?

442 What is the name of the natural limestone escarpment just west of the city Mâcon?

443 Heading south from the Mâconnais, what is the name of the next Burgundian wine region?

444 What is the red wine grape used to produce Beaujolais AOP?

445 The next quality step above the basic Beaujolais AOP is called what?

446 Name two Premier Cru and two Grand Cru villages in the Beaujolais region.

447 What is the next quality step up from Beaujolais-Villages AOP?

448 Which Beaujolais Cru was the first granted AOP?

449 What was the most recent village designated as Cru?

450 Which Cru Beaujolais village does not belong? Brouilly; Ardèche; Chénas; Morgon; Fleurie; Moulin-à-Vent.

451 Name three of the five remaining Cru Beaujolais AOPs in addition to the ones listed above.

452 What Cru Beaujolais Cru is perfect for Valentine's Day?

---

437 False. (Mâcon-Villages AOP is a *white wine only* appellation, exclusively from Chardonnay).

438 1971. (This appellation is adjacent to the Pouilly-Fuissé AOP).

439 Pinot Noir and Gamay Noir (The Pinot Noir offers elegance & the Gamay is more fruit forward).

440 Tête de Cru; Vieilles Vignes; Les Clos; Les Brûlés; Les Combettes. (This property is owned by the Vincent family).

441 Pouilly, Fuissé, Chaintré, Solutré and Vergisson. (Pouilly-Loché & Pouilly-Vinzelles are neighboring villages).

442 The rock of Solutré. (This is a very imposing stone structure dominating the landscape).

443 Beaujolais. (Officially part of the Rhône administrative region, but geographically considered part of Burgundy).

444 Gamay Noir. (Better suited to the granitic soils of the region that retard vine vigor).

445 Beaujolais-Villages AOP. (Must originate in the northernmost 38 villages of the region).

446 There are no Premier Cru or Grand Cru villages in the Beaujolais region. The term is simply *Cru*.

447 Cru Beaujolais. (These are ten different villages producing the highest quality in the northern part of the region).

448 Moulin-a-Vent (windmill, in English) in 1936. (This is perhaps the most recognized Cru).

449 Régnié. (Achieved Cru status in 1988).

450 Ardèche. (This is part of the Rhône département).

451 Juliénas, St.-Amour, Chiroubles, Régnié, Côte de Brouilly.

452 St.-Amour. (The wine for lovers).

453 What is the largest producing Cru Beaujolais?

454 What is the smallest producing Cru in Beaujolais?

455 Which producer in Beaujolais is owned by the producer Maison/Domaine Louis Latour?

456 Château de Poncié in Beaujolais was founded in 949 AD. What was their original Latin name?

457 Name the popular unaged version of Beaujolais released around Thanksgiving?

458 What year was Beaujolais Nouveau introduced in France?

459 In 1985 the release date was changed from November 15th to what date?

460 What is another term used for Beaujolais Nouveau?

461 Whole berry fermentation is a popular production method used in Beaujolais. What is the technical term for this?

462 Briefly describe the *carbonic maceration* fermentation technique.

453 Brouilly. (This AOP produces about 20% of all Crus combined, at ≈ 8 million bottles from over 3,000 acres).

454 Chénas. (The vineyards cover less than 1 square mile, producing approximately 1.5 million bottles).

455 Henry Fessy. (Formed in 1888, the family owns 172 acres, and produces all 10 Cru and Beaujolais-Villages).

456 Villa Ponciago. (They are based in Fleurie producing several bottlings of Fleurie, and other Cru).

457 Beaujolais Nouveau. (A highly quaffable, light and fruity red wine).

458 1951. (Several producers would rush the new vintage to Paris for parties starting November 15th).

459 3rd Thursday in November. (George Duboeuf was the top marketer. "Le Beaujolais Nouveau est Arrivée").

460 Beaujolais en Primeur. (The term is just another way of saying new or first regarding the *EARLY* release).

461 Carbonic Maceration. (Macération Carbonique in French).

462 *Whole clusters of uncrushed grapes are placed in a sealed vat, the weight breaking the skins of the grapes on the bottom. In turn, CO_2 is created, causing other grapes to ferment at the intracellular level.*

FRANCE

NORTHERN RHÔNE VALLEY AOC

463 How many red wine varieties are permitted in the northern Rhône Valley AOPs? Name them.

464 What is the parentage of the Syrah grape?

465 What three white grapes are permitted in northern Rhône Valley AOPs?

466 What is the bedrock geology formation in the northern Rhône Valley?

467 How many acres is the AOP and monopole Château Grillet?

468 How any acres of Viognier were planted in the northern Rhône Valley in 1968? 35; 60; 95, 125

469 Name a top producer in Condrieu.

470 Name the two bottlings of Condrieu produced by Delas Frères.

471 What are the only two northern Rhône AOPs on the east side of the Rhône River?

---

463 Only one, Syrah. (In several AOPs, small amounts of white grapes may be blended with Syrah).

464 Mondeuse Blanche (Savoie) X Red Dureza (Ardèche or northern Rhône Valley)

465 Viognier, Marsanne and Roussanne. (Viognier alone in Condrieu and Château Grillet.)

466 Granite. (This is perfect for growing the Syrah grape).

467 8.6 acres. (This property is owned by François Pinault who also owns Château Latour, Clos de Tart, etc.).

468 ≈ 35 acres. (Due to just a few producers post-WWII, Viognier hectarage dwindled, now on the rebound).

469 Yves Cuilleron. (Also, Guigal, Georges Vernay, André Perret, René Rostaing and Pierre Gaillard).

470 Clos Boucher (5-acre property) and La Galopine (Blended from 4 vineyard plots).

471 Hermitage and Crozes-Hermitage. (The other six AOPs are on the west side of the river).

472 Which AOP from the question above makes more affordable wines?

473 Provide a short aromatic description for northern Rhône Valley wines from Viognier, Roussanne and Marsanne.

474 What is the northernmost AOP in the northern Rhône Valley?

475 Name the two vineyard parcels in Côte-Rôtie that many producers may use on their labels.

476 Name the important village in the AOP of Côte-Rôtie?

477 Name the 40-mile long AOP on the west side of the Rhône River?

478 Just south of Cornas AOP lies another "St." wine. What is it?

479 Which of these AOPs has more acreage planted to grapes, Cornas or Saint-Péray?

480 Rank these AOPs from smallest to largest in acreage: St.-Joseph, Hermitage, Crozes-Hermitage.

481 True or False? Cornas AOP only produces white wines.

482 Translate to English Jean-Luc Colombo's wines from Cornas. Les Ruchets, La Louvée, Vallon de l'Aigle, Terres Brûlées.

483 Name the three Côte-Rôtie AOP "La-La-La" wines from Domaine Guigal.

484 In the mid-18th century, some Bordelaise châteaux added wine from what Rhône region to add body and color?

485 What is the name of the business center town in Hermitage?

486 What is the size in acres of the famous Hermitage AOP?

487 What domaine owns the famous *La Chapelle* vineyard in Hermitage AOP?

488 In Hermitage AOP, what percentage of production is red wine versus white wine?

---

472 Crozes-Hermitage. (Production is 90% red wine (Syrah) and 10% white wine (Roussanne and Marsanne).

473 Viognier: Peach/pear; Roussanne: Apricot; Marsanne: Marzipan/pineapple.

474 Côte-Rôtie. (This AOP, along with Hermitage, makes some of the highest quality and longest-lived wines).

475 Côte Blonde and Côte Brune. (The former is limestone/sand, the latter is darker clay/iron, hence the names).

476 Ampuis. (Located on the river, Marcel Guigal purchased and renovated Château d'Ampuis, and is now a label).

477 St.-Joseph. (Some of the Northern Rhône's best values, ≈ 90% Syrah and 10% Marsanne and Roussanne).

478 St.-Péray AOP. (Marsanne and Roussanne contribute to a remarkably high percentage of whites made here).

479 Cornas. (225 acres) Saint-Péray has 150 acres.

480 Hermitage (345 acres), St.-Joseph (2,100 acres), Crozes-Hermitage (3,000 acres).

481 False. (Exclusively red wines from the Syrah grape).

482 The Beehives (5.4 acres), The She Wolf, (2 acres), Valley of the Eagle (< 1 acre), Burnt Earth (11 acres).

483 La Landonne, La Mouline, La Turque. (These wines are among the finest produced in France).

484 Hermitage. (Check out the question in the Bordeaux section: Historical 19th Century Cuvée).

485 Tain-l'Hermitage. (This quaint village offers exciting restaurants, delectable chocolates, and of course wine).

486 ≈ 345 acres. (A smaller AOP but some of the finest red and white French wines are produced here).

487 Maison Paul Jaboulet Aîné. (Named for the small chapel on the top of the hill).

488 Red wine approximately 75%, and white wine approximately 25%.

489 Name the famous domaine and négociant who uses Braille on their labels?

490 What is the name of the sweet white wine produced in Hermitage?

489 Michel Chapoutier. (Since 1996, the labels were started to help the vision impaired identify wine labels).

490 Vin de Paille. (Marsanne grapes are harvested and shriveled on straw mats to concentrate the sugars)

FRANCE

SOUTHERN RHÔNE VALLEY

491 What is the best-known appellation from this region?

492 How was this name Châteauneuf-du-Pape derived?

493 How many grapes are permitted to make Châteauneuf-du-Pape AOP?

494 Approximately how many acres does Châteauneuf-du-Pape AOP cover? 2,500; 4,200; 7,900; 9,200; 14,400.

495 What are the two popular Châteauneuf-du-Pape producers that claim to use all 13 grapes every year?

496 What family owns Château de Beaucastel?

497 What is the name of the large round vineyard stones in the Châteauneuf-du-Pape AOP?

498 Which does not belong? Fortia; St.-Préfert; Vinsobres; La Gardine; Château La Nerthe; Chateau Rayas; Vieux Télégraphe.

499 Name the largest volume AOP in the area, producing affordable red, white, and rosé wines.

---

491 Châteauneuf-du-Pape AOP. (New house of the Pope).

492 In 1305, Frenchman Pope Clément V moved the Papal seat to Avignon, France.

493 13. (18 if you consider color variations of some grapes, including blanc, noir, or gris).

494 ≈ 7,900. (There are around 320 growers in the AOP and produce ≈ 14 M/bottles per year).

495 Château de Beaucastel and Clos des Papes.

496 La Famille Perrin. (They also own the popular branded wine *La Vielle Ferme*.)

497 Galets Roulées. (They absorb heat, aid in drainage, and are 1.8-million-year-old Alpine glacial material).

498 Vinsobres. (It is an AOP in the southern Rhône, the other six are Châteauneuf-du-Pape producers).

499 Côtes du Rhône AOP. (Côtes du Rhône-Villages AOP bottlings offer a higher level of quality).

500 How many villages are entitled to the Côtes du Rhône-Villages AOP?

501 G-S-M on a wine label from the southern Rhône Valley (and elsewhere) means what?

502 What does VDN stand for?

503 Name a popular VDN wine from this area.

504 What two terms are used for sparkling wines produced in the Rhône Valley?

505 What is the Rosé only AOP in the Southern Rhône Valley?

506 Where is the Tavel wine region located?

507 Which is not a Tavel producer? Château d'Aqueria; Château Leroy et Fils; Domaine de la Mordorée; Domaine l'Anglore.

508 Name the two very similar AOPs just northeast of Châteauneuf-du-Pape.

509 What elevated natural landmark can be viewed from most of the region?

500 22. (This AOP produces red and white wines and was granted appellation status in 1966).

501 A blend of Grenache-Syrah-Mourvèdre. (The three key quality red wine grapes of the area).

502 Vins Doux Naturels. (A sweet white or red wine made by arresting fermentation by adding alcohol while sugar remains).

503 Muscat de Beaumes-de-Venise AOP. (The grape is Muscat, known as Moscato in Italy).

504 Crémant de Die and Clairette de Die. (Two different production techniques).

505 Tavel. (An unusual Rosé only AOP typically made from Grenache, Syrah, Mourvèdre and Cinsault).

506 Across the river from Châteauneuf-du-Pape, and just north of the city of Avignon.

507 Château Leroy et Fils. (A fictitious name).

508 Vacqueyras and Gigondas. (These are great alternatives to the more familiar Châteauneuf-du-Pape).

509 Mont Ventoux. (This is a 6,263-foot-high mountain ideal for biking and hiking).

FRANCE

LOIRE VALLEY

510 True of False? The Loire Valley is home to some of the most elaborate castles in France.

511 Approximately how many miles long is the Loire River?

512 What are the four major wine regions along the in the Loire, each containing numerous AOPs?

513 True or False? The Loire Valley produces more white wines than red wines.

514 What is the westernmost Loire AOP around the city of Nantes?

515 What is the official name of the grape used to make Muscadet?

516 Muscadet has three sub-AOPs. Name them.

517 A common production technique in Muscadet involves extended yeast contact with the wine. Name the procedure.

518 Common in the production of Loire Valley white wine and elsewhere, what is the French term for stirring the lees?

---

510 True. (A few examples: Chambord, Chenonceau, Samur, Azay le Rideau, Cheverny, Blois).

511 629 miles. (The longest river in France, offering climatic differences and varied soil compositions).

512 From west to east: Pays Nantais, Anjou-Saumur, Touraine, Central Vineyards.

513 True. (Almost half of the production is white, with the balance being rosé, red, and sparkling).

514 Muscadet. (Due to its proximity to the Atlantic Ocean, it is a perfect seafood/shellfish compliment).

515 Melon de Bourgogne. (This grape originated in Burgundy, or Bourgogne, hence the name).

516 Muscadet Sèvre-et-Maine AOP; Muscadet-Côteaux de la Loire AOP and Muscadet Côtes de Grandlieu AOP.

517 Sur Lie. (On the lees (or spent yeast cells). This adds complexity and texture to the wine).

518 Bâtonnage. (This action keeps yeast suspended and creates additional texture and complexity).

519 What are the most planted white and red wine grape varieties in the Anjou region?

520 What grape variety is used to produce Savennières AOP within the Anjou region?

521 Within the Savennières AOP, name two estates that have their own sub-appellations.

522 Who is the owner of the monopole Coulée de Serrant?

523 What is the Loire Valley's first official Grand Cru?

524 What is the other AOP southeast from Quarts de Chaume making very similar wines?

525 True or False? Pink wine plays a very minor role in the Anjou region.

526 What AOP is at the center of sparkling from the Loire Valley?

527 From a quality standpoint, what is the name of the next level up from Saumur Brut AOP?

528 The next wine growing district heading east from Anjou and Saumur is called what?

529 What is arguably the most famous red wine produced in Touraine?

530 In addition to Chinon AOP, what are two more Touraine AOPs made from Cabernet Franc?

531 Further east, yet still in Touraine, name two white wine AOPs made from Chenin Blanc.

532 What Loire Valley AOP was the first to introduce the now trendy category of sparklers called Pét-Nat?

533 True or False? The style of Vouvray is always dry.

534 True or False? Sancerre AOP produces white wines only.

535 What grape is used in the production of Sancerre Blanc and its cross river neighbor, Pouilly-Fumé AOP?

---

519 *Chenin Blanc* (very versatile in style) and *Cabernet Franc* (lighter and higher in acid than wines from Bordeaux).

520 Chenin Blanc. (Although its wines are often semi-sweet in style, Savennières AOP is bone dry).

521 Coulée de Serrant (17 acres) and Roche aux Moines (81 acres).

522 Nicolas Joly. (One of pioneers of biodynamic viticulture).

523 Quarts de Chaume AOP. (Sweet, late-harvest wine made from 72 acres by approximately 20 producers).

524 Bonnezeaux. (Quite a bit larger at approximately 247 acres).

525 False. (Much pink wine is made under the Rosé d'Anjou, Rosé de Loire and Cabernet d'Anjou AOPs).

526 Saumur AOP. (Traditional method wine made in both white or rosé options).

527 Crémant de Loire AOP. (Lower yields, hand harvesting, and at least one year of lees aging).

528 Touraine. (The vineyards are located north and south of the Loire and Vienne rivers).

529 Chinon AOP. (This wine is made from the Cabernet Franc grape variety).

530 Bourgueil (More structured than Chinon) and St.-Nicolas-de-Bourgueil (a touch lighter than Chinon).

531 Vouvray and Montlouis. (Vouvray is on the north side and Montlouis is on the south side of the Loire River).

532 Montlouis AOP. (Or Pétillant Naturel. Made by the Ancestral Method, with some residual sugar in the wine).

533 False. (Options include dry, off-dry, medium-dry (demi-sec), sweet (moelleux) and sparkling).

534 False. (In addition to white, Sancerre rosé and Sancerre rouge are also produced from Pinot Noir).

535 Sauvignon Blanc. (Although different soil compositions create different aroma and flavor profiles).

536 Which wine estate in the village of Pouilly-sur-Loire has a Disneyland styled castle on their property?

537 Which is out of place? Quincy, Les Mesnil, Reuilly and Menatou-Salon.

536 Château du Nozet de Ladoucette. (This estate makes ultra-premium Pouilly-Fumé wines).

537 Les Mesnil. (This is a Champagne village, and the others are AOPS located southwest of Sancerre).

FRANCE

ALSACE

538 Alsace is separated from what country by what river.

539 True or False? The climate of Alsace during the growing season is dry and sunny with warm days and cool nights.

540 What mountain range has a "rain shadow" effect on Alsace, making the weather dry during the growing season?

541 True or False? Alsace is known for its wide variety of soil types.

542 How many wine producers are there in Alsace? 150; 325; 690; 1,000; 1,236.

543 What is the northernmost large city in Alsace?

544 True or False? Grape varieties are never listed on the front labels of wines from Alsace.

545 Which grape is out of place? Muscat, Gewurztraminer, Sémillon, Pinot Gris, Riesling.

546 Which does not belong? Hugel, Trimbach, Prüm, Zind-Humbrecht, Marcel Deiss.

---

538 Germany. The Rhine River. (Throughout history, Alsace has belonged to both countries at various times).

539 True. (The perfect climate for the rich, dry, food friendly white wines produced here).

540 The Vosges Mountains. (The best vineyards of Alsace are planted on the eastern foothills of the Vosges).

541 True. (There are more than twenty major soil formations, with several diversified terroirs).

542 There are approximately 1,000 wine producers in Alsace, and over 4,500 grape growers.

543 Strasbourg. (Home to one of France's many famous cathedrals).

544 False. (They are almost always listed unless the wine is a blend of more than one variety).

545 Sémillon. (Although French (Bordeaux), it is not grown in Alsace).

546 Prüm. (A popular producer in the Mosel area of Germany; the rest are producers in Alsace).

547 Which is out of place? Léon Beyer; Leitz; Marc Kreydenweiss; André Ostertag; Rolly Gassmann; Josmeyer; J-B Adam.

548 Which is out of place? Fritz Haag; Bott-Geyl; Paul Blanck; Domaine Weinbach; Kuentz-Bas, Lucien Albrecht.

549 What is out of place? Rangen; Geisberg; Himmelreich; Saering; Brand; Kessler.

550 Which estate owner in Alsace is also a Master of Wine (MW)?

551 Which estate produces the line of wines Cuvée des Comtes d'Eguisheim?

552 Approximately how many miles is the region of Alsace running north/south?

553 What is traditional method sparkling wine called in Alsace?

554 What is the name of the famous village located in the geographic center of Alsace?

555 What are the two départments that compose the wine region of Alsace?

556 What year did Alsace achieve AOP status?

557 What year were the *Grand Cru* vineyards classified?

558 What percentage of all Alsace wines produced are from Grand Cru vineyards? 1%; 4%; 9%; 16%; or 22%

559 What is the term for late harvest wine from Alsace?

560 Since 1984, what is the minimum potential alcohol level for Vendange Tardive wines?

561 What is the term for botrytis affected wine from Alsace?

562 Since 1984, what is the minimum potential alcohol level for Sélection de Grains Nobles wines?

563 Who has the largest privately owned estate in Alsace?

---

547 Leitz. (Weingut Johannes Leitz is based in Rüdesheim, (Rheingau) Germany, and the others are from Alsace).

548 Fritz Haag. (Haag is based in the Mosel, Germany and the others are from Alsace).

549 Himmelreich. (A vineyard in the village of Graach, Germany; the others are Alsace Grand Cru vineyards).

550 Olivier Humbrecht. (Olivier was the first French national to achieve MW status in 1989).

551 Domaine Léon Beyer. (This series produces Riesling, Pinot Gris and Gewurztraminer).

552 Over 60 miles. (Alsace has both French and German influences in wine, food, architecture and people).

553 Crémant d'Alsace. (Made in both white and rosé versions, Crémant is defined as bottle fermentation).

554 Colmar. (This village is slightly north of the two wine villages of Ribeauvillé and Riquewihr).

555 *Bas-Rhin* (lower elevation to the north) and *Haut-Rhin* (to the south, and home to the best vineyards).

556 1962. (Unique in France, over 95% of the wines have the grape listed but without a specific place name).

557 1983. (Starting with 25 vineyards; currently there are 51).

558 4%. (With minor exception, Grand Cru wines are made from Riesling, Gewurztraminer, Pinot Gris or Muscat).

559 *Vendange Tardive* (Late harvest grapes are riper, with more sugar accumulation. Style ranges from dry to sweet.)

560 13.0 % Alcohol. (As the grapes mature on the vine, sugar increases, allowing for higher potential alcohol).

561 *Sélection de Grains Nobles*. (Botrytized means the noble rot has punctured the skins, leaving sweet raisins).

562 15.2 % Alcohol. (Botrytis dehydrates the grapes and concentrates sugars, allowing for higher potential alcohol).

563 Domaines Schlumberger. (Over 340 acres, half of which are in Grand Cru vineyards).

——————— FRANCE ———————

564 Name two of the four Grand Cru vineyards in which Schlumberger has ownership.

565 The prestigious "Clos Ste. Hune" vineyard owned by Trimbach is a parcel within which Grand Cru vineyard?

566 Trimbach also produces a Riesling called "Cuvée Frédéric Émile." It is sourced from what two Grand Cru vineyards.

567 What vineyard was the first to be designated Grand Cru?

568 What is the smallest Grand Cru vineyard?

569 What is the most widely planted grape variety in Alsace?

570 What is the difference between the Sylvaner grape and the Silvaner grape?

564 Saering, Kitterlé, Kessler and Speigel.

565 Rosacker. (Rosacker is not named on the label).

566 Osterberg and Geisberg. (Frédéric Émile took Trimbach to the next level in the mid-19th century).

567 Schlossberg. (Also, the largest Grand Cru vineyard at 198 acres).

568 Kanzlerberg. (Less than 10 acres located in the municipality of Bergheim).

569 Riesling. (Wine styles range from bone dry → Vendange Tardive → Sélection de Grains Nobles).

570 It is the same grape. (Sylvaner is the French spelling and Silvaner is the German spelling).

FRANCE

LANGUEDOC & ROUSSILLON

571 Name the famous medieval fortified city in the western Languedoc, west of Narbonne.

572 True or False? The Languedoc and Roussillon regions together produce more wine than any other French region.

573 Which is out of place? Minervois AOP, St.-Chinian AOP, Barsac AOP, La Clape AOP, Fitou AOP.

574 What area in the Languedoc was producing sparkling wine before the region of Champagne?

575 What year was the sparkling wine of Limoux purportedly introduced?

576 What appellation is more specific than Côtes du Roussillon AOP?

577 Which one is out of place? Rivesaltes, Maury, Beaumes-de-Venise, Banyuls.

578 Name the Languedoc winemaker with a connection to the Rugby Club of Narbonne?

---

571 Carcassonne. (A major tourist attraction, drawing 3 million visitors annually).

572 True. (And more organic production than any other region as well).

573 Barsac AOP. (Located in Bordeaux. The rest are in the Languedoc).

574 Limoux. (The grapes include Mauzac; Chenin Blanc; Chardonnay; Clairette).

575 1531. (Produced by the monks at the Abbey of Saint-Hilaire).

576 Côtes du Roussillon-Villages AOP. (The rules stipulate lower yields and higher alcohol levels).

577 Beaumes-de-Venise. (It is in the southern Rhône and the others are from Roussillon).

578 Gérard Bertrand. (A former pro rugby player and captain of Stade Français, and deeply passionate winemaker).

579 Name the 1,300-acre estate in Corbières owned by the Barons de Rothschild (Lafite) family.

580 Name three AOPs from Languedoc and Roussillon that have Muscat in their title.

579 Château d'Aussières. (Wine has been made here since Roman times).

580 Muscat de Frontignan, Muscat de Rivesaltes, Muscat de St.-Jean de Minervois.

—————— FRANCE ——————

FRANCE

PROVENCE, CORSICA, JURA, SAVOIE

581 What is the large city of commerce anchoring Provence?

582 *Rolle* is a white wine grape grown in Provence. What is it called in Languedoc and Italy?

583 Which winery is out of place? Domaine Ott, Château d'Esclans, Domaine du Tavel, Château La Gordonne.

584 What is the catch-all AOP for most of Provençal Rosé wines?

585 Aubert de Villaine (DRC) and Jacques Seysses (Dujac) formed a partnership in Provence in 1989 called what?

586 What is the principle red wine variety grown in Bandol?

587 What are the three grapes used to produce *white* Bandol?

588 Name the most popular winery from Bandol?

589 True or False? Corsica is a landlocked vineyard area just south of Bordeaux.

---

581 Marseille. (Other vacation spots include Nice, Cannes, Antibes, Toulon, and Saint-Tropez).

582 Vermentino. (Vermentino in Italy grows in Bolgheri, Liguria, and Sardinia).

583 Domaine du Tavel. (If this label did exist, it would come from the southern Rhône, the others are Provence).

584 Côtes de Provence AOP. (This appellation covers about 50,000 acres, and about 80% of production is rosé).

585 Triennes. (They produce St.-Auguste (Cabernet/Syrah); Ste. Fleur (Viognier); and a great rosé.)

586 Mourvèdre. (Wines must contain a minimum of 51% Mourvèdre, with Grenache and Cinsault).

587 Clairette, Bourboulenc, and Ugni Blanc.

588 Domaine Tempier. (Also, Château Pradeaux, Domaine de la Terrebrune and Domaine le Galantin).

589 False. (It is a French owned island in the Mediterranean, southeast of Marseille).

590 Although difficult to spell and pronounce, what red wine variety is the most planted in Corsica?

591 Name the famous wine region of northern Corsica.

592 Which producer in does not belong? Stéphane Tissot, Pierre Trousseau, Jean-François Ganevat, Pierre Overnoy.

593 True or False? The wine region of Jura is located east of Burgundy.

594 What are the two best known white wine varieties planted in Jura?

595 Name the three best known red wine varieties planted in Jura.

596 Name the all-encompassing AOP of Jura.

597 What is the name of the sherry-like wine that Jura is noted for?

598 Who was the famous scientist that was born in the Jura, in the town of Arbois?

599 Is Savoie more mountainous than Jura?

600 What are the two key red wine varieties grown in Savoie?

601 What are two key white wine varieties grown in Savoie?

590 Nielluccio. (Another name for Tuscany's Sangiovese).

591 Patrimonio. (Wine styles are Nielluccio, Rhône-styled reds and rich Muscat-based VDNs).

592 Pierre Trousseau. (A made-up name; the others are top producers in the Jura).

593 True. (The region is located near the rise of the Jurassic foothills approaching the Alps).

594 Chardonnay and Savagnin (also known as Traminer).

595 Poulsard, Pinot Noir and Trousseau.

596 Côtes du Jura AOP.

597 Vin Jaune. (The wine is matured in barrels under a layer of yeast, *flor* in Jerez.)

598 Louis Pasteur. (Credited with understanding the role of yeast in wine production. His museum is in the city).

599 Yes. (The microclimates of high elevation allow several unique styles of wine).

600 Mondeuse (planted before the Romans) and *Persan*.

601 Jacquère. (50% of all plantings, floral/fruity); Altesse. (Age-worthy white grape with more complexity)

FRANCE

WINES OF SOUTHWEST FRANCE

The Southwest is a region comprised of several lesser known AOPs.

As Bordeaux is nearby, the same grapes plus indigenous varieties are used for wine.

602 What is the style Monbazillac AOP wines?

603 How does the grape blend in Monbazillac differ from the similar blends of Sauternes and Barsac?

604 What AOP is out of place? Cahors, Gaillac, Jurançon, Pic St.-Loup, Tursan, Madiran.

605 What AOP is out of place? Bergerac, Chavignol, Pécharmant, Montravel, Monbazillac.

606 What AOP is out of place? Maury, Côtes de Duras, Rosette, Buzet, Irouléguy.

607 What red wine variety is out of place? Tannat, Fer Servadou, Malbec, Cabernet Sauvignon, Grenache, Merlot.

---

602 Sweet white wine, like but more affordable than better known Sauternes and Barsac.

603 Many producers here use more Muscadelle in their blends plus Sémillon and Sauvignon Blanc.

604 Pic St.-Loup. (This AOP is in the eastern Languedoc; the others are in Southwest France).

605 Chavignol. (This is a village in the Sancerre AOP in the Loire Valley; the others are in Southwest France).

606 Maury. (Maury is a fortified Vin Doux Naturel in Roussillon, the others are in Southwest France).

607 Grenache. (Grenache is not approved for Southwest AOPs and the others are.)

FRANCE

COGNAC

Cognac is an appellation in France, yet unlike any other regions previously discussed. This is because the product here is not wine, but a distilled spirit, a type of brandy called cognac. The reason it is included here is that unlike most spirits, cognac is grape based (and it is one of my passions).

608 True or False? All brandy is cognac.

609 True or False? Cognac is an AOP in France located in the central-southwest part of the country.

610 Does the cognac region border on the Atlantic Ocean?

611 Is cognac only the name of the spirit?

612 What was the name of the first cognac firm? In what year was it founded?

613 What are the top two growing regions in cognac called?

614 When you see the term champagne here, does this reference the champagne region?

---

608 False. (The reverse: all cognac is brandy. Brandy is made in many countries; cognac is exclusive to France).

609 True. (Bordeaux lies directly to the south, and the Loire Valley is further north).

610 The lesser quality vineyards do extend to the ocean; however, the prime vineyards are inland to the east.

611 No. (It is named for the village of Cognac).

612 Augier, established in 1643. (This French family was first to recognize the grapes and terroir of cognac).

613 *Grande Champagne* (The top-quality region) and *Petite Champagne* (Ranking a close second in quality).

614 No. (Champagne comes from the Latin word *campania*, meaning open fields).

615 The total cognac growing region equates to how many total acres? 87k, 124k, 215k, 260k, 355k.

616 What term on a cognac label is used when Grande Champagne and Petite Champagne are blended?

617 What year was the term *Fine* established?

618 Name the primary grape used to make cognac?

619 What grape was dominant in cognac production prior to phylloxera scourge in the 1870s?

620 What type of still is required by law for cognac distillation?

621 Water evaporates at 212° F. At what point does alcohol evaporate?

622 How many distillations is Cognac required to go through?

623 What is the heat source that takes the initial base wine from liquid to vapor?

624 During the second distillation from vapor to liquid, what final procedure of purification eliminates negative compounds?

625 In the cognac region harvesting is usually done by October or November. When must distillation be complete?

626 After the double distillation has occurred, what is the next step for the eau de vie in the life of a cognac?

627 What type of French oak is most used for cognac production?

628 What are the benefits of the oak from these two forests above, important in Cognac aging?

629 What is the French name for above ground storage building used for cognac during their first year of aging?

---

615 ≈ 215,000 acres. (There are ≈ 5k grape growers, and ≈ 200 small distilleries or co-ops).

616 Fine. (Pronounced feen. The only qualifier here is that the blend must be a minimum of 51% Grande).

617 1938. (Blending the two allows an option should bad weather affect vineyards within either region).

618 Ugni Blanc. (AKA St.-Émilion des Charente, or Trebbiano in Italy. ≈ 90 – 95% of production is from this grape).

619 Folle Blanche. (Ugni Blanc became favored due to higher acidity, necessary for good quality cognac).

620 A copper Alembic pot still that also utilizes a swan's neck configuration as part of the process.

621 173° F. (Congeners evaporate before ethyl alcohol removing negative acetaldehydes. See last book chapter).

622 Two. (The concept is to collect the final distillation in its most purified form).

623 Coal and wood were used for centuries, but now natural gas is allowed.

624 The heads (first) and tails (last) are removed. (Only the *coeur* (heart) is retained, the purest part of the distillate).

625 March 31st of the following year. (Then oak aging for a minimum for two years, but often much longer).

626 Aging. (Done in oak barrels this step brings color, complexity, and bouquet over time to the final product).

627 Limousin (from forests around the city of Limoges) but Tronçais is also used.

628 Both are porous, allowing alcohol to evaporate, yet no harsh wood tannins are imparted.

629 *Chai*. (This term is also used in Bordeaux).

630 In the below ground cellar, the aging cognac gently evaporates and reforms on the ceiling. What is this known as?

631 Cognac is a very labor-intensive process. How many bottles of base wine does it take to create a bottle of Cognac?

632 What is the French term for the cognac cellar master? (Also used elsewhere in other wine regions in France).

633 Prior to bottling, barrels are blended to create a consistent house style. What other steps may occur before bottling?

634 What does VS stand for on cognac labels, and what is the age statement?

635 What does VSOP stand for, and what is the age statement?

636 What does XO stand for, and what is the age statement?

637 What are the four largest cognac houses in terms of production?

638 Name the popular blend of brandy and unfermented grape juice from the Cognac region.

639 Name the other popular French brandy located south of Cognac.

630 The Angel's Share. (French: Part des Anges). Between 3-4% of total liquid, creates a black mold on the ceiling).

631 Ten. (Double distillation involves extensive concentration creating a distillate from the base wine).

632 Maître d'Chais. (Master tasters and blenders, replicating the house style year after year.)

633 Distilled water may be added to reduce the alcohol level, and caramel may be added to achieve proper color.

634 VS is Very Special. (The entry level of quality with at least two years aging, but often more).

635 VSOP is Very Superior Old Pale. (Some say the S means Special, with 4 ½ years aging, but often much more).

636 XO is Extra Old. (Also, may be called Napoleon, with ≈ 6 years aging, and often more up to 20 - 25 years).

637 Hennessy, Rémy Martin, Martell and Courvoisier. (There are hundreds more small producers and co-ops).

638 Pineau des Charente. (A sweet aperitif of unaged cognac and must (unfermented grape juice).

639 Armagnac. (Older than Cognac in origin but being landlocked, prevented trade with northern Europe)

FRANCE

ARMAGNAC

Like Cognac, Armagnac is an appellation in France for a distilled spirit, a type of brandy.

640 Where in France is the Armagnac region located?

641 In addition to the Armagnac, what gourmet food is also produced in Gascony?

642 How many acres of grapevines make up the Armagnac region? 10,600; 12,800; 15,900, 27,000

643 Between Cognac and Armagnac, which is the larger volume region?

644 Three grapes are permitted in the production of cognac. How many grapes are allowed in Armagnac production?

645 What three regions comprise the Armagnac AOP?

646 How long has Armagnac been produced?

---

640 Armagnac is a brandy from southwest France, in the region of Gascony.

641 *Foie Gras*, the fattened liver of geese.

642 There are ≈ 12,800 acres of grapevines in the Armagnac region.

643 Cognac by far with ≈ 215,000 acres planted, versus ≈ 12,800 planted in Armagnac.

644 Ten. (Including a French American hybrid, Baco 22-A.)

645 Bas-Armagnac, Haut-Armagnac and Ténarèze.

646 ≈ 700 years. (Definitely France's oldest brandy).

647 True or False? Once the young Armagnac spirit is placed in oak barrels, it remains there until bottling.

648 Oak aging changes the aromatics of Armagnac through micro-oxygenation. Can you name a few aromatic adjectives?

649 True or False? Prior to bottling, it is illegal to add any components that may change the flavor profile of Armagnac.

650 There is a relatively new Armagnac category that is not wood aged. What is this called?

651 Name two producers of Armagnac.

647 False. (Then is placed sequentially in two additional barrels, each more neutral than the previous).

648 Vanilla, caramel, dried fruits, apricot, floral, toffee, nuttiness.

649 False. Caramel (color), corn syrup (sweetness) and water (lowers alcohol) may be added.

650 Blanche Armagnac. (This may be served neat or possibly more versatile in cocktails

651 Château de Tariquet, Sempé, Darroze, Laubade, Castarède, de Montal, Janneau, Danflou and others.

CHAPTER 5

ITALY

Italy is an exceptionally diverse wine producing country. From north to south, east to west, and the islands, the vast amount of wine grapes and wine styles is second to none. Distinctive terroirs with both indigenous and international grape varieties give Italy variety unmatched by any other country.

General questions relating to Italian wines will start the dialog, followed by these broad regions:

Tuscany
Piedmont & Wines of the Northwest
Northeast Italy
Central Italy
Southern Italy & The Islands

ITALY

GENERAL QUESTIONS

1   What is the name for wine in Italian?

2   What Italian words translate these wine colors? White, red, rosé.

3   What Italian words translate these wine styles? Sweet, sparkling, semi-sparkling.

4   Speaking of sparklers, what Italian sparkling wine has enjoyed huge growth over the past decade?

5   True or False? Italy only produces red wines.

6   Approximately how many vineyards are in Italy?

7   How many varieties of wine grapes are planted in Italy?

8   In 2010 a *new* Italian/European Union classification was created. What are the new categories?

9   DOP may contain what two sets of letters indicating quality wines?

---

1   *Vino.* (The original term for common table wine was Vino di Tavola, now it is officially called Vino d'Italia)
2   Bianco, rosso, rosato.
3   Dolce, spumante, frizzante.
4   Prosecco. (This refreshing wine has taken the wine world by storm. (More info in the Northeast chapter).
5   False. (A large percentage is red, but all types of wine are produced here).
6   ≈ 1 Million. (Although this is an impossible number to calculate, it is often used).
7   ≈ 350 - 500. (Another impossible calculation as regional names may differ, & new indigenous grapes are found).
8   *Vino* (generic wines); *Varietali* (varietal wines); *IGP* (indicated geographical protection); *DOP* (protected origin)
9   DOCG and DOC.

10 What does DOCG, the highest level of quality, stand for?

11 How many DOCG zones are there?

12 What does DOC, the second highest level of quality, stand for?

13 How many DOC zones are there?

14 What other 3 letter classification defines the broadest category of Italian wines?

15 Name the Italian wine book published annually that describes and ranks producers and their wines.

16 The country of Italy is surrounded by five seas. Name three of them.

17 Name the two primary Italian island regions located in in the Mediterranean Sea.

18 Which is not a red wine variety from Italy? Sangiovese; Primitivo; Nebbiolo; Corvina; Vernaccia; Barbera; Aglianico.

19 *Tougher*: What is not a red wine variety from Italy? Nerello Mascalese; Teroldego; Garganega; Raboso; Schiava; Refosco.

20 Which is not a white wine variety from Italy? Trebbiano; Greco; Nero d'Avola; Moscato; Verdicchio; Fiano; Traminer.

21 *Tougher*: What is not a white wine grape from Italy? Gialla; Grillo; Freisa; Coda di Volpe; Erbaluce; Pecorino; Catarrato.

---

10 (*Denominazione di Origine Controllata e Garantita*, or controlled and guaranteed place of origin in English).

11 77. (The takeaway here is that these are zones so every producer in the zone is classified DOCG).

12 (Denominazione di Origine Controllata, or controlled and place of origin in English).

13 ≈ 333. (The takeaway here is that these are zones, so every producer in the zone is classified DOC).

14 IGT. (Indicazione Geografica Tipica). These occur all over Italy and include the Super Tuscans.

15 *Gambero Rosso*. (The rankings are in the form of wine glasses from 1 to Tre Bicchieri (1 to 3 glasses).

16 All five: Mediterranean, Ionian, Tyrrhenian, Adriatic, Ligurian.

17 Sicily (*Sicilia* in Italian) just west of Calabria, and Sardinia (*Sardegna* in Italian) northwest of Sicily.

18 Vernaccia. (A white grape variety from Tuscany used to make Vernaccia di San Gimignano).

19 Garganega. (A white wine grape from the Veneto region of Italy).

20 Nero d'Avola. (The most important red wine variety grown in Sicily).

21 Freisa. (A red wine variety grown in Piedmont).

ITALY

TUSCANY

22   In English, the spelling for the wine region is Tuscany. How is it spelled (and pronounced) in Italian?

23   What is the most famous wine produced in Tuscany?

24   What are the three quality levels of wine from the Chianti Classico zone?

25   What is the predominant red wine variety used in the production of Chianti?

26   Approximately how many acres of vines comprise the entire Chianti zone? 15,500; 27,480, 38,000, 52,450.

27   Is Chianti a DOC or DOCG zone?

28   Geographically, the Chianti Classico region is the large oval shaped land mass in-between which two cities?

29   The original Chianti zone was geographically delimited in what year?

---

22   Toscana. (Toh-SCAHNA).
23   Chianti. (The most famous area is Chianti Classico, the original heart of wine production).
24   Chianti Classico; Chianti Classico Riserva; Gran Selezione.
25   Sangiovese. (It is also the most widely planted red wine variety in Italy).
26   ≈ 38,000 acres. (This number includes Chianti Classico).
27   DOCG. (As is Chianti Classico, which has its own separate status as DOCG).
28   Florence (Firenze) to the north, and Siena to the south, about 30 miles apart).
29   1716. (The first defined wine region in the world).

30 The original "recipe" for Chianti mandated two dark-skinned grapes and two white. What were the dark grapes?

31 What were the white grapes used in the blend?

32 Currently what red wine varieties may be used in the production of Chianti?

33 Which winery is out of place? Antinori; Fèlsina; Monsanto; Ruffino; Biondi Santi; Castello di Ama; Rocca della Macìe.

34 What family owns the famous historic Castello di Brolio in Chianti Classico?

35 How do Ruffino Chianti Classico Riservas "tan label" and "gold label" differ?

36 Which family owns the Nipozzano Estate in Chianti?

37 Which wine is not made by Castello di Querceto? Il Picchio, La Corte, Il Sole di Alessandro, La Solatìa, Romantic.

38 Name the seven sub-zones of Chianti DOCG. All append their respective names to the Chianti designation.

39 True or False. Super Tuscans must contain at least 50% Sangiovese in the blends.

40 Casalvento and Livernano wineries are both owned by the Cuillo family in Radda-in-Chianti. Name some of their labels?

41 Name some examples of Super Tuscan wines.

42 Tenuta San Guido is a property on the Tyrrhenian coast (near Bolgheri) and is known for what special wine?

43 Sassicaia's second label and third label wines are called what?

44 How did Sassicaia get it name?

---

30 Sangiovese and Canaiolo. (Minimum/maximum percentages however have changed over the centuries).
31 Malvasia Bianca and Trebbiano Toscana. (After 1995, white grapes were no longer allowed in Chianti).
32 Sangiovese (80-100%), Canaiolo Nero, Colorino, Cabernet Sauvignon, and Merlot.
33 Biondi Santi. (Located in Montalcino; the others are in Chianti Classico).
34 The Ricasoli Family. (The majestic castle has been in the family since 1141, over 8 centuries).
35 Tan label is produced every vintage, and Oro (gold label) is only produced in great vintages.
36 Frescobaldi. (This estate is in Chianti Rufina. Frescobaldi owns several properties throughout Tuscany).
37 La Solatìa. (This is a tenuta owned by Ruffino, and the others are wines from Castello di Querceto).
38 Rufina, Colli Aretini, Colli Fiorentini, Colli Senesi, Colline Pisane, Montalbano and Montespertoli.
39 False. (There are no such rules. However, they are typically based on either Sangiovese or a Bordeaux variety).
40 Chianti Classico, Chianti Classico Riserva, Janus, L'Anima, Jupiter, Grappa, Rosé, Dream, (sparkling).
41 Sassicaia, Ornellaia, Tignanello, Masseto, Solaia, Le Pergole Torte, Flaccianello, Tinscvil, Monte Antico, etc.
42 Sassicaia. (The wine is based on Bordeaux varieties and was founded by Mario Incisa della Rocchetta).
43 Following the Bordelaise model, Guidalberto is the second label, and Le Difese is the third label.
44 It is the name of the vineyard. The 42-acre site is named due to the stony soil. Stone (*sassi* in Italian).

———— ITALY ————

45 Ornellaia is a Super Tuscan originally produced by Ludovico Antinori. What is the name of the Merlot-based wine?

46 Ornellaia's second and third label wines are called what?

47 Montevertine is an estate located in Radda. Sergio Manetti restored his ancestral property. What is their flagship wine?

48 Super Tuscan wines may come from anywhere in Tuscany, however what western part of Tuscany is the birthplace?

49 Name the famous Castello di Fonterutoli property in the Maremma?

50 Guado al Tasso is the Antinori owned property in Bolgheri. They make superb wines, including Scalabrone. What is that?

51 What is the name of the of the first DOCG zone awarded in the Maremma?

52 Fill in the blank. Brunello di _____.

53 True or False? Brunello di Montalcino is one of Italy's most age worthy red wines.

54 What is the DOC wine like Brunello di Montalcino but less expensive?

55 Which estate is credited as being the original producer of Brunello di Montalcino?

56 Name the other, similar DOCG located near Brunello di Montalcino.

57 What is the local name for Sangiovese used to produce Vino Nobile di Montepulciano DOCG?

58 How did Vino Nobile di Montepulciano DOCG get its name?

59 Which is out of place? La Braccesca, Greppone Mazzi, Il Poggione, Castelgiacondo, Biondi Santi, Argiano.

---

45 Masseto. (This is a high-quality wine grown on a specific clay-rich site now owned by Frescobaldi).

46 Following the Bordelaise model, Le Serre Nuove is the second label, and Le Volte is the third label.

47 Le Pergole Torte. (First made in 1976, this is made from 100% Sangiovese).

48 Bolgheri (A relatively new but prestigious Italian appellation in the Maremma along the coast).

49 Belguardo. (The Mazzei family purchased the property in the mid-1990s and today produce six wines).

50 Rosato. (Their rosé named after a local 18th century bandit. It is a Cabernet, Merlot, Syrah blend).

51 Morellino di Scanscano. (Morellino is the local name for Sangiovese, and Scansano is the name of the town).

52 Montalcino. (A Tuscan DOCG zone, Brunello is the local name for Sangiovese, and Montalcino is the town).

53 True. (Well-made Brunello di Montalcino ages well for decades).

54 Rosso di Montalcino. (Less aging, and lighter in body).

55 Biondi Santi. (The estate is 49 acres in size and was founded in 1840.)

56 Vino Nobile di Montepulciano DOCG. (Be careful not to confuse the two similar village names).

57 Prugnolo Gentile. (Sangiovese due to its importance in multiple regions, has many local names).

58 The Medici family coined the name, *Wine for Nobles* in English for wine from the village of Montepulciano.

59 La Braccesca. (This estate is in Montepulciano; the others are Montalcino producers).

60 What is out of place? Poliziano; Avignonesi; Fontodi; Carpineto; La Braccesca; Dei.

61 Another DOCG zone west of Florence is Carmignano. Name the most famous historical estate.

62 Who is the owner of Villa Capezzana?

63 What is the only DOCG white wine produced in Tuscany?

64 In addition to producing Vernaccia di San Gimignano, what winery produces Terre d Tufi?

65 Besides wine, what other consumable product is often produced by Tuscan wineries?

66 What is the name of the sweet white wine produced by numerous Tuscan wineries?

60 Fontodi. (This is a producer in Chianti Classico, and the others are producers of Vino Nobile di Montepulciano).

61 Villa di Cappezzana. (This winery was originally a Medici family villa. Their hunting lodge was Barco Reale).

62 Count Ugo Contini Buonacossi. (This family still produces more than half of the DOC zone wines of the area).

63 Vernaccia di San Gimignano. (Vernaccia is the variety, San Gimignano is the town, west of Chianti Classico).

64 Teruzzi & Puthod. (This wine is an IGT blend of Vernaccia and Chardonnay plus aromatic grapes).

65 Olive oil. (The olive tree is one of the oldest on the planet.).

66 Vin Santo. ("Holy Wine" made from Malvasia and Trebbiano.)

———— ITALY ————

ITALY

PIEDMONT & NORTHWEST ITALY

67   In English, this region is spelled Piedmont. How is it spelled in Italian?

68   What geographical area of Italy is home to Piedmont?

69   What is the rare food delicacy harvested in Piedmont?

70   The two most famous DOCG wine zones in Piedmont start with the letter "B." What are they?

71   Which zone is larger, Barolo or Barbaresco?

72   What grape variety is used to produce Barolo DOCG and Barbaresco DOCG?

73   Barolo and Barbaresco are the most expensive expression of Nebbiolo. What are the more affordable alternatives?

74   Name the iconic Barbaresco winemaker who also makes wine from Barolo and has two estates in Tuscany?

75   Name the three-vineyard designated Barbaresco wines produced by the Gaja family.

---

67 Piemonte. (Translation *foothills*, as in the foothills of the Alps).

68 Northwest Italy. (In this northern latitude the weather is cold, wet, and fog is common).

69 White Truffles. (Alba is the epicenter of the autumn harvest. Delicious thinly shaved over fresh pasta).

70 Barolo and Barbaresco. (These red wines are among the finest produced worldwide).

71 Barolo. (Barolo produces approximately three times more wine than neighboring Barbaresco).

72 Nebbiolo. (Piedmont's premier variety, and one of the most celebrated in Italy).

73 Nebbiolo d'Alba, Langhe Nebbiolo, Gattinara, Ghemme, etc.

74 Angelo Gaja. (The Tuscan estates are Pieve di Santa Restituta in Montalcino and Ca' Marcanda in Bolgheri).

75 Sorì San Lorenzo, Sorì Tildin and Costa Russi.

76 Which winery does not produce Barolo? Bruno Rocca, Ceretto, Foradori, Elio Altare, Aldo Conterno, Vietti.

77 Oscar Farinetti recently purchased the Fontanafredda winery in Piedmont. What is another of his Barolo properties?

78 ≈ 50 miles north of Barolo/Barbaresco is an ancient region called Alto Piemonte. Name two popular wines from here?

79 What Gattinara producer bottles his wine in a uniquely shaped indented bottle?

80 Ghemme and Gattinara, are made from Nebbiolo. What is the local name for this variety?

81 In addition to Nebbiolo, what are Piedmont's other red wine varieties?

82 Two DOC/G zones for Barbera are Barbera d'Asti and Barbera d'Alba. What is the 3rd zone for Barbera?

83 What is the derivation of the grape name Dolcetto?

84 In addition to those already discussed, name two more red wine varieties from the Asti region.

85 What are the three most popular white wine varieties grown in Piedmont?

86 Name another white wine variety and its linked town in Piedmont that achieved DOCG status in 2010.

87 From a bubbly standpoint, what is the difference between Asti and Moscato d'Asti?

88 What is the red, sparkling, sweet wine produced in Piemonte?

89 Gavi is a popular white wine from the town of the same name. What are the four possibilities of label nomenclature?

90 Arneis (little rascal) is a popular white variety (and wine) of the region. What is the associated DOCG?

---

76 Foradori. (Elisabetta Foradori is based in Trentino-Alto Adige and specializes in Teroldego.)

77 Giacomo Borgogno. (Farinetti is also behind *Eataly*, the gourmet Italian market concept).

78 Gattinara and Ghemme. (Both are DOCG Nebbiolo-based wines in the hills of Novarra).

79 Travaglini. (Introduced in 1958, the indents purportedly catch sediment, negating decanting).

80 Spanna. (Production rules allow for the addition of Uva Rara and Vespolina along with Spanna).

81 Barbera. (The most widely planted in the region) and Dolcetto.

82 Barbera del Monferrato. (A benefit here is other non-Piemontese grapes may be blended, unlike Alba and Asti).

83 Sweet little one. (This is a misnomer as the resulting wines are not sweet, with some tannin and low acidity).

84 Freisa d'Asti (rustic flavor profile); Grignolino d'Asti (light bodied for warm weather drinking).

85 Cortese (Gavi), Arneis, and Moscato (Asti and Moscato d'Asti).

86 Erbaluce di Caluso. (Wine styles range from still to sparkling to passito).

87 Asti is spumante ("*Foaming*" - fully sparkling) and Moscato d'Asti is frizzante (lightly sparkling).

88 Brachetto d'Acqui. (Brachetto is the name of the variety, and Acqui is the village name).

89 Gavi, Gavi di Gavi, Gavi dei Gavi (religious connotation) and Cortese di Gavi (Cortese is the variety for all).

90 Roero Arneis DOCG. (Grown in the hills northwest of Alba.)

91 What is the name of the famous aromatized wine produced in Piedmont?

92 The large area east of Piedmont containing the city of Milan is Lombardy. What wine is this area best known for?

93 Which is not a Franciacorta producer? Ferghettina, Ferrari, Berlucchi, Ca' del Bosco or Bellavista.

94 There is a version of Franciacorta that uses only white grapes. What is this category called?

91 Vermouth. (Available in both dry (white) or sweet (red) versions.

92 Franciacorta DOCG. (Exclusively for traditional method sparkling wine.)

93 Ferrari. (Although a producer of top-quality sparkling wine, Ferrari is based in Trentino).

94 Satèn. (Normally Chardonnay dominates this blend, but up to 50% may be Pinot Blanc).

ITALY

NORTHEAST ITALY

95 What are the three primary wine growing regions of northeast Italy?

96 What is the name of the Veneto's most popular sparkling wine?

97 Most Prosecco is produced utilizing the *Charmat* bubble producing system. What is the original name for the process?

98 What is the typical number of atmospheres of pressure in a bottle of Prosecco?

99 True or False? Prosecco may only be produced in The Veneto region.

100 There are two quality levels of Prosecco, one is DOC and the other DOCG. What is the full name of the latter?

101 What year was Prosecco Superiore given DOCG status?

102 The higher elevation zone of Valdobbiadene contains an ultra-premium sub-zone. What is the name?

---

95 The Veneto, Trentino-Alto Adige (Südtirol in German) and Friuli-Venezia Giulia.

96 Prosecco. (Glera is the predominant grape variety).

97 Martinotti Process. (Federico Martinotti started it in 1895, and Eugène Charmat improved it in 1907).

98 ≈ 3 atmospheres (45 psi pressure) versus ≈ 6 atmospheres for Champagne (90 psi).

99 False. (Although the vast majority comes from Veneto, it may also be made in Friuli-Venezia Giulia).

100 Prosecco Superiore. (Must come from the sub-regions of Valdobbiadene, Conegliano or Asolo).

101 2009. (The DOCG zones are in superior growing areas).

102 Cartizze. Full name Superiore di Cartizze Valdobbiadene DOCG. (≈ 265 acres are owned by ≈ 140 owners.).

103 Who is not a Prosecco producer? Mionetto, Nino Franco, Villa Sandi, Borgoluce, Lamborghini, Mongarda, Masottina, Syltbar.

104 The province of Verona is in southwestern Veneto. Name four wines produced here.

105 Most Soave is classified DOC, yet four DOCGs exist. What are they?

106 What is the primary grape variety grown in Soave?

107 Valpolicella is a popular red wine produced here. What varieties may be used in production?

108 There is a winery production step that adds more intensity to common Valpolicella. What is it called?

109 True or False? Righetti is a famous wine producing family that specializes in Soave Classico.

110 Amarone della Valpolicella Classico DOCG is the most famous of wines from the Veneto. Briefly describe the production process.

111 In Amarone production, what is the process of air drying the grapes called?

112 Modern Amarone is typically fermented to dryness. What is the sweet style called?

113 Which winery is out of place? Bertani, Allegrini, Mionetto, Quintarelli, Dal Forno Romano, Masi.

114 Friuli-Venezia Giulia produces some of the northeast's finest white wines. What grapes are used?

115 In 1977, an artistic Friulian winemaker named Silvio Jermann created Italy's first cult white wine. What was it?

116 What are the names of the two hilly DOC zones beginning with "C" in Friuli?

117 What Friuli-based winery makes the following wines? Terre Alte, Abbazia di Rosazzo, Vertigo, Sossó, Picolit.

---

103 They are all producers of Prosecco, and in some cases, they make other wines too.

104 Soave, Bardolino, Valpolicella, and Amarone della Valpolicella Classico, among others.

105 Soave Superiore, Soave Superiore Classico, Recioto di Soave, Recioto di Soave Classico.

106 Garganega. (Trebbiano di Soave, among others, may be blended with Garganega.)

107 Corvina, Rondinella, Molinara, Corvinone and Oseleta grapes.

108 Ripasso. (The juice is re-fermented on the skins of Amarone, adding extra body to the wine).

109 False. (Righetti is a Valpolicella producer, making several wines including the flagship Amarone (Capitel de Roari).

110 The grapes are harvested and allowed to dry out in a climate-controlled room for 3 - 4 months before pressing.

111 Appassimento. (The fruit is dried out on racks or in plastic bins – losing 35% of their volume).

112 Recioto della Valpolicella. (Recioto has up to 50 g/l residual sugar, Amarone is typically 5 – 7 g/l.)

113 Mionetto. (A Prosecco producer. The others are Amarone/Valpolicella producers).

114 Pinot Grigio, Friulano, Picolit, Ribolla Gialla, Pinot Bianco, Sauvignon Blanc, Chardonnay.

115 Vintage Tunina. (A blend of several indigenous and international grapes. Perfect with white truffles).

116 Collio (hills) and Colli Orientali del Friuli (east facing hills). These eastern areas border Slovenia.

117 Livio Felluga. (Livio passed at the ripe old age of 102, but the next two generation carry on his good work).

118 True or False? Trentino is the southern half of Trentino-Alto Adige.

119 What type of wine is made under the Trentodoc appellation?

120 True or False? Trentodoc may also produce sparkling wines Franciacorta and Prosecco.

121 Alto Adige is the northernmost region in northeast Italy. What is the name of the mountains of the region?

118 True. (Trentino is named for the village of Trento, and Alto "upper" Adige is the river valley to the north).

119 Traditional Method sparkling wine (Chardonnay, Pinot Nero, Pinot Bianco and Meunier are allowed.)

120 False. (Franciacorta is exclusive to Lombardy and Prosecco to Veneto and Friuli-Venezia Giulia).

121 The Dolomites. (In Italian, *Dolomiti*.)

ITALY

CENTRAL ITALY

122 Emilia-Romagna wine region is north and east of Tuscany. What is the gastronomic center of Emilia-Romagna?

123 What is the most popular wine from Emilia-Romagna?

124 True or False? All Lambrusco is sweet.

125 Who does not produce Lambrusco? Pederzana, Lini Oreste, Labrusca, Piccola, Medici Ermete.

126 What was the first Italian white wine to achieve DOCG status?

127 What region is to the east and south of Tuscany?

128 What is the best-known white wine from Umbria?

129 What is the name of the Chardonnay/Grechetto blended wine produced at Antinori's Castello della Sala?

130 What are the two DOCG red wines from Umbria?

---

122 Bologna. (This is the largest city and home to many cultural and cuisine-based adventures).

123 Lambrusco. (There are several denominations, all made from the grape Lambrusco).

124 False. (There are *Dolce* (sweet), *Amabile* (slightly sweet) and *Secco* (dry) versions of Lambrusco.

125 Labrusca. (Labrusca is a vine species native to North America; Concord is a typical Labrusca variety.)

126 Albana di Romagna. (DOC in 1967, and DOCG in 1987).

127 Umbria. (One of of the very few of Italy's landlocked regions).

128 Orvieto. (Made primarily from Grechetto and Trebbiano grapes).

129 Cervaro della Sala. (First made in 1985, Cervaro was the name of the original owners of Castello della Sala).

130 Sagrantino di Montefalco and Torgiano Rosso Riserva.

131 What year did Sagrantino di Montefalco achieve DOC status? What year did it become DOCG?

132 The Marches (Pronounced MAHR-Kay) region is on the Adriatic coast. What is the name of the local white wine?

133 Abruzzo is just south of The Marches. What are the primary red and white wines produced here?

131 1979, 1992. (Sagrantino is derived from *sacred*, and the grape produces a powerful and intense red wine).

132 Verdicchio (both grape and wine. Two DOC zones: Verdicchio dei Castelli di Jesi, Verdicchio di Matelica).

133 Montepulciano d'Abruzzo (red) Trebbiano d'Abruzzo (white.)

ITALY

SOUTHERN ITALY & THE ISLANDS

Southern Italy contains the regions of Campania, Basilicata, Calabria and Puglia

134 Campania is home to Naples, the Amalfi Coast and the ruins of Pompeii. Name two white wines produced in Campania.

135 Who is credited with commercializing Marsala as a wine region on Sicily's western end?

136 Sardinia, Italy's other island region further west in the Mediterranean, has one DOCG region. What is it?

137 Sardinia also produces wines from a red wine variety called Cannonau. What is the French name for this grape?

138 What are the two DOCGs for red wines from Campania?

139 List two of Campania's top producers.

140 Name two white wines produced by at the Feudi di San Gregorio estate.

141 Basilicata is south of Campania and has one significant DOC red wine. What is it?

---

134 Fiano di Avellino (variety/town); and Greco di Tufo (grape/soil type) are both DOCG.

135 John Woodhouse. (An 18th century Englishman. The thirsty English were forever in search of new wine regions.)

136 Vermentino di Gallura. (This is a fresh, dry white wine made from the Vermentino variety).

137 Grenache. (Garnacha in Spain).

138 Taurasi and Aglianico del Taburno. (Both made from the Aglianico variety).

139 Feudi di San Gregorio, Mastroberardino; Villa Matilde; Montevetrano; Masciarelli; Terradora.

140 Greco di Tufo DOCG, Fiano di Avellino DOCG, Falanghina DOC.

141 Aglianico del Vulture. (the grapes are grown on the slopes of an extinct volcano).

142 Apulia (Puglia in Italian) is a region located in Italy's southeast. What variety grown here is synonymous with Zinfandel?

143 In addition to Primitivo, what is another red wine variety grown in Puglia's Salento peninsula?

144 The Antinori family invested in Puglia in 1998. What is the name of the winery?

145 Italy has two island regions, Sicily (Sicilia) and Sardinia (Sardegna.) Which is closest to the mainland?

146 What is the name of Sicily's only DOCG wine?

147 What red wine variety from Sicily is notably grown in the volcanic soil slopes of Mt. Etna?

148 What variety is responsible for the dry white wine Etna Bianco Superiore?

149 What Moscato wine is grown on an island off Sicily closer to the African mainland than that of Italy?

142 Primitivo. (Also known as Crljenak Kaštelanski and Tribidrag).

143 Negroamaro. (Meaning dark and bitter in Italian. It is the primary variety in Salice Salentino DOC.)

144 Tormaresca. (Two estates: Bocca di Lupo in Castel del Monte; Masseria Maime in upper Salento).

145 Sicily. (Just two miles separate Sicily from the rest of Italy).

146 Cerasuolo di Vittoria. (A red wine made from varieties Nero d'Avola and Frappato).

147 Nerello Mascalese. (Etna is an active volcano and erupts occasionally, making viticulture a bit dangerous).

148 Carricante. (The wine shows a well-defined minerality and floral aromatics).

149 Moscato di Pantelleria. (Moscato (Muscat of Alexandria) is known as Zibibbo on the island of Pantelleria.

CHAPTER 6

GERMANY

For most, it is a rigorous exercise to learn about Germany's wine regions, grape varieties, classifications, and stylistic differences. Coupled with long multi-syllabic names in difficult to read Gothic lettering, many just give up and move on to less complex countries. German wine has always been one of my passions, so to make this easier, I have broken the questions down into two headings. Level one is the basics, and level two is a more in-depth study of the wines from Germany.

GERMANY

GENERAL QUESTIONS – LEVEL 1

150 True or False? Germany's vineyards are always located on flatlands.

151 Who has more acres planted to grapevines, the region of Bordeaux, France, or the entire country of Germany?

152 Are the wine regions of Germany positioned in the eastern or western part of the country?

153 Name the most popular German wine imported into the United States in the 1960s and 1970s?

154 Name another once popular German wine that appeared after Blue Nun?

155 Another once popular wine featured a label with a black cat and city tower. What was the name of this wine?

156 What % of all German wine produced is white wine?

157 What percentage of Germany's vineyard area is planted to Riesling, Germany's signature variety?

---

150 False. (Although ≈ 20% of vineyards are located on flatlands, ≈ 80% are on hillsides or mountains).

151 Bordeaux. (Germany has ≈ 250,000 acres planted, and Bordeaux has ≈ 300,000 acres).

152 In the western part. (The German wine regions border France and partially Luxembourg).

153 Blue Nun Liebfraumilch. (First released in 1923 by H. Sichel Söhne).

154 Black Tower. (The black ceramic, square shouldered bottle became a popular alternative).

155 Zeller Schwarze Katz. (From the town of Zell in the Mosel, in English, the Black Cat of Zell).

156 ≈ 80%. (The balance is red and some rosé; the cool climate is more conducive to white wine varieties).

157 ≈ 25%. (Riesling is planted on the best sites, 75% of the acreage is planted to grapes for volume production).

158 Approximately how many total acres are planted to Riesling in Germany?

159 Name 1 dark-skinned grape grown in Germany.

160 True or False? Most German wine producers own very large parcels of vineyards.

161 What recent phenomenon allows Germany to produce riper grapes than in the past?

162 True or False? Most German wines are sweet.

163 Name the 2 terms for drier styles of German wine?

164 What is another name often used instead of the less popular term Halbtrocken?

165 Many German Rieslings have a considerable amount of sugar. What other component balances the sweetness?

166 What is the German term for sparkling wine?

167 What term is used for sparkling wine produced from German producers only?

168 Name the two broad classifications for German wines.

169 Where is the world's largest wooden wine barrel located?

170 Historically, how could a consumer from a distance determine which wine was Mosel and which was Rhine?

171 Hock is a dated term the English coined for German white wine. What is the derivation of the term?

172 What soil type is predominant in the Mosel?

173 Which estate in Germany was the first to bottle a Spätlese (late harvest) wine?

174 How many acres make up the Schloss Johannisberg estate in the Rheingau?

---

158 50,000 acres. (Riesling is Germany's most widely planted variety).

159 Spätburgunder (Pinot Noir); Dornfelder; Portugieser.

160 False. (The average vineyard size is less than 3 acres).

161 Climate Change. (The downside is that it is harder to produce Eiswein, which is made from frozen grapes.)

162 False. (The popular assumption is that all German wine is sweet, but ≈ 70% of German wines are dry.)

163 Trocken (Dry); Halbtrocken (half dry.)

164 Feinherb (This term is not officially recognized under German or EU law).

165 Acid. (High acidity offsets the sugar, making the wine taste less sweet).

166 Sekt. (Basic Sekt may be made from inexpensive juice imported from Italy and elsewhere).

167 Deutscher Sekt. (German sparkling wine only. A small portion of the Sekt category).

168 *Tafelwein*. (Table wine, not often seen in the US). *Qualitätswein* (Quality Wine).

169 Heidelberg, Germany. (Built in 1751, it measures 7 meters high X 8.5 meters wide, and holds 58,124 gallons).

170 Rhine wines were sold in brown bottles, and Mosel wines were sold in green bottles.

171 Hock (Hoch in German) was taken from the village of Hochheim am Main in the Rheingau.

172 Devonian Blue Slate. (Paleozoic Era ≈ 416-358 million years ago. Great sun reflectivity on steep slopes).

173 Schloss Johannisberg. (In 1755, the monks could not harvest until the Abbot returned. The wine was delicious).

174 86 acres. (In addition to the first Spätlese, they were also first to bottle an Auslese in 1787.)

GERMANY

GENERAL QUESTIONS – LEVEL 2

175 Terms for measuring sugar levels at harvest include °Brix and °Baumé. What is the German term?

176 In addition to the Riesling grape, name two additional white wine grapes grown in Germany.

177 Müller-Thurgau grape is a crossing between which two other grapes?

178 What is the Silvaner X Gutedel (Chasselas in France & Switzerland) cross called?

179 In German, what term is used for the official "quality wine growing regions"?

180 How many Anbaugebiete are there in Germany?

181 Name five of the most internationally recognized Anbaugebiete of Germany?

182 Which Anbaugebiet is the largest in acreage? Which is the smallest?

183 Anbaugebiete contain large, official sub-regions called what?

184 Within a Bereich, what is the German term for a collection of vineyard sites?

---

175 °Öchsle. (Based on specific gravity or density, realize that this measurement determines *potential alcohol*).

176 Müller-Thurgau, Grauburgunder (Pinot Gris), Weissburgunder (Pinot Blanc), Silvaner (Sylvaner in Alsace).

177 Riesling X Madeleine Royale. (Crossed in 1882 by Dr. Hermann Müller, ripening before Riesling X Silvaner).

178 Nobling. (In the early 20th century, Silvaner was the most planted grape in Germany).

179 Anbaugebiet (singular). Anbaugebiete (plural).

180 13. (Eleven are in southwestern Germany, with two in northeast Germany).

181 Mosel, Rheingau, Rheinhessen, Nahe, Pfalz. (The others are less well-known).

182 Rheinhessen (≈ 27,000 acres). Hessische Bergstrasse (≈ 460 acres).

183 Bereich (singular). Bereiche (plural). (There are 39 of them within the 13 Anbaugebiete).

184 Grosslage. Grosslagen plural. (A grouped selection of vineyard sites. There are 160 of them).

185 Within a grosslage, single vineyard sites are called what?

186 Gemeinde is German for village (Gemeinden-plural.) Name three gemeinden in the Mosel Anbaugebiet.

187 On labels, the Gemeinde is often linked to the einzellage. Name two well-known examples in the Mosel.

188 Approximately how many grape growers are in Piesporter Goldtröpfchen?

189 Which Anbaugebiet has the greatest number of Einzellagen?

190 What was one of the factors that the German Wine Law of 1971 changed and simplified?

191 What was the previous name for the Mosel Anbaugebiet? (The new name occurred in time for the 2007 vintage).

192 What was the previous name for the Pfalz? (The name change occurred in 1995).

193 What are the two levels of Qualitätswein (Quality wine)?

194 What year was Qualitätswein mit Prädikat (QmP - old term) change to Prädikatswein?

195 From a production standpoint, what is a major difference between Qualitätswein and Prädikatswein?

196 Name the Prädikate classifications in order of ripeness of grapes at harvest?

197 What year was the first Trockenbeerenauslese produced?

198 Name three well-known Mosel producers.

199 What year did Deinhard & Co. produce a Bernkasteler Doctor Brut Sekt?

200 In my collection is a Dr. Thanisch Berncasteler Doctor und Gaben Christwein Eiswein 1970. What is Christwein?

---

185 Einzellage (singular), einzellagen (plural.)

186 Piesport, Wehlen, Graach, Bernkastel, Ürzig, Erden, Trittenheim. (Grammar: ER is added to the village).

187 Piesporter Goldtröpfchen, Bernkastler Doctor, etc. ("Er" is possessive; Doctor belongs to Bernkasteler.)

188 ≈ 350. (A lot, but it is a large vineyard, and many growers own relatively small parcels).

189 Mosel. (With a total of 507, followed by Rheinhessen with 442).

190 It reduced the ≈ 25,000 Einzellagen (vineyards) to the current 2,715, which anyone can memorize!

191 Mosel-Saar-Ruwer. (The Mosel (Moselle in French) is the main river and the other two are tributaries).

192 Rheinpfalz or (Palatinate, which had historical significance).

193 Level 1. Qualitätswein. (Quality wine). Formally Qualitätswein Bestimmter Anbaugebiete (QbA).
    Level 2. Prädikatswein. (Quality wine with special distinctions. Formally Qualitätswein mit Prädikat (QmP).

194 2007. (This makes the Qualitätswein and Prädikatswein easier to comprehend (and pronounce.)

195 Chaptalization (sugar addition pre-fermentation) is allowed in Qualitätswein, but not in Prädikatswein.

196 Kabinett, Spätlese, Auslese, Beerenauslese (BA), Trockenbeernauslese (TBA), Eiswein (Ice wine).

197 1921. (From the Bernkasteler Doctor, two producers, Dr. Thanisch and Bischöflichen Weingüter).

198 J.J. Prüm, Fritz Haag, Dr. Loosen, J.J. Christoffel, St. Urbans-Hof, Von Hovel, Wegeler, Willi Schaefer, etc.

199 1978. (This rare bottle celebrates Deinhard's 100th Anniversary 1882-1982. 18,578 bottles were produced).

200 The grapes were harvested on Christmas Eve (1970 was the last vintage allowing Christwein on the label).

201 Observant readers will note label spellings of Dr. Thanisch's Berncastel and Bernkastel. What is the difference?

202 What is the size of the Berncasteler Doctor vineyard?

203 Which vineyard is out of place? Maximin Grünhauser, Ayler Kupp, Scharzhofberger, Ockfener Bockstein.

204 What family owns the famous Scharzhofberg vineyard in the Saar?

205 Schloss means castle in English. Name two famous estates in the Rheingau with schloss in their names.

206 Which vineyard is out of place? Niersteiner Hipping; Forster Jusitengarten; Oppenheimer Herrenberg.

207 Which producer is out of place? Hermann Dönnhoff, Schlossgut Diel, Emrich-Schönleber, Gunderloch.

208 Franken wines are often packaged in a uniquely shaped bottle. What is the name of the bottle?

209 The term *Ortsteil* means what in German viticulture?

210 What is the name of the grower's association that has an eagle with a cluster of grapes as their logo?

211 What are the top two levels of the VDP classification called Grosse Lage (Note: No association with grosslage).

212 Which producer is out of place? Dr. von Basserman-Jordan, Müller-Catoir, Dr. Bürklin Wolf, Selbach-Oster, Dartling.

213 What is the name of the steepest inclined vineyard in Germany (and the world)?

---

201 Berncastel is used only for the Doctor labels, Bernkastel is used for the labels Lay, Graben, Badstube. etc.

202 8.1 acres. (Doctor is arguably the top vineyard site in Germany, located in the Mosel).

203 Maximin Grünhauser. (This is in the Ruwer, and the others are in the Saar).

204 Weingut Egon Müller, Scharzhof. (This 20-acre vineyard produces some of the most expensive German wines).

205 Schloss Johannisberg, Schloss Vollrads.

206 Forster Jusitengarten. (It is in the Pfalz, and the others are in the Rheinhessen).

207 Gunderloch. (They are in the Rheinhessen, the others are in the Nahe).

208 Bocksbeutel. (This flagon shaped bottle is like the Mateus bottle from Portugal).

209 A historic walled vineyard plot. Examples: Steinberg, Schloss Johannisberg, Schloss Vollrads.

210 VDP (Verband Deutscher Prädikatsweingüter) 200 members producing Germany's highest quality wine.

211 *Grosse Gewächs* (Grand Cru Vineyards, dry wines) and *Erste Gewächs* (Premier Cru Vineyards).

212 Selbach-Oster. (They are based in the Mosel, and the others are producers from the Pfalz).

213 Calmont Bremm. (The Calmont vineyard is a 65° incline slope in the village of Bremm, Mosel).

Here is a real geeky final German wine trivia question:

214 Which wine had the longest name on the smallest bottle label back in the 1960s (we had it on The Breakers wine list).

214 Eitelsbacher Karthäuserhofberg Sang. (To achieve the small label criteria, it was a narrow neck label).

CHAPTER 7

AUSTRIA

AUSTRIA

THE WINES OF AUSTRIA

1   True or False? Like Germany, the wine growing regions in Austria are in the western part of the country.

2   Name the major river along which many wine regions are located in the northern part of the country.

3   How many acres are planted to grapevines in Austria? 27,500, 76,800, 123,000, 181,000, 240,000.

4   What is the name of Austria's appellation system?

5   How many DACs currently exist in Austria?

6   Why is the capital city of Vienna important in viticultural discussions?

7   Within the city limits of Vienna there are several wine tasting rooms open to the public. What are they called?

---

1   False. (The soil and climate of eastern Austria are ideal for viticulture. The west is too cold and mountainous).

2   The Danube. (Called the Donau in German.)

3   ≈ 123,000 acres. (This is roughly 1% of the world's total vineyard acreage).

4   DAC. (Districtus Austriae Controllatus). Controlled Wine Districts of Austria.

5   17. (These regulations identify not only geographical areas, but grape varieties that match the soil and climate).

6   Vienna (Wien) is the only capital in the world that has grapevines planted (1,574 acres) within the city limits.

7   Heurige. (Plural is Heurigen, and the recent wine releases are offered, along with some local bites).

8 What white wine DAC incorporates the vineyards of Wien?

9 What are the three major regional wine growing areas in Austria? (One in the north, and the other two in the south).

10 What percentage of all wine made in Austria is white?

11 Name the predominant two high quality white varieties grown in lower Austria.

12 Name three red wine varieties grown in Austria.

13 Dr. Zweigelt crossed Blaufränkisch and St. Laurent in 1922. What was the original name for the grape?

14 What is the name of the large DAC north of Vienna, yet still contained within Niederösterreich?

15 The western part of Niederösterreich has three famous high-quality wine growing areas in Austria. Name them.

16 The Wachau has its own classification for wines based on ripeness at harvest. Name the three levels.

17 What is the Wachau's entry level term for grape ripeness/alcohol, and what is the alcohol range?

18 Name the Wachau's mid-level term for grape ripeness/alcohol, and what is the alcohol range?

19 Name the Wachau's highest level term for grape ripeness/alcohol, and what is the alcohol range?

20 Which producer is out of place? Hirtzberger, Martin Nigl, Nikolaihoff, FX Pichler, Emmerich Knoll.

21 What is the derivation of the names Kremstal and Kamptal?

---

8 Wiener Gemischter Satz. (Min. three grapes planted in a field blend with no grape exceeding 50% of the blend).

9 Lower Austria. (Niederösterreich-notable white wines), Burgenland (red, dessert) and Styria (Dry white wines).

10 ≈ 66%. (Although a larger percentage is white, Austria produces notable red wines as well).

11 Grüner Veltliner. (Most widely planted) and Riesling (grown in the top vineyard sites).

12 Blaufränkisch (spicy, brash); St. (Sankt) Laurent (fruit forward); Zweigelt (a crossing of the previous two).

13 Rotburger. (With a spelling too similar to the German grape Rotberger, the name was changed in the 1970s).

14 Weinviertel DAC. (This extensive area produces fruit forward, light, and delicate red and white wines).

15 Wachau, Kremstal DAC and Kamptal DAC.

16 Steinfeder, Federspiel, Smaragd.

17 Steinfeder. (< 11.5% Alcohol). Steinfeder is name of a local grass around the vineyards.

18 Federspiel. (11.5% - 12.5% alcohol). Federspiel is a falconer's tool.

19 Smaragd. (> 12.5% alcohol). Smaragd is a type lizard that prefers the warmest areas of the vineyard.

20 Martin Nigl. (Nigl is based in the Kremstal DAC, and the other producers are in Wachau).

21 Krems and Kamp are names of towns, and *tal* translates to valley. Vineyards are on the valley hillsides.

22 Which producer is out of place? Willi Bründlmayer, Schloss Gobelsburg, Sepp Moser, Fred Loimer, Josef Hirsch.

23 Name two of the notable hillside vineyards just east of the city of Langenlois in Kamptal.

24 What is the Austrian term for a single vineyard site?

25 The measurement for sugar levels in the grapes at harvest in Germany is called Öchsle. What is the Austrian term?

26 Name two DACs contained within Burgenland.

27 Name the shallow lake surrounded by Burgenland and its DACs?

28 Name the most notable producer in Neusiedlersee DAC famous for dessert wines.

29 Burgenland is not known for Grüner Veltliner or Riesling. Name two popular white grapes grown in Burgenland.

30 Name the most famous historic town in Neusiedler-Hügelland known for high Prädikat wines.

31 What country borders Burgenland to the east?

32 What is the local name for Chardonnay in the Styria region in southern Austria?

22 Sepp Moser. (Moser is based in Kremstal, and the others are in Kamptal).

23 Heiligenstein, Renner, Lamm, Gaisberg, Offenberg, Grub.

24 Ried. (This term must appear on the label followed by the name of the vineyard.)

25 KMW. (Klosterneuburger Mostwaage). 1 KMW^0 = 5^0 Öchsle. This is used to indicate the wine's potential alcohol).

26 Neusiedlersee, Leithaberg, Mittleburgenland, Eisenberg, Rosalia.

27 Lake Neusiedl; Neusiedlersee DAC is named for it. (Notable for botrytized dessert wines due to humid climate).

28 Kracher. (The passing of Father Alois propelled his son Gerhard to take the company to the next level).

29 Furmint; Muskateller (Muscat); Weissburgunder (Pinot Blanc); Neuberger; Welschriesling (Not Riesling).

30 Rust. (Their Trockenbeerenauslesen have a local name called Ruster Ausbruch).

31 Hungary. (With a similar climate, Hungary produces notable botrytized dessert wines as well).

32 Morillon. (The versatility of the grape produces crisp dry wines as well as dessert-style whites).

CHAPTER 8

SPAIN

SPAIN

THE WINES OF SPAIN

1   True or False? For centuries, Spain has led the wine world with the highest quality wines available.

2   Beginning in 1986, what primary factor led to an advancement in quality in Spanish wine?

3   What are the two highest official quality levels for Spanish wine.

4   How many DOCa regions currently exist? Name them.

5   How many DO regions currently exist?

6   What is the official term for high quality single estate appellations?

7   The vines in the hotter and drier areas of Spain are usually planted far apart. What is the reason for this?

8   True or False? Spain has the most acreage planted to grapevines in Europe.

9   What are the two most widely planted wine grapes in Spain?

---

1   False. (Spain is a relative newcomer to the game of world class wines).

2   Joining the European Union (EU) led to many advancements in quality to reach EU standards.

3   Denominación de Origen Calificada (DOCa) and Denominación de Origen (DO)

4   Two. Rioja, granted in 1991 and Priorat, granted in 2003. (Two of the most famous wine regions of Spain).

5   More than 70. (This number is growing steadily).

6   *Vinos de Pago.* (This was established in 2003.)

7   Lack of enough groundwater and/or rainfall. (Irrigation is not approved for many European wine regions).

8   True. (However, France and Italy produce more wine.)

9   Airén (white wine variety widely used for brandy production) and Tempranillo (red wine variety.)

10 Which of the following grapes is not native to Spain? Albariño, Cariñena, Vermentino, Verdejo, Macabeo.

11 Where does the Verdejo grape get its name?

12 Which wine grape variety listed is not native to Spain? Tempranillo, Picpoul, Garnacha, Monastrell.

13 The red wine variety Garnacha is known as what in France.

14 Which wine is not from Northwest of Spain? Ribeiro; Ribeira Sacra; Valdeorras; Jerez; Bierzo.

15 Galicia is in northwest Spain, on the Atlantic coast. What is the most famous wine from this area?

16 What is Spain's best-known wine region, famous for red wine?

17 Rioja has three subregions. What are they?

18 What age statements may be listed on Rioja wine labels?

19 Define the minimum total aging requirements for each of the above.

20 Which was the first established commercial bodega in Rioja?

21 Which producers are not in Rioja? Muga; Lopez de Heredia; Marqués de Riscal; Scala Dei; Riojannas; Martinez Bujanda.

22 Who is the largest landowner in Rioja DOCa?

23 West of Rioja, there is a notable wine region called Ribera del Duero. What is the English translation of the name?

24 What Ribera del Duero winery established in 1864 produces the region's most famous and expensive red wine?

---

10 Vermentino. (Vermentino is native to Italy and France.)

11 Verde is green in Spanish. (This white wine variety is grown in Rueda and comparable to Sauvignon Blanc).

12 Picpoul. (This white wine variety is native to southern France).

13 Grenache. (Many varieties native to Spain are also grown in southern France and have been for centuries).

14 Jerez. (Produced in Andalusia, in the south, also known as Sherry, an English corruption of Jerez).

15 Albariño from the Rías Baixas appellation. (Both grape and wine are known as Albariño).

16 Rioja. (The modern era dates to the 1860s, when wineries such as Marqués de Riscal were established).

17 Rioja Alta (most well-known wineries); Rioja Oriental (formerly Rioja Baja); Rioja Alavesa (highest elevation).

18 Joven; Crianza; Reserva; Gran Reserva.

19 Joven (none); Crianza (24 mos.); Reserva (36 mos.); Gran Reserva (60 mos.).

20 Marqués de Murrieta (founded in 1852).

21 Scala Dei. (That winery is in Priorat, and the others are in Rioja).

22 Bodegas Faustino. (They own over 1,600 acres of vineyards. They are responsible for 34% of Rioja Gran Reserva).

23 Ribera means "riverbank" and Duero is the name of the famous river.

24 Vega Sicilia. (The estate of 250 acres is planted to Tinto Fino (Tempranillo), and Bordeaux varieties).

———— SPAIN ————

25   What do the two words Vega Sicilia translate to?

26   Name the two top wines produced by Vega Sicilia.

27   Vega Sicilia's Álvarez family also owns a sister winery with a more modern approach to winemaking. Name the winery?

28   What is the name of another notable Ribera del Duero winery led by Alejandro Fernández?

29   Which is not a Ribera del Duero winery? Legaris, Dominio de Pingus, Ramon Bilbao, Emilio Moro.

30   Southwest of Ribera del Duero lies Rueda, a region known primarily for white wine. What grape is used for production?

31   Just west of Reuda is Toro. What famous Louis Vuitton Moët Hennessy-owned winery is located here?

32   The areas of Reuda, Ribera del Duero, Bierzo, Arribes, Tierra de Léon and Toro are contained within which larger area?

33   The city of Barcelona is located within what major Spanish wine region.

34   Penedès is a sub-region of Catalonia. What is the predominant wine produced here?

35   Name the two largest Cava producers.

36   What are the three predominant grapes used in Cava production?

37   What famous Spanish wine family is based in Vilafranca del Penedès near Barcelona?

38   Which Torres wine is not produced in Catalonia? Sangre de Toro; Coronas; Verdeo; Vina Esmeralda; Viña Sol.

39   South of the Penedès is the high-quality red wine region Priorat. When did this region get worldwide attention?

---

25 Vega means fertile lowlands, and Sicilia refers to a local revered saint.

26 *Unico*. (The Gran Reserva is typically released more than 10 years after the vintage). *Valbuena 5°* (aged 5 years).

27 Alión. (A few miles away from Vega Sicilia, Alión is 100% Tempranillo aged in new French oak).

28 Tinto Pesquera. (Founded in 1972, just before Ribera del Duero began to be internationally recognized).

29 Ramon Bilbao. (That estate is in Rioja, and the others are in Ribera del Duero).

30 Verdejo. (Rioja producer Marqués de Riscal moved their white wine production to Rueda in the 1970s).

31 Numanthia. (The 200-acre estate makes three red wines; Termes; Numanthia, Termanthia).

32 Castilla Y Léon. (This large region is very historical and cultural and home to many castles and monasteries).

33 Catalonia (Catalunya), located in northeastern Spain on the Mediterranean coast).

34 Cava. (This is Spain's most widely produced traditional method sparkling wine, made like champagne).

35 Codorniu and Freixenet. (These wines are more affordable than champagne and offer both value and quality).

36 Macabeo ≈ 35% total plantings, Xarel-lo ≈ 25%, Parellada ≈20%.

37 Torres. (Although based in Penedès, Torres makes wines from premium wine regions throughout Spain).

38 Verdeo. (Made from the Verdejo grape, this wine is produced in Reuda).

39 In the 1980s. (Before that the region was primarily known for inexpensive bulk wine).

40 Which two winemakers are recognized as pioneers of high-quality wine in Priorat?

41 Who does not produce wines from Priorat? Clos Mogador, Lancer's, Clos Erasmus, Clos Martinet, Clos Daphne.

42 The very southern part of Spain is called Andalucía. What wine style is the region most famous for?

43 Name the three sub-regions of Jerez.

44 What is the predominant grape used to make sherry?

45 Which is not a type of sherry? Manzanilla, Fino, Port, Amontillado, Oloroso, Cream.

46 True or False? Controlled oxidation and fractional blending are both used in sherry production.

47 What is the name of the system employed in sherry for fractional blending?

48 What term is used for the stacking of barrels for the Solera system defining the rows from top to bottom?

49 Name two well-known sherry brands.

50 Name two sherry producers. These are the companies that make some of the brands above.

40 Alvaro Palacios and René Barbier. (Today, there are over 100 wineries in Priorat).

41 Lancer's. (This is an inexpensive rosé from Portugal, the rest are high quality wineries in Priorat).

42 Sherry. "Sherry" is an English corruption of the word Jerez (hay-reth) and is a famous type of fortified wine.

43 Jerez de la Frontera, Sanlúcar de Barrameda, El Puerto de Santa Maria.

44 Palomino. (This grape is ≈ 90% of planted grapes).

45 Port. (Port is produced in Portugal, and the others are styles of sherry).

46 True. (Unusual in wine production, oxidation benefits Sherry, and blending creates a uniform house style).

47 The Solera System. (The maturing process blending several vintages in stacked barrels, from top to bottom).

48 Criadera. (The youngest wine starts at the top and is gradually blended with the mature wine at the bottom).

49 Harvey's Bristol Cream, Tio Pepe, Dry Sack, Lustau, etc.

50 González Byass, Pedro Domecq, Williams & Humbert, Savory & James, Osborne, etc.

——————— SPAIN ———————

CHAPTER 9

PORTUGAL

PORTUGAL

THE WINES OF PORTUGAL

51 What is the wine classification system used in Portugal?

52 True or False? Most Portuguese wines are made from well-known international varieties.

53 What is arguably the most well-known Portuguese red wine variety?

54 True or False? Portugal makes red wines exclusively.

55 What Portuguese term is used to indicate a sparkling wine?

56 What wine Portuguese region claims the title as the world's oldest defined wine region?

57 Besides winemaking, what other related industry is prevalent in southern Portugal?

58 What Portuguese region is home to port wine?

59 The Port producing area has a name that signifies the intense heat of where the grapes are grown. What is the term?

60 When one states port is a fortified wine, what does this mean?

---

51 DOC. (Denominação de Origem Controlada; it resembles the French AOP system).

52 False. (Most wines are made from indigenous varieties, offering unique flavor profiles).

53 Touriga Nacional. (Despite low yields, the grape is used in Port production and wine from the Dão region).

54 False. (Although most of the production is red, there are several versions of white wine, both dry and sweet).

55 Espumante. (Sparkling wines are made by the traditional, Charmat, and transfer methods).

56 The Douro. (The year was 1756. Named after the Douro river, the same river is called Duero in Spain).

57 Cork production. (Due to an abundance of oak forests, Portugal is the largest supplier of cork worldwide).

58 The Douro Valley. (While justifiably famous for port, about 50% of production is still wine).

59 The Douro Bake. (Among the warmest European wine zones. Thick-skinned port varieties can handle the heat).

60 Aguardente (neutral grape spirit) is added increasing the wine's alcoholic strength.

——— SPAIN ———

61 Where did the name port originate?

62 What is the name of the city across the river from Oporto?

63 Oporto is some distance west of the vineyards. From west to east what are the 3 wine growing districts?

64 Name 2 of the major grape varieties used to make Port.

65 In total, how many different grapes can make Port?

66 What have the Portuguese devised in the Douro Valley to manage working very steeply planted vineyard sites?

67 Port houses (and other regions) use a word for their wine producing estates or farms. What is that term?

68 England has a historical role in the creation of port wine. Name a few port producers of English origin.

69 What are the 2 basic types of Port?

70 Name 3 types of Ruby Port.

71 Which Port house was the first to release a rosé (rosado) port?

72 Name two ruby reserve ports. (Producer's name and the proprietary name of the wine).

73 In addition to the producers above, which is out of place? Churchill; Cálem; Delaforce; Berwick; Burmester.

74 Name the upscale Six Grapes label by W. & J. Graham's.

75 What is Late-Bottled Vintage Port?

76 Define the category of Vintage Port.

---

61 Oporto. (This is the name of the city on the Atlantic Ocean and the Douro river, where Port is shipped).

62 Vila Nova de Gaia. (This is where port wines are matured, prior to being shipped from Oporto).

63 *Baixo Corgo* (lower Corgo river), *Cima Corgo* (Upper Corgo river) and *Douro Superior.*

64 Touriga Nacional, Touriga Franca, Tinta Barroca, Tinto Cão, Tinta Roriz.

65 ≈ 30 grapes are recommended, but up to ≈ 82 are permitted. (Most blends use a combination of the 5 above).

66 Terraces. (This aids in easier farming practices and mitigates the effects of soil erosion).

67 Quinta. (The quinta is followed by a family name or the estate name. EX. Quinta do Noval).

68 Warre's, Croft, Graham, Dow, Cockburn, Sandeman, Taylor-Fladgate.

69 *Ruby Port.* (Deep red in color). *Tawny Port.* (The color tawny (orange/brown).

70 Ruby, Ruby Reserve, Late-Bottled Vintage (LBV), Vintage, Single-Quinta Vintage.

71 Croft. (Named *Pink* and positioned as an apéritif as opposed to service with dessert).

72 Sandeman Founder's Reserve; Graham's Six Grapes; Fonseca's Bin 27; Cockburn's Special Reserve).

73 Berwick. (Berwick is made up, and the remainder are official Port houses).

74 Six Grapes, Old Vines, Special Edition. (The 1st release is based on the 2011 vintage, from their top five quintas).

75 This is a Ruby Port from a single vintage, but it is in oak barrels longer (4-6 years) than a true Vintage Port.

76 This is the highest quality level, and only made in great years. Two years in oak, and long maturation in bottle.

77   True or False? Vintage Port should be drunk directly after release because it's the best quality port.

78   True or False? Once opened, Vintage Port may last for months in the bottle because it is such a high-quality product.

79   How does fortification allow port to be both sweet and high alcohol?

80   Tawny port is a different category of port, matured longer in oak cask. Name two types of high-quality tawny port.

81   Is there such a thing as white port?

82   Setúbal is a peninsula southeast of the Portuguese capitol of Lisbon. Name the oldest table wine producer located here?

83   Name another famous dessert style wine from Setúbal.

84   Heading north, we encounter the region of Bairrada on the Atlantic Ocean. What is the indigenous red wine grape?

85   Just east of Bairrada is the Dão (named after the river) wine region. Name a red wine variety grown here.

86   Name the highest quality white wine variety from Dão (some say highest quality in all of Portugal.)

87   Name the largest wine growing area in southeastern Portugal?

88   Following World War II, what two Portuguese wines took the world by surprise? (Hint, they are both rosé wines).

89   What is the most popular type of wine from the northernmost part of Portugal bordering Spain?

90   Vinho Verde is often mis-pronounced due to its Portuguese origin. What is the correct pronunciation?

---

77   False. (Vintage Port is meant to be aged in bottle for years, if not decades, to reach proper maturity).

78   False. (The bottle should be consumed within two weeks before it loses its freshness).

79   When spirits are added to fermenting juice, the high alcohol content stops fermentation while sugar remains.

80   Aged tawny port (10, 20, 30 or 40 years) and Colheita, a single vintage aged tawny port.

81   Yes. (The production methods are the same as Ruby Port, but only white grape varieties are used).

82   José Maria da Fonseca. (Founded in 1834, this firm makes both the Periquita and Lancer's brands).

83   Moscatel de Setúbal. (Fortified Muscat of Alexandria often has a faint orange color).

84   Baga. (With trademark high acid and tannin, some liken the wine style to that made from Italy's Nebbiolo).

85   Jaen is the most widely planted, followed by Touriga Nacional, then Tinta Roriz.

86   Encruzado. (This grape makes high acid wine with full body and high complexity).

87   Alentejo. (This is home to many red and white varieties, creating truly diverse styles of wines.)

88   *Mateus* (created in 1942), & *Lancers* (created in 1944). These two wines have sold billions of bottles.

89   Vinho Verde. (Green Wine, in Portuguese. Green indicates young, defining the wine's youth, not color).

90   Veeng-yo Vaird. (In the Spanish language, verde is pronounced Ver-Day).

——————   PORTUGAL   ——————

91 True or False? Vinho Verde is exclusive a white wine.

92 Several grapes are used or blended to produce Vinho Verde. Which one is considered highest in quality?

93 What is the southernmost wine region (and popular vacation spot) in Portugal?

94 Name the island region of Portugal located about 600 miles off the coast of Morocco.

95 Name the commercial and business city center of Madeira.

96 What are the four styles of varietally named Madeira?

97 Name two Madeira producers.

98 Name the process of gently heating Madeira in tanks over several months to replicate the canteiro method.

99 What is the most widely planted Madeira grape variety?

91 False. (Actually, more red wine than white is produced, but white is the main export style).

92 Alvarinho. (Known as Albariño across the Minho River in Rías Baíxas in Spain).

93 Algarve. (Most wine is sold as Vinho Regional, but the four DOCs are Lagoa, Portimao, Tavira and Lagos).

94 Madeira. (When the Portuguese arrived in the 15th Century, they burned the forests and planted vines).

95 Funchal. (Located on the southernmost part of the island, this port city has a very dynamic history).

96 Sercial, Verdelho, Boal and Malvasia (Malmsey). (These go from lighter and drier to full, rich and sweet).

97 Blandy's, Cossart Gordon, Madeira Wine Company, Henriques & Henriques, Vinhos Barbeito among others.

98 Estufagem. (Higher quality Madeira is made via the canteiro process.)

99 Tinta Negra. (This disease resistant grape was planted after the phylloxera epidemic of the 1870s).

PART III

OTHER EUROPEAN COUNTRIES

Hungary

Greece

Switzerland

England

CHAPTER 10

HUNGARY

THE WINES OF HUNGARY

1   Which country does not border Hungary? Serbia; Romania; Poland; Croatia.

2   Which large country borders Hungary to the north?

3   Budapest is the capital of Hungary. What river flows through it?

4   True or False? Historically, Hungary was the 3rd country to classify vineyards in 1853.

5   Although Hungary has been producing wine for over 1,000 years, what changed the industry in 1949?

6   After 1989, foreign investment and technology gained hold. Name some of the international grapes now used.

7   What is the Hungarian word for wine?

8   How many wine growing districts are in Hungary?

---

1   Poland. (Poland has one country spaced between their borders, but the other countries border Hungary).
2   Slovakia. (Slovakia is the country that separates Hungary from Poland).
3   The Danube. (A continuation of the Lower Austria wine region).
4   False. (They were the 1st country to classify their vineyards in 1700).
5   Communist rule. (The state-owned monopoly shifted quality wines to bulk production. It changed back in 1989).
6   Whites: Chardonnay; Sauvignon Blanc; Pinot Gris. Reds: Cabernet Sauvignon; Pinot Noir; Merlot.
7   Bor. (The word has middle Persian origins).
8   22. (The most popular are: Tokaj, Eger, Somoló, Sopron, Badascony, etc.).

9 Hungary makes wine primarily from indigenous grape varieties. Name one of the most popular.

10 One of the most popular red wines produced in Hungary is *Bull's Blood*. What is the Hungarian translation?

11 What varieties are used to produce Bull's Blood?

12 What term is used for protection for consumers for the Hungarian wine industry?

13 What is the most famous dessert wine produced in Hungary?

14 Tokaj, Tokaji, Tokay, what do the terms mean?

15 To achieve high levels of sugar concentration, what naturally occurring substance affects the grapes around harvest?

16 Tokaji Aszú dessert wines rank the levels of sweetness with a scale called what?

17 The scale goes from 3 to 6 Puttonyos, 6 being the sweetest. What are the 3 to 6 Puttonyos residual sugar levels?

18 There are two higher levels of sweetness called what?

19 Name two well-known Tokaji producers?

20 Which famous wine author is also part owner of the Royal Tokaji Wine Company?

9 Whites: Furmint, Hárslevelű, Juhfark; Reds: Kadarka, Kékfrankos.

10 Egri Bikavér. (In the 1500s during skirmishes, the Egers drank copious amounts to intimidate opponents).

11 Kekfrankos and Kadarka. (The wine region of Eger is between Budapest and Tokaj).

12 Districtus Hungaricus Controllatus (DHC). (Like other countries, a regulating agency to benefit consumers).

13 Tokaji Aszú. (This is one of the highest-quality and most recognized dessert wines worldwide).

14 Tokaj is the name of the village. Tokaji means from the region. Tokay is the English version of Tokaji

15 Botrytis Cinerea. (A beneficial mold (aszú) attaches to the grape, puncturing it, and water evaporates).

16 Puttonyos. (A *puttony* was the traditional basket for the harvested aszú (botrytized) grapes).

17 3 Putonyos: 60 – 90 g/L RS; 4 Putonyos: 90-120 g/L RS; 5 Putonyos: 120-150 g/L RS; 6 Putonyos: 150-180 g/L RS.

18 Tokaji Aszú Eszencia (180-450 g/L RS); Tokaji Eszencia (450-900 g/L RS). The more common term is Essencia.

19 Royal Tokaji Wine Company, Oremus, Disznókö, Szepsy, Dereszla, Pajzos, etc.

20 Hugh Johnson. (Author of the popular World Atlas of Wine, among other books).

CHAPTER 11

GREECE

THE WINES OF GREECE

21 What label change has assisted Greece in increasing their wine sales?

22 Who was the Greek God of wine?

23 What three countries border Greece to the north?

24 What country borders Greece to the east?

25 Greece has a large land mass; however, many islands and seas border the boundaries. Name the three seas.

26 Name two white wine varieties grown in Greece.

27 Name two red wine varieties grown in Greece.

28 Name the most famous historic white wine produced in Greece.

29 Which grape variety is most often used to produce Retsina?

---

21 Latin words and terms have replaced some of the more challenging traditional Greek nomenclature).
22 Dionysus. (The gift of wine from Dionysus aided in social interaction and intellectual discussions).
23 Albania, Macedonia, and Bulgaria. (From west to east in direction).
24 Turkey. (Turkey is a large country with several wine producing areas of its own).
25 Ionian Sea on the west, Aegean Sea to the east and the all-encompassing Mediterranean to the south.
26 Moschofilero, Savatiano, Assyrtiko, Roditis, Malagousia, Robola; etc.
27 Mavrodaphne, Agiorgitiko, Xinomavaro, Negoska, Mandilaria, Limnio, etc.
28 Retsina. (Historically pine resin was added for flavor and to retard oxidation.)
29 Savatiano. (The most planted variety in Greece, particularly in Central Greece and including the Attika region).

30 Name the large wine growing area in northern Greece.

31 Name the large wine growing area in southern Greece.

32 Name two of the Greek wine producing islands located in the Aegean Sea.

33 Name two well-known wineries in Greece.

30 Macedonia. (The top region contained within is Náoussa, home to several top Greek wine producers).

31 Peloponnese. (Contained within are the wine regions of Neméa, Pátra, Mantinía, etc.

32 Santorini, Rhodes, Crete, Samos, Páros, etc.

33 Boutari, Sigalas, Semeli, Gerovassiliou, Gentilini, Tselepos, Karanika, Pavlidis, Gaia, Mercouri; etc.

CHAPTER 12

SWITZERLAND

THE WINES OF SWITZERLAND

34 What 4 wine countries does Switzerland border?

35 What two famous wine rivers originate here, and flow towards other countries?

36 The Swiss use *Cantons* (provinces) as geographical sub-regions. There are 26. Name two of the French speaking cantons?

37 What is the Italian speaking canton?

38 What is the most famous of these aforementioned wine-producing cantons?

39 True or False? Because Switzerland is so mountainous, most production is by large co-operative wineries.

40 True or False? At last count, there was about 60 different wine varieties grown in Switzerland.

41 What is the widely planted wine variety in Switzerland?

42 In addition to wine, what other popular consumer product is Switzerland known for?

---

34 France, Italy, Germany and Austria.

35 The Rhine River heads north towards Germany, and the Rhône River heads west towards France.

36 Valais, Vaud, Geneva (Genève), Neuchâtel (Three Lakes). (These cantons border France).

37 Ticino. (Located in the southern part of the country bordering Italy).

38 Valais. (There are over 12,000 acres dedicated to viticulture in this canton).

39 False. (Of the county's ≈ 36,000 acres of vineyards, by far the majority are small family plots).

40 False. (Reports show ≈ 250 different grapes grown in Switzerland, many in small family vineyards).

41 The white wine variety Chasselas. (Known as Fendant in the Valais).

42 Milk chocolate (created in 1879 Daniel Peter and Henri Nestlé.) But don't forget cheese and watches.

CHAPTER 13

ENGLAND

THE WINES OF ENGLAND

43 What global phenomenon has allowed England to increase their viticultural footprint?

44 True or False? Most of the vineyards and wineries are in the extreme northwest part of England.

45 Name two of the leading counties for viticulture.

46 How many vineyards are there currently in England and neighboring Wales?

47 What particular style of English wine closely emulates a famous French wine style?

48 What primary soil type in southern England is the same as in Champagne?

49 First planted in 1988, what estate is at the forefront of the English sparkling wine movement?

50 What famous Champagne house owns Domaine Evremond in Kent?

---

43 Climate change. (Long considered too cold and rainy, England now has more than 7,000 acres of vineyard).

44 False. (Most estates are in the southern half of the country, where it is warmer).

45 East Sussex, West Sussex, Surrey, Kent, Hampshire.

46 ≈ 600. (This number is growing yearly.)

47 Traditional method sparkling Wine. (Chardonnay, Pinot Noir, and Meunier all grow well in England).

48 Chalk/limestone soil that exists in Champagne (and much of France) is also part of the English landscape.

49 Nyetimber. (Located in Sussex, this estate put English fizz on the map after achieving numerous accolades).

50 Taittinger. (The Taittinger family and English partner Hatch-Mansfield are planting 40 ha. to vines in Kent).

51　Name the Pommery Champagne project in England.

52　Name the two largest wine producers in England?

The theme of this publication is wine trivia coupled with wine education. In my opinion, it is not necessary from a trivia standpoint to cover every wine producing country on the globe, just the consumer based popular ones. If you wish to further educate yourselves, please consider the following central and eastern European countries:

Slovenia; Slovakia; Croatia; Balkans; Czechia; Romania; Bulgaria; Moldova; Ukraine; Crimea; Russia; Armenia; Georgia, Cyprus; Turkey; Israel; Lebanon; etc.

51　Louis Pommery England. (The 100-acre estate is in Pinglestone in Alresford, Hampshire).

52　Denbies Wine Estate (Surrey) and Chapel Down (Kent).

PART IV

SOUTHERN HEMISPHERE

CHAPTER 14

AUSTRALIA

THE WINES OF AUSTRALIA

1   True or False? Southern hemisphere temperatures at the same latitudes are identical to the northern hemisphere.

2   True or False? The wine industry in Australia is very recent, starting in the 1940s.

3   True or False? Australia has absolutely embraced the screwcap closure for many of its bottles.

4   In the early to mid-2000s, what term was given to inexpensive Australian wines with cute animals on the labels?

5   Bin number labeling is another labeling format used by Australian wineries. Name two wineries that do this.

6   Name one popular winery today that was established in the 1800s.

7   Approximately how many Australian wineries are currently in operation?

8   Name the wine producing island 260 miles off the coast of southeast Australia.

---

1   False. (The southern hemisphere is colder at the same latitudes due to Antarctica's cold influences).

2   False. (The Australian wine industry dates to the early 19th Century).

3   True. (According to published data, ≈ 95% - 98% of the wines are bottled under screwcaps).

4   Critter Wines. (Led by the popular [yellow tail] brand, many more followed suit).

5   Penfolds Bin 389, 407, 707 and Lindemans Bin 65, among others.

6   Penfolds, Lindemans, Orlando, Seppelt, Henschke, etc.

7   ≈ 2,500. (The majority are in South Australia).

8   Tasmania. (Although several types of wines are made here, sparkling wines are most notable).

——— SOUTHERN HEMISPHERE ———

9   Australia produce a significant amount of sweet wines. What term do they used as a generic for sweet wines?

10 What is Australia's annual top wine award?

11 What is the most popular red wine variety grown in Australia?

12 What is the 2nd most planted red wine variety in Australia?

13 In order, what are the three most widely planted white wine varieties?

14 True or False? Australia now ranks 18th in worldwide production.

15 Rank Australia's four primary wine producing states in order by total volume of wine produced.

16 Name the largest city in the state of Victoria?

17 What is the largest city in the state of New South Wales?

18 Name the most populous city in the state of Western Australia.

19 Name two of the primary sub-regions of the large South Australia state.

20 The bulk of Australia's vineyards are concentrated in three large regions in SE Australia. What are their names?

21 Among the most revered wines from Australia, Grange is made by Penfolds. What was the original name of this wine?

22 In what year was Grange Hermitage created, and by whom?

23 Regarding Penfolds, they own among the oldest Cabernet Sauvignon vineyards in the world. Name the plot of land.

24 Which winery based in Western Australia displays *Art Series* on their labels? (Aside from regular bottlings).

---

9   Stickies. (These may or may not be fortified, and grapes include Muscat, Sémillon, Muscadelle, etc.).

10 The Jimmy Watson Trophy. (This award is for the best 1-year old red wine. First awarded in 1962).

11 Shiraz. (Known as Syrah in most of the rest of the world).

12 Cabernet Sauvignon. (This is often a stand-alone grape or may be blended with Merlot, Shiraz, etc).

13 Chardonnay, Sauvignon Blanc, Sémillon.

14 False. (Australia is currently ranked 5th in following Italy, Spain, France, and the US).

15 South Australia, New South Wales, Victoria and Western Australia.

16 Melbourne. (This coastal city is very cultural with lures of art museums and music attractions).

17 Sidney. (Australia's most populous city, also known for culture).

18 Perth. (Perth is the cultural center of the west coast. Great beaches and art museums).

19 Barossa Valley, Coonawarra, Adelaide Hills, Clare Valley, Eden Valley, McLaren Vale, etc.

20 Riverland, Murray-Darling (2 rivers), and Riverina. (These contribute ≈ 60% of total Australian production).

21 Grange Hermitage. (Hermitage was dropped as it is an official and famous appellation in the northern Rhône).

22 In 1951 by Max Schubert of Penfolds. (His concept was to create a premium red blend a la Bordeaux).

23 Block 42 Kalimna. (The 10-acre parcel, planted in the 1880s, was only released six times since 1953).

24 Leeuwin Estate. (Based in Margaret River, their museum houses over 150 paintings since the 1987 label).

——————— SOUTHERN HEMISPHERE ———————

25 Which winery bottles the famous Hill of Grace single vineyard wine?

26 Two other special Shiraz bottlings are called The Laird and The Armagh. Name each producer of these wines.

27 Which winery in Western Australia is owned by Estates & Wines (LVMH)?

28 What is the name of the oldest winery in Victoria, and one of the five oldest wineries in Australia?

29 Name the Shiraz flagship wine produced at Clarendon Hills Winery.

30 Which Yarra Valley winery, founded in 1971, uses the name Quintet for their red wine blend?

31 Which wine is *not* made by d'Arenberg winery? Dead Arm, Laughing Magpie, Aussie's Dream, Footbolt, Dry Dam.

32 Which wine is *not* made by Mollydooker? Blue Eyed Boy, Two Left Thumbs, Velvet Glove, Gigglepot, The Boxer.

25 Henschke. (This 100 % Shiraz vineyard is in Eden Valley in South Australia).

26 The Laird (from Torbreck winery, Barossa Valley) and The Armagh (Jim Barry Winery, Clare Valley).

27 Cape Mentelle. (One of the pioneer wineries in Western Australia specializing in Cabernet Sauvignon).

28 Château Tahbilk. (Founded in 1860, this winery specializes in northern Rhône white wine varieties).

29 Astralis. (Definition: *Pertaining to the Stars*. Founded in 1990, the Astralis Vineyard has 80-year-old vines).

30 Mount Mary Vineyard. (Quintet is the perfect name for a wine made from the five Bordeaux varieties).

31 Aussie's Dream. (d'Arenberg was founded in 1912 in the McLaren Vale and they label imaginatively)

32 Two Left Thumbs. (Mollydooker was founded in 1991 in McLaren Vale by newlyweds Sarah and Sparky Marquis)

CHAPTER 15

NEW ZEALAND

THE WINES OF NEW ZEALAND

33 What was the first declared wine vintage in New Zealand?

34 How far from New Zealand is Australia in air miles? 450, 900, 1,300, 1,800, 2,100.

35 What is the capital of New Zealand? Sidney, Auckland, Wellington, Christchurch, Canterbury, Cloudy Bay.

36 What % of the world's wine supply is generated out of New Zealand? 1%, 10%, 15%, 20%.

37 How many acres of vines are planted in New Zealand? 44,000, 68,000, 98,000, 165,000.

38 New Zealand is divided into how many islands?

39 What body of water separates the North Island from the South Island?

40 Name the two most important wine regions on the South Island.

41 What is unique about the vineyards of Central Otago?

42 What year is recognized as New Zealand's first vintage for commercial Sauvignon Blanc?

---

33 1836. (However, many consider their wine industry as new, due to international recognition in recent decades).

34 1,343 miles from Sidney to Auckland. (Many think a closer proximity, but the flight is about 3 hours).

35 Wellington. (Located on the southern part of the North Island and granted title in 1865).

36 1%. (New Zealand wines are extremely popular today, but it is not a large volume producer).

37 ≈ 98,000 acres. (In 1990 there were only 11,000 - 12,000 acres; steady growth since).

38 Two. The North Island and The South Island.

39 The Cook Strait. (Named after James Cook, the first European explorer to sail through it in 1770).

40 Marlborough (in the north, known for Sauvignon Blanc) and Central Otago (south end, known for Pinot Noir).

41 They are the most southernly vineyards worldwide. (A close second is the Patagonia region in Argentina).

42 1973. (Matua Winery, under the direction of Bill and Ross Spence, created the category).

SOUTHERN HEMISPHERE

43   Name two of the North Island's wine growing areas.

44   Name the three most planted varieties in New Zealand.

45   As recently as the early 1990s, what was the most planted variety in New Zealand?

46   How many wineries exist in New Zealand?

47   True or False? Most of New Zealand's wines are exported.

48   What name does not belong? Craggy Range, Greywacke, Felton Road, Ayers Rock, Ata Rangi, Wairau River.

43   Gisborne, Hawke's Bay, Martinborough/Wairarapa, etc.

44   Sauvignon Blanc (≈ 60% of plantings, and almost 90% of exports), Pinot Noir, Chardonnay.

45   Müller-Thurgau. (Today there are very few plantings remaining, due to the popularity of Sauvignon Blanc).

46   ≈ 700 + (This number has dramatically increased in recent years).

47   True. (About 90% is exported. The United States, United Kingdom and Australia are the top three markets).

48   Ayers Rock. (This is a notable landmark in Australia; the rest are wineries in New Zealand).

CHAPTER 16

CHILE

THE WINES OF CHILE

49 The country of Chile is on which side of the Andes Mountains?

50 Define the approximate length and width of Chile.

51 What is the capital of Chile, and where is it located?

52 Who were the first people to plant wine varieties in Chile?

53 What is still the most popular originally Spanish variety used for mass produced wines in Chile?

54 Which variety is by far the most widely planted in Chile?

55 In addition to Cabernet Sauvignon and Merlot, name another red wine variety originally from Bordeaux.

56 What name was used before 1998 for Carménère, prior to governmental approval of the name?

---

49 The west side. (The Andes form the boundary between Chile (west) and Argentina (east).

50 ≈ 4,000 miles long and 93 miles wide at its narrowest point.

51 Santiago. (Santiago is slightly inland from the coast, and almost at the midpoint of the country).

52 The Spanish explorers. (They brought vine cuttings from Mexico; the first vines were planted in 1551).

53 País. (Also known as Criolla in Argentina and Mission (Misión in Mexico) in California).

54 Cabernet Sauvignon. (≈ 80% of all plantings are Cabernet Sauvignon, followed by many others).

55 Carménère. (First released by Viña Carmen in 1996. Many other wineries followed suit).

56 Grande Vidure. (The variety was misidentified as Merlot before being correctly identified as Carménère).

——————— SOUTHERN HEMISPHERE ———————

57 What scourge ravaged European vineyards beginning in the late 19th Century, but did not affect Chile?

58 What is the name of the desert in northern Chile?

59 What weather pattern plays a role in Chile's Central Valley regarding viticultural decisions?

60 Name the two northernmost wine regions of Chile, not included in the Central Valley?

61 Name the northern wine region containing the largest mountain peak area in the Andes chain?

62 Name two of the wine regions just south of Aconcagua and west of Santiago on the Pacific coast?

63 Name the large central region containing most of Chile's viticultural industry.

64 How many miles long is the Central Valley wine producing area in Chile? 225, 560, 750, 870.

65 There are two wine regions within the Rapel Valley beginning with the letter "C". Name them.

66 Name three wine districts in southern Chile, south of the Central Valley?

67 There is also a very new, small, wet, and cold climate wine region over 500 miles south of Santiago. Name it.

68 What is the largest winery in Chile?

69 Name the joint venture wine that was created in 1995 between Robert Mondavi and Eduardo Chadwick (of Errazuriz).

70 Name the flagship red wine blend made by Errazuriz Winery?

71 Viña Concha Y Toro created a joint venture in the 1990s with which winery? Name the wine.

---

57 Phylloxera. (The Pacific, Andes, northern desert, and cold Patagonia effectively kept phylloxera out of Chile).

58 Atacama Desert. (This desert extends from northern Chile into Bolivia as it approaches the equator).

59 The Humbolt Current. (The cold water/air comes up from Antarctica cooling the warm eastern vineyards).

60 Elqui. (Grapes for Pisco and Syrah). Limari. (Originally Pisco country, now Chardonnay, Sauvignon Blanc).

61 Aconcagua. (This east-west region extends from the coast toward the mountains).

62 Casablanca, San Antonio, Leyda.

63 The Central Valley. (Sub-regions from north to south: Maipo Valley, Rapel Valley, Curicó Valley, Maule Valley).

64 870. (This large north-south area *does not* include some wine regions in the extreme north and south of Chile).

65 Colchagua Valley and Cachapoal Valley. (These regions produce a variety of high-quality wine).

66 Itata (País variety), Bío-Bío (Aromatic French and German varieties); Malleco (Chardonnay and Pinot Noir).

67 Osorno. (Sandwiched between two rivers, stylistic versions of Riesling, sparklers, and Pinot Noir have started).

68 Viña Concha Y Toro. (Founded in 1883 by Don Melchor in a suburb of Santiago called Pirque (Maipo Valley).

69 Seña. (A premium Bordeaux blend from Aconcagua Valley).

70 Don Maximiano, Founder's Reserve. (A Bordeaux blend including Carménère, sourced from Aconcagua Valley).

71 With Château Mouton Rothschild. First vintage was 1996. (Almaviva.)

72 What winery is owned by Domaines Barons de Rothschild (Lafite)?

73 What family owns the Clos Apalta winery in the Colchagua Valley?

74 Which winery does not belong? Clos Apalta, Causiño-Macul, Neyen, Montes, Los Vascos, Viu Manent.

72 Viña Los Vascos. (Based in Colchagua Valley, the flagship wine is *Le Dix* (Premium Bordeaux red blend).

73 Alexandra Marnier Lapostolle. (A member of the family that owns the liqueur Grand Marnier).

74 Causiño-Macul. (This winery is in the Maipo Valley, and the others are in Colchagua Valley)

CHAPTER 17

ARGENTINA

THE WINES OF ARGENTINA

75 Harvest in the northern hemisphere takes place between August and October. When is the harvest in Argentina/Chile?

76 What is the highest peak in the Andes Mountain range?

77 What is the name of the major wine producing area in Argentina?

78 What red wine variety is the most widely cultivated in Argentina?

79 Why are vineyards commonly planted at elevations of 3,000 feet and higher in Mendoza?

80 Argentina is a New World wine country. In what century were the first vineyards planted.

81 What year was Malbec introduced to Argentine vineyards?

82 Many know Malbec as a Bordeaux variety. Name another French region where Malbec has a primary role.

83 In addition to Malbec, name some other popular red wine varieties planted in Argentina.

---

75 Late winter/early spring. (Between February and April.)

76 Mount Aconcagua. (The highest point in the western hemisphere at almost 23,000 feet).

77 Mendoza. (Mendoza is the name the city also contained within the province of Mendoza).

78 Malbec. (Like Chile's Carménère, Malbec plays a greater role in Argentina than it does in Bordeaux.)

79 Climate. (Lower elevations are too warm to produce top quality wine.)

80 The 16th century. (Spanish conquistadors brought vine cuttings from Chile and Mexico.)

81 1853. (Other French varieties such as Cabernet Sauvignon were also introduced in the mid-19th century).

82 Cahors. (Cahors is in southwest France and produces very dark and intense wines from Malbec.)

83 Bonarda, Cabernet Sauvignon, Syrah, Merlot, Tempranillo. (Bonarda is the #2 most planted variety.)

——— SOUTHERN HEMISPHERE ———

84 What is widely considered the "signature" white wine variety in Argentina?

85 Name a few aromatic attributes of the Torrontés grape variety.

86 True or False? If a grape variety is listed on an Argentine wine label, the contents must be 100% of that variety.

87 Name the northernmost wine growing region in Argentina.

88 Name the wine region located south of Salta and north of Mendoza.

89 Name the relatively new wine growing district northeast of San Juan?

90 Name the two popular wine regions in the northern part of the larger Mendoza district.

91 Name the southernmost wine region in Argentina?

92 Which does not belong? Santa Julia; Catena Zapata, Zuccardi, Rutini, Salentein, Clos de los Siete, Masi Tupungato.

93 The famous Spanish cava producer Raventós Codorníu owns a winery in Argentina. Name the winery?

94 A union of two wineries in 1999 created the Cheval des Andes Winery in Mendoza. Who are the two owners?

95 World famous consultant Michel Rolland is a partner in what Argentine winery?

96 Paul Hobbs is a famous winemaker in Napa Valley and beyond. Name his winery in Argentina.

97 Which winery does not belong? Bodega Norton, Achaval Ferrer, Catena Zapata, Cheval des Andes, Miguel Torres.

---

84 Torrontés. (There are three Torrontés varieties, of which Torrontés Riojano is most common).

85 Highly aromatic, floral and grapey, like Muscat/Moscato (one of its parent varieties.)

86 False. (85% is the minimum, which happens to conform to international standards.)

87 Salta. (The wine region is known for top quality Torrontés.)

88 San Juan. (Second in Malbec production to Mendoza.)

89 La Rioja. (Best known for Torrontés and home to the well-known co-operative winery La Riojana).

90 Luján de Cuyo. (South of the city of Mendoza). Valle de Uco. (Uco Valley).

91 Patagonia. (A cold climate region influenced by Antarctica, and promising for Pinot Noir).

92 Catena Zapata. (This winery is based in Luján de Cuyo, and the others are based in the Uco Valley).

93 Séptima. (Bodega Séptima in Mendoza is farming 900 acres at an elevation of 1,050 feet).

94 Terrazas de los Andes and Château Cheval Blanc (Premier Grand Cru Classé "A") in St.-Émilion.

95 Clos de los Siete. (Four wineries add their blending components to create Clos de los Siete from Uco Valley).

96 Viña Cobos. (Sourcing grapes from Luján de Cuyo and Valle de Uco within Mendoza.

97 Miguel Torres Winery. (Miguel Torres Winery is based in Chile, and the rest are in Argentina).

——————— SOUTHERN HEMISPHERE ———————

CHAPTER 18

URUGUAY

THE WINES OF URUGUAY

98   What 2 countries border Uruguay?

99   How many wineries are in Uruguay?

100   Name the most popular red wine variety grown in Uruguay.

101   Tannat offers a health benefit when consumed moderately. What is it?

102   Which producer won a Top 100 Wine Spectator Award for the first time for the Tannat grape?

---

98   Argentina to the west and Brazil to the north. (Uruguay is a small country compared to the other two).

99   ≈ 270. (The bulk of the wineries are in the southern part of the country around Montevideo).

100   Tannat. (Tannat is another variety of French origin; the key variety in the appellation of Madiran.)

101   Tannat has among the highest levels of phenolic antioxidant properties, especially resveratrol.

102   Bodega Garzon, Tannat, *Reserve*, 2015. (The wine was selected in 2017 for the #41 position).

CHAPTER 19

BRAZIL

THE WINES OF BRAZIL

103 What was the first Brazilian wine region to be recognized as a quality wine growing district?

104 Name the new popular region in the northeast part of the country?

105 What is a unique viticultural phenomenon about Vale do São Francisco at this latitude near the equator?

106 What is the name of the largest premium wine producer in Brazil?

---

103 Serra Gaucha. (This wine region is in the southern part of the country in the state of Rio Grande do Sol).

104 Vale do São Francisco. (This is in the extreme north just inland from the Atlantic Ocean).

105 It is possible to have two separate harvests in the vineyards. (Irrigation and ripening heat cycles are responsible).

106 Miolo. (With major production in Vale dos Vinhedos and Campagna wine regions.

——— SOUTHERN HEMISPHERE ———

CHAPTER 20

SOUTH AFRICA

THE WINES OF SOUTH AFRICA

107 What year was the first wine vintage for South Africa (SA)?

108 What European country colonized SA?

109 What event in SA changed the political landscape of the country in 1994?

110 How many wineries are in South Africa? 145; 360; 542; 612; 850.

111 What is the number one grape in terms of volume grown in SA?

112 SA leads the world in production of Chenin Blanc. What country is number two?

113 What two white wine varieties follow the Chenin Blanc in terms of planting volume?

114 What is the *local* name for Chenin Blanc in SA?

115 Name two popular red wine varieties grown in South Africa.

---

107 1659. (Cape Town was founded in 1652, and the first harvest just a few years later).

108 The Netherlands. (The Dutch influence lives on in architecture and language).

109 Nelson Mandela was elected president, ending Apartheid and re-opening commerce with the world.

110 ≈ 542. (This number includes individual wineries and co-ops. There are ≈ 3,000 vineyards farmed).

111 Chenin Blanc. (This grape represents almost 20% of total plantings).

112 France. (In particular, the Chenin-based appellations in the Loire Valley such as Vouvray).

113 Colombard and Sauvignon Blanc. (White varieties account for 55% of the total SA production.)

114 Steen. (This name is derived from the Afrikaans word "*hoeksteen*" or cornerstone of the SA wine industry).

115 Cabernet Sauvignon, Shiraz (Syrah), Pinotage. (Some of the best wines are Bordeaux blends.)

——————— SOUTHERN HEMISPHERE ———————

116 What is Pinotage?

117 What is SA's official geographical appellation system called?

118 The WO system divides growing regions how many categories?

119 Name the geographically largest WO region in SA.

120 Name two Regions contained within the Western Cape Geographical Unit.

121 What is the arguably the most famous premium wine District in South Africa?

122 Name the Ward responsible for South Africa's most popular sweet wines.

123 Constantia is made using which grape variety?

124 Name the famous geological formation in Constantia overlooking many vineyards.

125 What winery does not belong? Kanonkop, Meerlust, Mulderbosch, Rust en Vrede, Graham Beck, Ken Forrester.

126 Meerlust (SA) and Inglenook (Napa Valley) make a blended red wine with the same name. Name it.

127 The very historic Glenelly Winery in Stellenbosch was purchased in 2003 by whom?

128 *Tough question*: What is the difference between Glen Carlou and Jean Carlu?

116 A variety created in 1925 by crossing varieties Pinot Noir and Cinsault (also known as Hermitage).

117 Wine of Origin (WO). (SA's wine regions were defined under the Wine of Origin Act of 1973.)

118 Four. (From least to most specific: Geographical Units, Regions, Districts and Wards.

119 Western Cape. (This Geographical Unit contains numerous Regions, Districts and Wards.)

120 Breede River Valley, Cape South Coast, Coastal Region, Klein Karoo and Olifants River.

121 Stellenbosch. (Located east of Cape Town and home to many of the top-quality wine producers).

122 Constantia. (In the 1800s, *Vin de Constance* was as well-regarded as Sauternes and other famous sweet wines.)

123 Muscat. (Vin de Constance was a favorite of King Frederick the Great of Germany and Napoléon Bonaparte).

124 Table Mountain. (Table Mountain is within a beautiful, forested national park.)

125 Graham Beck. (Graham Beck is in Franschhoek, and the rest are based in Stellenbosch).

126 Rubicon. (Named after Julius Caesar crossing the Rubicon in 49 BC; no turning back).

127 May de Lencquesaing. (Former owner of Château Pichon Longueville, Comtesse de Lalande in Bordeaux).

128 Glen Carlou is a winery in Paarl, and Jean Carlu painted the 1924 Château Mouton Rothschild label).

PART V

SAKÉ

_____

The perennial question: Is Saké beer or wine?

The answer: It is neither beer nor wine. It is a unique beverage that with its own identity. The similarity to beer is that saké is brewed from grain (rice) and the starch in rice must be converted to fermentable sugars. Yet sake's alcohol level is higher than beer, like that of wine. However, there are many differences in the making of sake from either beverage to merit its own chapter.

SAKÉ

GENERAL QUESTIONS

1   What is the correct way to pronounce Saké?

2   When toasting, and an *ochoko* (small porcelain drinking cup) is raised, what is the term used as "cheers"?

3   What is the small ceramic decanter used to pour saké into an ochoko, or the square wood *masu* called?

4   True or False? Saké is always meant to be served hot (often heated in a microwave oven.)

5   True or False? All Saké is sweet.

6   True or False? Saké is brewed only from rice.

7   Name one of the roughly 60 types of rice used in the production of saké.

8   In addition to rice, what are the other three ingredients used to make pure saké?

9   I think everybody understands the first few ingredients, but what is koji all about?

---

1   Sah-**Keh** is correct, versus the commonly used **sah**-Key. (Note the accent over the é.)

2   *Kanpai.* (The term literally means "dry cup", meaning drink it all, or bottoms up).

3   *Tokkuri.* (These are made from different materials and may mitigate temperature fluctuations.

4   False. (Though this is still a common practice, saké is usually served chilled in a white wine glass).

5   False. (Like wine, sake styles range from dry to sweet).

6   True. (No other grain is ever used).

7   Yamada Nishiki, Gohyakumangoku, Koshi Tanrei, Omachi, Miyamanishiki.

8   Water, yeast and koji (mold).

9   Koji is a mold that converts starch molecules in rice to fermentable sugar.

——— SAKÉ ———

10 To prepare the raw material, first the rice is dried then milled (polished.) What is the purpose of this?

11 What is the Japanese term for this polishing/milling process of the rice kernels?

12 In saké production, what steps follow polishing the rice kernels?

13 Following washing, what is the next step in saké production?

14 Where do the steamed rice, koji, water and yeast come together?

15 Is pasteurization a step in saké production?

16 There is a type of saké that is not pasteurized. What is the term for this?

17 What category of saké is made from rice; water; yeast; and koji with no added alcohol or anything else?

18 What is the term for the premium category of saké with any quantity of alcohol added?

19 What is the saké quality term if the polishing has achieved at least 60% of the original kernel?

20 What is the term for Ginjo with no added alcohol?

21 What is the saké quality term if the polishing has achieved at least 50% of the original kernel?

22 What is the term for Daiginjo with no added alcohol?

23 What term for saké that reaches the highest alcohol levels of 18+ alcohol by volume?

24 What term is used for cloudy saké?

25 What is the term for aged saké?

26 Most saké labels have a numeric scale both above and below 0. What is this scale called?

---

10 Polishing removes the outer layers of the rice grain, leaving only pure starch.

11 Seimaibuai. (This word appears on many bottles, especially those imported from Japan).

12 Washing and soaking. (This removes any impurities and allows the rice to absorb some water.)

13 Steaming. (This labor-intensive step uses a kettle or a belt system to prepare the rice for fermentation.)

14 Moto Tank. (Here the yeast feed on the sugar in the rice and fermentation begins).

15 Yes. (This takes place after filtration and just before the bottling stage).

16 Nama-zaké. (Without pasteurization, micro-organisms remain active, offering a very fresh style.)

17 *Junmai* (literally meaning pure.)

18 *Honjozo*. (The alcohol enhances the aromas and flavors and adds body and texture).

19 *Ginjo*. (This is a premium category and may be Junmai or not.)

20 *Junmai Ginjo*. (This is also a premium category, Ginjo, with no added alcohol.)

21 *Daiginjo*. (The highest premium category, , highly polished rice plus alcohol added).

22 *Junmai Daiginjo*. (The highest premium category, highly polished rice with no added alcohol).

23 *Genshu*. (Most saké is diluted with water to around 14% alcohol. Genshu is undiluted.

24 *Nigori*. (The result of minimal filtration allowing a highly textured, often slightly sweet style.)

25 *Koshu*. (After 7 or 8 years of age, Koshu takes on a Madeira-like color and complexity.)

26 Saké Meter Value (SMV.) Above 0 is increasingly dry, below 0 increasingly sweet.

27 What are the three standard bottle sizes for Japanese Saké?

28 What is the Japanese name for a saké brewery?

27 300 ml., 720 ml., 1.8 liter. (Options for US producers include 375 ml., 750 ml., etc.).

28 *Kura.* (The ≈ 1,800 Kura use diverse water sources and rice strains creating over 10,000 saké options).

PART VI

FERMENTATION SCIENCE & VITICULTURE

This final section is important, yet novices may find it overwhelming. For me, it was challenging to format. My concept throughout the book embodies a phrase I describe as concise wine learning. Science questions (and answers) are often much more complicated, but I've done my best to be concise. Although I have spent decades studying wine biochemistry and microbiology, I am self-taught. My stint at the Robert Mondavi Winery during harvest (including lab work) in 1981, a few courses at University of California, Davis, with wine microbiologist Lisa Van de Water, tutoring from winemakers and good friends Greg La Follette (scores of multi-year technical data email exchanges) and Rollin Soles, and numerous podcasts were my only professional training. Some of the headings listed below may overlap with other categories due to the complexity of the subject matter.

"Wine is sunlight held together by water."
Galileo Galilei

FERMENTATION SCIENCE & VITICULTURE

PRIMARY & SECONDARY FERMENTATION

1. What is the science of winemaking called?

2. Primary fermentation is a very natural and ancient chemical sequence. On one line describe the process.

3. What term is used for the grape solids remaining after fermentation?

4. The chemical equation for sugar to alcohol conversion looks complicated: $C_6H_{12}O_6 \rightarrow 2C_2H_5OH + 2CO_2$.

5. Who discovered and explained the process of sugar to alcohol conversion in wine?

6. What is the definition of a "stuck fermentation?"

7. Although not a disorder as much as a stumbling block, a stuck fermentation is often caused by what two factors?

PRIMARY & SECONDARY FERMENTATION

1. Oenology. (Oenologists must have a strong background in microbiology and biochemistry for lab work).

2. The synthesis of sugar into alcohol. (This happens naturally. Wild yeasts consuming fruit sugar = fermentation.)

3. Pomace. (This is removed and may be used as organic compost, or distilled into industrial alcohol, etc.)

4. Sugar ($C_6H_{12}O_6$) converts via action of yeast to ethanol (C_2H_5OH) and carbon dioxide (CO_2.)

5. Louis Pasteur. (Through the lens of a microscope, in the 1850s Pasteur observed yeast as the catalyst).

6. When fermentation stops during the process, leaving an unfinished wine susceptible to microbial spoilage.

7. Insufficient yeast nutrition and a rapid drop/or rise in fermentation temperatures. Both inhibit the action of yeast.

PRIMARY & SECONDARY FERMENTATION, Cont.

8   Ethyl alcohol (ethanol) is the primary alcohol found in wine. Name two more higher alcohols.

9   What is a fermentation lock, and what is its function?

10 Many wines go through a secondary fermentation after the primary fermentation. What is the name of this process?

11 In addition to softening acidity and adding body to the mouthfeel, what are additional attributes of MLF?

12 What attributes does MLF impart to the aromatics and mouthfeel in the final wine?

13 What is a chemical compound created during MLF leaving the cream/butter impressions?

14 True or False? Sugar accumulation and acid decomposition are parallel processes, but don't progress at the same rate.

15 True or False? MLF always takes place after primary fermentation in the cellar.

16 Which factor inhibits MLF? Low pH, high alcohol, high sulfate levels, low tank temperatures.

17 Leuconostoc Oeni has always been recognized as a beneficial genus of MLF bacterium. What is the more recent name?

18 There are basically two types of fermentation strategies regarding the presence of oxygen. What are they?

19 Name a couple of reductive steps to reduce oxygen and its effects during the fermentation process.

20 Name a couple of oxidative steps to increase oxygen and its effects during fermentation and aging.

21 List some benefits of stainless-steel fermenters.

PRIMARY & SECONDARY FERMENTATION, Cont.

8 Methanol, isoamyl alcohol, butanol, propanol, etc. (These are not meant for consumption and are toxic.)
9 A fermentation lock is a device on top of a fermentation vessel. It is a one-way valve letting carbon dioxide out.
10 Malolactic Fermentation. (MLF is a bacterial process converting tart malic acid into softer lactic acid).
11 It can add color stability to red wines and improve microbial stability.
12 Buttery, creamy aromas and flavors, lower acidity and higher pH.
13 Diacetyl. A byproduct of fermentation. Levels increase when MLF occurs after primary fermentation.
14 True. (As grapes ripen, sugar levels rise and acids are lost through respiration at a different pace).
15 False. (MLF may take place during or after primary fermentation. Warmer temperature is needed for MLF).
16 All these factors inhibit MLF.
17 Oenococcus Oeni. (Taxonomy studies has determined this genus is more specific to wine acid decomposition).
18 Reductive and oxidative. (The former allows very little oxygen ingress, and the latter allows larger amounts).
19 Think Riesling: Cool to cold fermentations; no MLF so acidity is retained; stainless steel fermenters; no new oak.
20 Barrel fermentation (porosity → micro-ox); warm temperature fermentations, MLF encouraged, barrel aged.
21 It is a strong material, easily cleaned and sanitized, corrosion resistant, and may be wrapped with coolant.

PRIMARY & SECONDARY FERMENTATION, Cont.

22 What is the French term for stainless steel used in primary fermentation?

23 In addition to stainless steel and oak barrels, name another popular material used for fermentation tanks.

24 Concrete eggs are a newer innovation on ancient convex vessels like amphorae. Name two benefits of concrete eggs.

25 Three categories of aromas/tastes exist in wine: Primary, secondary and tertiary. Where do primary ones originate?

26 Where do secondary aromas and taste originate?

27 Where do tertiary aromas and flavors originate?

SUGARS

28 How is sugar accumulation initiated during the growing season?

29 Sugar is the grape component necessary for fermentation to take place. Do sugars originate in the grapes?

30 What enzyme is responsible for transferring sugar from leaves to the grape?

31 Prior to berry absorption, invertase also reduces the sucrose into what?

32 How do glucose and fructose (monosaccharides) offer an advantage over sucrose (a disaccharide)?

33 When measuring sugar level in grapes prior to harvest, what term is widely used for this measurement?

PRIMARY & SECONDARY FERMENTATION, Cont.

22 Onyx. (Popular in Chablis, keeping fermentation temperatures cool and retaining fresh varietal character).

23 Concrete. (Epoxy-lined tanks are often seen in European cellars.)

24 Thick walls keep temperature constant, keep wines cool and concrete breathes (like oak), porosity $\rightarrow$ micro-ox.

25 Primary aromas and tastes originate from the grape itself, offering fruit-driven simplicity.

26 These aromas and flavors are produced by fermentation itself, and/or oak. Think yeasty, toast, baking spice, etc.

27 Tertiary components are the result of post-fermentation aging. Think oxidation, fruit development, bottle age.

SUGARS

28 By photosynthesis. (Green pigment-chlorophyll-uses sunlight energy to convert H_2O and CO_2 into sugar).

29 No. (Sugar accumulation begins in the leaves and is subsequently transferred to the grapes).

30 Invertase. (This enzyme transports sugar – sucrose – from leaf to grape).

31 The biosynthesis of sucrose creates two monosaccharides, glucose and fructose.

32 Glucose and fructose have just one molecule each and are easier for yeast to consume than sucrose).

33 Brix, measured in degrees brix. (This number is but one component used to determine when to harvest).

SUGARS, Cont.

34 Name 1 of the 2 ways that degrees brix is measured?

35 What is another option winemakers use to determine ripeness prior to harvest?

36 In cooler climates, it is legal add sugar to the must before fermentation. What is this called?

37 What are the origins of the term chaptalization?

38 Wine has two sets of components. 1: Sugar, acid, alcohol. 2: Pigments, flavors, tannin. Which group changes?

39 True or False? A fermentation that finishes totally dry, means the yeast has consumed every bit of available sugar.

YEAST

40 What is the catalyst that starts the fermentation process?

41 Approximately how many yeast cells can fit on the head of a pin? 450, 4,000, 10,500, 25,000, 40,000.

42 What is the full Latin term for yeast strains used in winemaking?

43 In addition to sugar to alcohol conversion, what are the two other major by-products of fermentation?

44 In addition to sugar, name the other yeast requirements for energy and reproduction.

45 Many wineries use laboratory bred yeast to create specific characteristics in wine. What is the other kind of yeast?

46 True or False? Spraying the vineyard with agrochemicals is harmless to ambient yeast.

SUGARS, Cont.

34 In the vineyard, a refractometer measures sugar content on a graduated slide. And by hydrometer in the lab.

35 Physiological ripeness of the grape, i.e., taste. (Woody stems, crunchy seeds, balance of acid and sugar.)

36 Enrichment or *chaptalization*. (This is done not to add sweetness but to allow for the proper level of alcohol).

37 Jean-Antoine Chaptal. (A French scientist who discovered this method.)

38 2. (Over time, these components change through biochemistry. Sugar, acid, and alcohol remain constant).

39 False. (Identifiable thresholds vary, but there is always some unfermentable pentose sugar.)

YEAST

40 Yeast cells. (These single celled fungal organisms consume natural grape sugars and create alcohol).

41 ≈ 40,000. (Although microscopic, we now know they are the tiny miracle workers turning grape juice into wine) .

42 Saccharomyces Cerevisiae. (Also known as baker's/brewer's yeast, it is a very efficient single cell organism).

43 Carbon dioxide (CO_2) and heat.(caloric migration).

44 Nitrogen, amino acids, phosphorus, biotin, and oxygen. (Yeasts contain enzymes and need these nutrients).

45 Ambient (AKA natural, wild or indigenous) yeast. These are naturally present in vineyard and winery.

46 False. (Chemicals used to combat disease and pests unintentionally affect other living things.)

YEAST, Cont.

47 What is the principal difference between ambient and commercial yeast strains?

48 What size winery is more likely to use commercial yeast: Small <10,000 cases Large >100,000 cases

49 Of the ≈ 1,000 volatile compounds found in wine approximately how many are from yeast? 11, 45, 200, 400, 600.

50 In addition to sugar breakdown, what is another function of yeast in winemaking?

51 Yeast continue to function up to what maximum level of alcohol, 9%, 12%, 16%, or 20%?

52 After the fermentation cycle and the yeast cells die, what is the next chemical sequence regarding the yeast?

53 In Champagne production, after primary has finished what is another favorable role that yeast provides?

54 When discussing yeast autolysis, this auto-digestion contain what compounds?

55 What is the French term for yeast stirring in a barrel or another container?

56 Although common with many white wines, what does bâtonnage provide for red wines?

ACIDS

57 True or False? All acids in wine originate in the grape.

58 Name two benefits that acids bring to wine.

59 Name three acids found in wine.

YEAST, Cont.

47 Ambient is unpredictable and commercial provides a predictable fermentation with normally less risk.

48 Large. Commercial yeasts provide specific characteristics and a reliable, complete fermentation.

49 400. (According to the *Science of Wine* by Jamie Good. A surprising number reflecting diversity of strains).

50 Lees aging after fermentation is complete. (This adds aromatic complexity and palate texture.)

51 16%. (Most yeast strains cannot survive higher alcohol levels.)

52 Autolysis. (The yeast's digestive enzymes metabolize yeast cells creating sourdough/mushroom aromas).

53 Yeast Autolysis. (This is a form of auto-digestion and spilling the nutrients of the yeast cells into the bottle).

54 Polysaccharides (long-chain sugars), amino acids, mannoproteins (reduce astringency) and fatty acids.

55 *Bâtonnage*. (This procedure increases complexity in the wine extracting additional flavor, aroma, and texture).

56 It softens tannins, stabilizes color, improves colloidal stability, reduces protein haze and enhances MLB.

ACIDS

57 False. (Some acids originate in the grape and others are the result of fermentation).

58 Acids bring freshness to the flavor profile. They also retard bacterial spoilage for stability.

59 Tartaric, malic, and succinic. (If MLF was performed, lactic acid is present as well).

ACIDS, Cont.

60   Does MLF affect tartaric acid?

61   Name one acid level laboratory index used to quantify ripeness in grapes.

62   If TA (Total Acidity) levels are too high, what is one way to reduce them?

63   Name another acid level laboratory index used to quantify ripeness in grapes.

64   In specific terms what do the letters pH mean?

65   Name the two broad categories of acids found in wine. (Hint: Not the names of specific acids).

66   Fixed acids in grapes fall during the ripening cycle. What is the reason for this?

67   What is a negative as acid levels drop in the grape during the ripening phase?

68   What is the salt contained in tartaric acid?

69   If a winery is in a hot climate, sugar levels in the berry are high and pH is also high. What is a remedy to decrease pH?

PIGMENTATION & TANNIN EXTRACTION

70   What is the name of the chemical compounds responsible for pigmentation in grape skins?

71   What is the French term describing the transformation of grapes as they approach ripeness?

72   Nearly all dark-skinned grapes contain clear juice. What is the French term for grapes with dark juice?

ACIDS, Cont.

60 No. (Tartaric acid remains constant. The biological acid decomposition occurs with malic acid only).

61 TA. (Total Acidity or Titratable Acidity).

62 De-acidification through addition of potassium bicarbonate or potassium or calcium carbonate.

63 pH. (pH measures the intensity of acid. Typical pH levels in finished wine are between 3.1 and 3.8)

64 Potential of Hydrogen. (pH Measures the concentration of hydrogen ions in solution.)

65 Volatile acidity and fixed acidity (Aromas in wine come from the vaporization of volatile acids.)

66 During the ripening cycle, the berry gets larger in size so the ratio of sugar-to-acid changes.

67 When acid levels drop, the pH levels rise increasing instability and the possibility of microbial disorders.

68 Potassium Bitartrate. (Commonly known as cream of tartar, used in baking).

69 Acidification. (In warmer climates, tartaric acid is commonly added to wine to raise acidity).

PIGMENTATION & TANNIN EXTRACTION

70 Anthocyanins. (During winemaking, these color compounds slowly leach out from skin to juice).

71 Véraison. (As grapes ripen, skins change color, berries soften, and stems get woody.)

72 *Teinturier.* (Alicante Bouschet is a notable example, typically used as a blending grape to add color.)

PIGMENTATION & TANNIN EXTRACTION, Cont.

73   True or False? If you heavily press a thin-skinned grape like Pinot Noir, you will get a deeply colored wine.

74   One technique used for color/tannin extraction is called "rack and return". What is the French term for this procedure?

75   A similar method for color and tannin extraction is called "pumping over". What is the French term for this procedure?

76   Another method of extraction is called punching down. What is the French term for this procedure?

77   What term is used when a small amount of white juice is added to a red wine ferment?

78   What are the two primary benefits of co-fermentation?

TANNIN AND ITS EFFECTS

79   Which of these are not benefits of tannin? Wine structure, salty flavor, mouthfeel, color stability, ageability.

80   In winemaking (or cooking) what term is used to soften solids in a liquid substrate over a certain period?

81   True or False? Both sense of smell and taste are used to assess tannin in wine, especially in a young wine.

82   Tannin is found in varying degrees in all red wines. What are the four principal sources of tannin?

83   Tannins, either from skins or seeds are combinations of compounds collectively called what?

PIGMENTATION & TANNIN EXTRACTION, Cont.

73 False. (A wine will never get a deeper color than the grape skins have to offer.)

74 Délestage. (The must is drained from the tank and pumped back on top of the skin cap, aiding extraction.)

75 Rémontage. (The must is pumped from the bottom of the tank and sprayed over the top of the skins.)

76 Pigeage. (The skins are pushed down into the juice manually or mechanically by a device on top of the tank).

77 Co-fermentation. (Ex: Côte-Rôtie, Syrah and Viognier. Up to 20% Viognier may be added in Côte-Rôtie).

78 It stabilizes the color of the finished wine, and Viognier adds aromatic complexity.

TANNIN AND ITS EFFECTS

79 Salty Flavor. (Of all the components in wine, salt (NaCl) is not one of them, nor derived from tannin.

80 Maceration. (In winemaking, the berries and seeds soften and are comingled with newly created must).

81 False. (Tannin is textural only. On the palate, high levels of tannin create an astringent, drying sensation.)

82 Grape skins, stems, seeds, and oak barrels. (Each contributes a slightly different form of tannin).

83 Flavanols. (These include catechins and epicatechins which often link up to form polymerized chains.)

TANNIN AND ITS EFFECTS, Cont.

84 If a winery does not de-stem and crush grapes, what procedure will they probably be using prior to fermentation?

85 What is the French term for de-stemming, or removing grapes from their stems?

86 Pre-fermentation maceration, or *macération pelliculaire* in French, is familiarly called what in California?

87 Tannins in young red wines are often overly astringent. What happens during bottle maturation that softens the wine?

88 Eventually, these long tannin chains fall out of solution as solid matter. What is this called?

89 During fermentation, name a technique used to soften tannin and improve stability in the wine?

90 Besides softening tannins and stabilizing phenols, name some of the other benefits of micro-oxygenation?

91 New oak barrels are charred slightly during construction. In wine, what gentler term is used instead of char?

92 What does a heavy toast on the barrel contribute to the wine?

ENZYMES

93 10 years after Pasteur understood the role of yeast in sugar decomposition, what else did he discover?

94 Name the group enzymes that encourage the conversion of glucose and fructose into ethyl alcohol (ethanol)?

TANNIN AND ITS EFFECTS, Cont.

84 Whole cluster pressing. (One goal is to make more delicate, less astringent wine.)
85 Égrappage. (Some wineries do partial or complete destemming depending upon the vintage parameters).
86 Cold soak. (Grapes are crushed, juice/skins are left in contact for a short period of time before fermentation.)
87 Polymerization. (Tannin molecules link together forming longer chains, softening the texture.)
88 Sediment. (This requires mature red wines to be decanted before serving to separate the wine from sediment.)
89 Micro-oxygenation. (Minute amounts of oxygen are introduced and dissolved in the wine.)
90 Improves color development, increases flavor complexity, reduces sulfur off-odors, reduces herbaceous notes.
91 Toast. (Winemakers request a specific level of toast on their barrels, ranging from light to heavy toast.)
92 A heavy toast adds layers of complexity including aromas of spice, vanilla, chocolate, smoke, roasted coffee, etc.

ENZYMES

93 That yeast were the catalysts, but deeper research showed enzymes within the yeast were responsible.
94 Zymase. (These enzymes are responsible for synthesizing both the 6-carbon monosaccharides).

ENZYMES, Cont.

95 Name the most basic enzyme that breaks down plant cell walls for red pigments during maceration?

96 In addition to pectin, name another polysaccharide chain embedded in fruit cell walls?

97 Pigment releasing enzymes like pectinase and sugar reduction hemicellulose continue working until what occurs?

98 What is another reason for using a pectic enzyme in addition to the cell breakdown for color absorption?

99 If choosing a partial MLF in a wine such as Chardonnay, in addition to SO_2 or filtration, what is an enzymic option?

100 After harvest, grapes and juice (phenolic compounds) in tank may start to oxidize or brown due to which enzyme?

101 What is the enzyme that breaks down ethanol in the liver?

SULFUR DIOXIDE - (SO_2) - AND ITS DERIVATIVES

102 Does sulfur appear on the periodic table of the elements?

103 What is the chemical equation that turns elemental sulfur (S) into sulfur dioxide?

104 What compounds are formed when SO_2 gas dissolves in water?

105 Historically, what was the first way sulfur was used winemaking?

106 True or False? Sulfur dioxide is a complex molecule.

107 Sulfur is an ancient and important asset in winemaking, List three benefits of sulfur dioxide?

ENZYMES, Cont.

95 Pectinase. (Pectin is a long chain polysaccharide (sugar molecule) that reinforces the fruit cell wall).

96 Hemicellulose. (This compound serves to cross-link cellulose fibers to support the plant structure).

97 They will continue breaking down cell walls until the rising alcohol level inactivates them.

98 Pectinase or pectinesterase reduces pectin via protein enzymes and in turn prevent pectin haze in the final wine.

99 Lysozyme. (This egg white sourced enzyme arrests bacterium prior to completed cycle, and just before bottling).

100 Polyphenol oxidase. (This compound negative effects are mitigated by an early SO_2 addition).

101 Alcohol Dehydrogenase. (Ethanol breaks down to acetaldehyde then acetate, allowing exit from the body).

SULFUR DIOXIDE - (SO_2) - AND ITS DERIVATIVES

102 Yes. (Sulfur is #16 on the table and is a non-metallic solid that is bright yellow in color at room temperature).

103 $S + O_2 \rightarrow SO_2$ (Elemental sulfur gains oxygen atoms (oxidized) as oxygen readily accepts electrons).

104 Sulfites. (These may negatively affect some people with allergic reactions like congestion, rash, hives, etc.).

105 The Romans burned sulfur wicks in empty barrels, freshening them and eliminating the smell of vinegar.

106 False. (It contains 1 sulfur atom and 2 double bonded oxygen atoms).

107 Antioxidant, antimicrobial, preserves aroma/flavor. (The small amount of SO_2 in wine is harmless to most).

SULFUR DIOXIDE - (SO$_2$) - AND ITS DERIVATIVES, Cont.

108 We often discuss sulfites as a beneficial component of sound wine. Is it only added during winemaking?

109 At what stages of the winemaking process is SO$_2$ used?

110 Name three chemical forms of sulfur dioxide that may be used during winemaking.

111 What vitamin may be used as an antioxidant alternative to SO$_2$ prior to bottling?

CLARIFICATION AND STABILIZATION OF WINE

112 One of the most elemental methods of separating solids from wine using gravity is called what?

113 What is the French term for allowing solid material to collect in a tank before racking for clarity? (Hint: de-sludging).

114 Name the two primary methods clarifying wine prior to bottling.

115 What are some of the materials used in the fining process?

116 True or False? Egg white fining is used for both red and white wine clarification.

117 Is there a fear of salmonella poisoning when raw egg whites are used as a fining agent?

118 If a wine is brilliantly clear after fined/filtered then suddenly turns hazy, what term may be used for this condition?

119 What is the most common remedy to eliminate (or lessen) a turbidity?

120 Another fining agent is obtained from the swim bladder of fish. What is this called?

SULFUR DIOXIDE - (SO$_2$) - AND ITS DERIVATIVES, Cont.

108 No. (Small amounts occur naturally during fermentation, so it is impossible to have a truly sulfite-free wine).

109 Crusher-stemmer, prior to and after fermentation (when necessary) and/or before bottling.

110 Sulfur dioxide gas; liquid sulfur dioxide; potassium metabisulfite crystals. ($K_2S_2O_5$).

111 Vitamin C (ascorbic acid.) (Because vitamin C does not inhibit enzymes in the must, it cannot be used earlier).

CLARIFICATION AND STABILIZATION OF WINE

112 Racking. (This may be done a few times prior to bottling and fulfills a double duty of aeration if desired).

113 Débourbage. (After this natural gravity function, enzymes clump material together prior to racking).

114 Fining and filtration. (In addition to achieving clarity, a second purpose of filtration is microbial stability.)

115 Egg whites, bentonite, casein. (All are removed through further clarification processes.)

116 False. Red wine only. (Egg whites remove harsh tannins in red wine, leaving soft tannins behind).

117 No. (If salmonella does exist, the high alcohol and low pH will kill any harmful pathogens.)

118 Turbidity. (Seen in red/white wine, an indication of protein haze, typically due to high temperatures).

119 Bentonite fining. (Bentonite attaches to proteins and sinks to the bottom of the tank, reducing haze).

120 Isinglass. (A positively charged gentle collagen, so may be used in conjunction with other agents).

CLARIFICATION AND STABILIZATION OF WINE, Cont.

121 In addition to clarity, fining has other benefits. What are they?

122 What process is performed before bottling to prevent potassium bitartrates crystals forming in the bottle?

CHEMICAL COMPOUNDS PRESENT IN WINES

123 Petrol is commonly used as a descriptor for Riesling. What chemical compound is responsible for this?

124 Is TDN more pronounced in cork finished bottles or twist off tops?

125 What is the chemical compound found in some underripe Cabernet Sauvignon and Sauvignon Blanc?

126 What is the peppery smelling chemical compound found in some northern Rhône Syrah, Grüner Veltliner, etc.)?

127 What volatile aromatic compounds are formed by a reaction of alcohols and acids?

128 These three pleasant smelling esters are reminiscent of which fruits? Benzyl acetate, isoamyl acetate, ethyl caprylate.

129 Name the group of chemical compounds responsible for fruit esters and floral aromatics of wine?

130 What is the group of organic chemical compounds resulting from the oxidation of alcohols?

131 What is the most prevalent aldehyde in all wines?

132 Name an ester that originates from the process of oak ageing wines.

CLARIFICATION AND STABILIZATION OF WINE, Cont.

121 Fining also removes off-aromas and may reduce astringency and bitterness.

122 Cold Stabilization. (Low temperatures cause the crystallization in the tank, the wine is then removed).

CHEMICAL COMPOUNDS PRESENT IN WINES

123 TDN (1,1,6-trimethyl-1,2-dihydronaphthalene. The aroma is intensified in mature Riesling).

124 Twist-off tops. (Natural cork absorbs TDN, resulting in lesser TDN intensity).

125 Pyrazine. (Pyrazine has an aromatic component that may be vegetative, green pepper, olive, dried sage, etc.).

126 Rotundone. (Also found in tubers and in the oils of black pepper, bell pepper, basil, thyme, rosemary, etc.).

127 Esters. (These compounds may occur during fermentation or post-fermentation).

128 Apples, bananas and pineapples. (The ester ethyl acetate smells unpleasantly of nail polish remover aromas).

129 Terpenes. (These lower molecular weight carbon-based compounds are more volatile and more aromatic).

130 Aldehydes. (Aldehydes take part in the polymerizations of tannin, so in turn play a role in the wine's texture).

131 Acetaldehyde. (Prior to ethanol formation, acetaldehyde is from yeast interaction with acetic acid bacteria).

132 Lactones. (Lactones are powerful and may impart aromas of spice, almonds, other nuts, and curry, etc.).

CHEMICAL COMPOUNDS PRESENT IN WINES, Cont.

133 Many know about diacetyl (the aroma of butter) as a by-product of MLF. Diacetyl is part of what larger group?

ALCOHOL

134 Ethanol is official name for wine alcohol. During the fermentation process, what other common alcohol is produced?

135 Who is credited with the understanding of glycerol and its function in the winemaking process?

136 True or false? Tears or viscosity (different terms for the same thing) in wine are totally dependent on glycerol.

137 What is the technical term for this surface tension action creating tears?

138 True or False? The body of a red wine is dictated by the glycerol level.

SULFITE HEADACHES – MYTHS

Everybody's biochemistry is different, so when coupled with wine's huge diversity of chemicals, headache origins vary.

139 A major wine labeling change occurred in America in 1988, adding what ominous sounding phrase to the back label?

140 Many consumers say, "I get headaches from red wine, but not from white wines." Is this a sulfite problem?

141 Why do red wines require less sulfite additions than white wines?

CHEMICAL COMPOUNDS PRESENT IN WINES, Cont.

133 Ketones. (Ketones are aroma compounds produced in exceedingly small quantities of which diacetyl is one).

ALCOHOL

134 Glycerol. (This is a clear, viscous carbohydrate that adds body to wine and may also have a pseudo-sweetness).

135 Louis Pasteur. (Also called glycerine, Pasteur knew it was a by-product, and it played a role in viscosity).

136 False. (Tears are caused by surface tension of the liquid and ethanol evaporation).

137 Gibbs-Marangoni Effect. (The interaction of alcohol, evaporation, water and surface tension + gravity).

138 False. (Another misconception. Body is determined by tannin, alcohol and intensity, not glycerol).

SULFITE HEADACHES – MYTHS

139 Contains Sulfites. (The small quantity of sulfites used in wine are completely harmless to most consumers.)

140 Probably not, as white wines generally have higher levels of added sulfites than red wines.

141 Red wines contain more compounds that protect against microbes and oxidation.

SULFITE HEADACHES – MYTHS, Cont.

142 A comparison: dried apricots contain ≈ 3,000 – 3,500 mg/L of sulfites. How much is in the average red wine?

143 Wine is a diuretic and therefore dehydrates the body, causing capillaries to constrict. What is one solution here?

144 Tannins release serotonin (a neurotransmitter in the nervous system) that constricts blood vessels. Headache?

145 When amino acids metabolize lactic acid bacteria what category of organic compounds are created?

146 Name two specific biogenic amines? (These compounds are natural and produced during the fermentation process).

147 Histamines are chemicals that are released when you have an allergic reaction. What is a solution here?

148 True or false? Consumers with higher levels of digestive enzymes that inactivate biogenic amines will have no ill effects like headaches.

THE BOTTOM LINE IS HEADACHES ARE NOT CAUSED BY SULFITES!

WINE FAULTS

149 The term cork taint has been frequently used in recent years but is abating. What is name of the chemical compound)?

150 In the winery, what else besides corks can be contaminated with TCA?

151 What is the name of a common spoilage yeast that begins with the letter B?

SULFITE HEADACHES – MYTHS, Cont.

142 50-75 mg/L. (The legal maximum of total amount of SO_2 allowed in red wine is 150 mg/L.)

143 Drink water. (Dehydration creates headaches, so hydrate before, during, and after drinking wine.)

144 Yes. (Serotonin is also found in the gastrointestinal tract *and dilate* vessels as a bi-phasal function).

145 Biogenic Amines. (These are probably the culprits of headaches, as red and some white wines go through MLF).

146 Histamine and tyramine. (These amines are compounded in the presence of alcohol.)

147 Try taking an antihistamine prior to drinking wine. (There are high levels of histamines in red wines).

148 True. (This is a principal reason why some consumers get red wine headaches and others do not).

WINE FAULTS

149 TCA. (2,4,6, Trichloroanisole. A powerful compound with a mildewy smell and taste that mutes wine aromas.)

150 Wood racks; wood beams, wood barrels; cardboard boxes; etc.

151 Brettanomyces, Brett for short. (Also known as dekkera bruxellensis.)

WINE FAULTS, Cont.

152 Some enjoy a touch of Brett, (like me), but the volume is impossible to control. Name some of the positive aromas?

153 Name some of the negative aromas associated with Brettanomyces.

154 Name a source in the winery that Brett feeds on.

155 What chemical compound resulting from wildfires contaminating grapes and wine is commonly called smoke taint?

156 What is the compound that over time converts alcohol in wine into vinegar?

157 What other compound (in small quantities) is acetobacter responsible for?

158 The smell of rotten eggs may occur if a sulfur gas forms during the fermentation process. Name this compound.

159 Name the class of compounds that deliver the negative sulfur aromatics like sewer; onion; garlic; and rotten eggs?

160 How do mercaptans differ from H_2S, in addition to the commonality of negative/offensive aromas displayed?

161 H_2S and mercaptans are disorders due to volatile sulfur compounds. What are the two aromatic differences?

162 If yeast nutrient levels are not maintained, the metabolic pathway may change into H_2S creation. What's a cure?

163 Which does not belong? Brettanomyces, lactobacillus, pediococcus, leuconostoc, acetobacter.

164 What is a negative of the MLB (malolactic bacteria) lactobacillus?

WINE FAULTS, Cont.

152 Smoked meat, clove, beef bouillon, glove leather, tobacco, truffle and other earthy, savory spices.
153 Barnyard, sweaty horse blanket, manure, band-aid, wet dog, gamey notes.
154 Cellulose (polysaccharide) in oak barrels, wines with high residual sugar and high pH concentration wines.
155 Guaiacol. (There are a few volatile phenol contributors, but the result is ash, smoky, char, and burnt aromas).
156 Acetobacter. (A group of bacteria that oxidatively convert ethanol into acetic acid).
157 Ethyl Acetate. (This compound may deliver the aroma of nail polish remover).
158 Hydrogen Sulfide (H_2S). (This fault may result from poor yeast metabolism).
159 Thiols. (Another name for mercaptans and offering negative smells like H_2S (hydrogen sulfide.)
160 H_2S is only one compound, and mercaptans are a whole host of odiferous sulfur containing compounds.
161 H_2S has rotten egg and sewer smells, and mercaptans may smell like rotten cabbage or burnt rubber.
162 Copper Sulfate ($CuSo_4$) addition. (H_2S will be removed by a $CuSo_4$ addition measured at 0.5 ppm.)
163 Leuconostoc. (This is a bacterium beneficial to MLF, and the others are spoilage yeasts and bacterium).
164 Resistance to alcohol creates acetic acid, and may create off-aromas reminiscent of sour milk.

OAK BARRELS

165 Oak barrels are widely used in winemaking. In which country are the best oak forests found?

166 Approximately how many different types of oak trees are grown worldwide?

167 At what age are oak trees harvested for wine barrels?

168 Burgundy and Bordeaux use different sized oak barrels for fermentation and aging. What sizes for each region?

169 Name the location of some of France's oak forests in France.

170 What is another traditional name for "barrel maker?"

171 Name three well-known French barrel manufacturers.

172 Why are wine barrels charred or "toasted" during assembly?

173 Of these oak treatment options, which are preferable: sawn or split; kiln or air dried; fire or steam bent staves?

174 Regarding barrel toasting, what are the aromas picked up with a light toast?

175 Same question for medium toast aromas.

176 Same question for temperatures over 400° F?

177 What is the French term for toasting barrels?

CORK & OTHER CLOSURES

178 What is the name of the often-indented irregular black lines found in natural cork?

OAK BARRELS

165 France. (Although many countries (including the US) worldwide produce food quality oak for barrels.

166 ≈ 400. (However only about 20 species are used for wine barrel production).

167 80 – 120 years old. (A mature oak tree will provide enough wood for two 225- liter barrels).

168 The traditional Burgundy barrel is 228 liters in capacity and Bordeaux barrels are 225 liters in capacity.

169 Limousin, Nevers, Allier, Tronçais and Vosges.

170 Cooper. (The barrel-making facility is called a cooperage.)

171 Darajou, Demptos, François Frères, Nadalie, Taransaud, Seguin-Moreau, Tonnelleries de Bourgogne.

172 To add aroma/flavor complexity via chemical compounds released via fire from the wood.

173 Split (releases less sap), air dried (sun/rain removes sap), desirable vanillin levels are higher in fire bent staves.

174 Straight forward simple oak aromas. (This open flame may be between 200 - 300° F).

175 Sweet or even honey aromas. (This range may be in the mid - 300° F).

176 Vanilla, spice, coffee, chocolate, nutty (depending on the toast level and temperature these may overlap).

177 Bousinage. (This is a very sophisticated science these days based on the reputation of coopers).

CORK & OTHER CLOSURES

178 Lenticels. (These thin-walled cells contain air. The fewer the lenticels, the better the cork quality.)

CORK & OTHER CLOSURES, Cont.

179 Name two of the major cork producing countries or islands.

180 What is the Latin term for the species of oak trees used in the production of cork for wine bottles?

181 How often do cork trees offer harvests?

182 Approximately how many thousands of corks may be harvested from a 200-year-old oak tree? 22, 58, 74, 100, 125.

183 Name three types of wine bottle closures.

184 What do the letters OTR mean when in discussions about cork and other closures?

185 What is a supposed negative of synthetic corks?

186 What is a supposed negative of screw cap closures?

187 What may be a negative to natural cork?

188 What is a benefit and a negative of engineered corks?

189 Why do champagne corks have between 1 - 3 discs at the base of the corks?

190 Considering the previous topic, if you close a still wine with a champagne cork, will it still form the mushroom shape?

VITICULTURE

191 What is the definition of viticulture?

CORK & OTHER CLOSURES, Cont.

179 Portugal (80% of the world's supply), Spain, France, Morocco, Algeria, Tunisia, Corsica, Sardinia, etc.

180 *Quercus Suber.* (The oak trees may have up to 12 - 15 bark harvests in their lifetimes.)

181 The first harvest is ≈ when the tree is 30 years old, then harvest may occur every 9 – 11 years.

182 100,000. (As there are many variables in this calculation, this is an approximate number).

183 Natural bark, engineered corks (agglomerated corks), synthetic corks, glass closures, screw caps.

184 Oxygen Transfer Rate. (All options should be determined by the of the winemaker's redox philosophy).

185 Some studies show these plastics have a high OTR, leading to early oxidation and wine spoilage.

186 A heavy carbon footprint due to coal energy costs to produce aluminum.

187 Still quite common, but it is a 400-year-old technology, introduced with the invention of bottles. Negatives: TCA.

188 The most affordable to produce, but the cork bits are glued together. They may also be tainted by TCA.

189 These are more elastic than the rest of the cork, designed to absorb CO_2, creating the mushroom shape.

190 No. (The CO_2 creates the expansion, so without the gas, the mushroom shape will not form).

VITICULTURE

191 The art and science of grape growing and everything else that is related to the farming aspect of the grapevine.

VITICULTURE, Cont.

192 Rose bushes are often seen planted at the end of each row of vines. What are three reasons for this?

193 Within the vine, name the two transport systems necessary for growth, health, and development.

194 What is the study within the science of botany identifying grapevines/grape leaves by their physical characteristics?

195 What compound makes up the vineyard spraying treatment called Bordeaux Mixture?

196 Which is out of place? Powdery mildew, Murphy's Stem Disorder, Pierce's Disease, leafroll virus, fanleaf degeneration.

197 How is Pierce's Disease spread in the vineyard?

198 Name one trellising method for maximizing sun exposure, allowing high levels of sugar accumulation.)

199 What is the colloquial term relating to the amount of time grapes remain on the vine prior to harvest?

200 What term is used when some grape clusters are cut off and dropped on the ground prior to the harvest dates?

201 What is the French term for the vine disorder causing poor fruit set following bad weather during flowering?

202 What is the other French term for abnormal bunch development due to bad weather during flowering?

203 What term is used for water rationing through limited irrigation?

204 In high quality wine production, what step is taken after the fruit is brought in to insure only top-quality fruit is used?

VITICULTURE, Cont.

192 1) Insect control. 2) Rose thorns deter plough horses from turning too quickly. 3) Appealing to the eye.

193 Xylem (delivers water/minerals from to leaves) and phloem (delivers sugar and amino acids through the plant.)

194 Ampelography. (Examines grape leaf formations, color, shapes, cluster configurations, DNA sequencing, etc.).

195 Copper sulfate. (This compound effectively combats mildew diseases in the vineyard.)

196 Murphy's Stem Disorder. (This is made up and the others are grapevine diseases).

197 Via the glassy-winged sharpshooter. (A small insect that spreads the bacterium from vine to vine).

198 Vertical Shoot Positioning (VSP). (The grapes are exposed to more sunlight, aiding ripening.)

199 Hang Time. (There are various reasons for extended hang time, but grape flavor concentration is common).

200 *Vendange Vert* in French, or Green Harvest. (This allows the remaining clusters to more easily achieve ripeness).

201 *Coulure.* (Also known as shatter, a smaller number of berries remain after flowering).

202 *Millerandage.* (Also known as shot berries or hens and chicks; uneven ripening and immature berries).

203 Reduced Deficit Irrigation (RDI). (Hydric stress keeps berry size small with highly concentrated flavors.)

204 Sorting. (Grapes are sent to a moving table where workers remove impurities and damaged grapes).

VITICULTURE, Cont.

205 Describe the calendar year of the grapevine, from after dormancy to crush pad.

206 Which Vitis vine species is out of place? Vinifera, labrusca, riparia, gerulaitis, rotundifolia.

207 Which grapes do not belong to Vitis vinifera? Chardonnay, Merlot, Riesling, Grenache, Pinot Noir, Cabernet Sauvignon.

208 In California, AxR-1 rootstock proved susceptible to phylloxera in the 1980s. What older rootstock is more tolerant?

209 AxR-1 is short for what?

210 Name the two primary methods used to attach bud wood to rootstock.

211 Name the two primary of vine training.

212 What are the two methods used to harvest wine grapes?

213 A mechanical harvester does the work of approximately how many vineyard workers?

214 What are some American species of grapes commonly grown in the mid-Atlantic states for wine production?

215 In relation to grape varieties, what is the difference between a crossing and a hybrid?

216 What are some examples of hybrid varieties created from crossbreeding French and American varieties?

217 In terms of grape varieties, what is the definition of a clone?

218 What are some specific reasons clones are propagated intentionally?

219 What term is used to describe the change from daytime to nighttime temperature?

VITICULTURE, Cont.

205 Budbreak, flowering, fruit set, ripening (or veraison), harvest.
206 Gerulaitis. (Vitas Gerulaitis was a world-famous tennis player in the 1970s).
207 They all belong to the European species Vitis vinifera. (Vitis is always capitalized and vinifera is lower case.)
208 Rupestris St. George. (Ironically, AxR-1 was recommended by scientists at UC Davis to replace St. George.)
209 Aramon x Rupestris Ganzin # 1. (A hybrid of Vitis vinifera (Aramon) and Vitis rupestris, an American species).
210 Field Budding (bud wood grafted to existing rootstock in vineyard) and bench grafting (in the nursery.)
211 Cane training (also known as Guyot) and cordon training..
212 Hand and Mechanical Harvesting. (Mechanical is best works on large, relatively flat land.)
213 About 60. (So, given economies of scale, for larger wineries this makes sense).
214 Niagara, Concord, Catawba, Scuppernong, Norton, Muscadine (No relation to Muscadet or Muscat.)
215 A crossing is a new variety from varieties of the same species. A hybrid is a new variety from different species.
216 Seyval Blanc, Baco Noir, Frontenac, Chambourcin, Vidal Blanc, Maréchal Foch, etc.
217 Clones are a genetic sub-type of a variety. They are propagated intentionally as well as naturally mutate.
218 Resistance to disease, bunch size, berry size, skin thickness, pigmentation, etc.
219 Diurnal range. (Warm daytime temperatures ripen fruit and cool evenings preserve acidity.)

VITICULTURE, Cont.

220 What country has the highest elevation vineyard in the world?

221 In what country is the oldest living grapevine on the planet located?

222 What country purportedly has the world's smallest vineyard in area?

223 A ton of grapes makes approximately how many bottles of wine?

VITICULTURE - NATURAL WINES

224 True or false? Natural wine is a new phenomenon, coming into being just fifteen years ago.

225 Name three characteristics that might qualify a wine as a natural wine.

226 Regarding the above practices, would these steps be considered minimal intervention or manipulation intervention?

227 Conventional grape farming uses chemical herbicides, fungicides, pesticides and fertilizers. Does organic farming?

228 What are some of the goals of sustainable farming?

229 How is biodynamic farming different from organic farming?

230 Who is considered the founder of biodynamic farming?

231 True or False? Organic and biodynamic farmers may add sulfur dioxide at all winemaking stages.

VITICULTURE, Cont.

220 Bolivia. (Carignan is planted as high as 9,000 feet above sea level.) Tibet has higher vineyards, but wines aren't commercial.

221 Slovenia. (Estimated to be between 350 – 400 years old and still bearing 75 – 120 pounds of grapes/year).

222 Canada. (An 11' x 7' plot in Toronto. The 26 Cabernet Franc vines in clay pots are brought indoors during winter).

223 ≈ 720 bottles. (This is an average, as grape size and juice volume vary.)

VITICULTURE - NATURAL WINES

224 False. (The category began gaining attention recently, but this method is thousands of years old.)

225 Organic/Biodynamically grown grapes, only native yeast used, little or no sulfites added, unfined/filtered.

226 Minimal intervention. (As little added to or subtracted from the wine as possible.)

227 No. (The first tenet of organic farming is no chemicals used in the vineyard.)

228 Carbon neutrality, clean energy; water conservation, recycling, support of employees; support community, etc.

229 Organic plus biodiverse ecosystem, following biodynamic calendar, use of herbal and other preparations, etc.

230 Rudolf Steiner. (An Austrian by birth, but not a viticulturalist.)

231 False. (SO_2 addition is only allowed after fermentation as a preservative, not before as an anti-microbial.)

VITICULTURE - NATURAL WINES, Cont.

232 What is the French term for minimizing without completely forbidding the use of chemicals in the vineyard?

233 Name two reasons for planting cover crops between vine rows.

234 What term is used to describe white wines fermented on their skins?

235 What type of fermentation vessel has been used in the country of Georgia since circa 6000 BC?

236 How do natural wines tastes compare to conventionally produced wines?

237 What is one of the reasons that natural wines are gaining popularity?

VITICULTURE - NATURAL WINES, Cont.

232 Lutte Raisonnée. (*The reasoned fight*. Eschewing chemicals while allowing that they are necessary on occasion.)

233 Erosion control, controls excessive water absorption, habitat for beneficial insects, provides nutrients.

234 Orange Wine. (White wine fermented in contact with skins, imparting an orange color to the wine.)

235 Qvevri. (These egg-shaped clay pots are sealed and buried underground for cooler temperatures).

236 Of course, tasting wine is very subjective, but fans observe more fruit-driven characteristics in natural wine.

237 The general trend towards healthier living. Natural wines are perceived to be better for you than conventionally made wines.

POSTSCRIPT

Years ago, my good friend Mark Ford asked me to tutor him on French wines. He commented, "I don't need to know everything about French wines; I just want to know more than my friends." Indeed, that phrase is why I wrote this book. Like anything else worthy of endeavour, regardless of why you begin the effort, learning something about wine will only increase your enjoyment of it.

G.S.

BOARD AND BENCH
PUBLISHING

Find this and all Board + Bench Ebooks at
www.imbiblioapp.com

**Best Drinks
Culture App
Gourman Awards**